The White Mark where we did much of our thinking and dreaming

NETTLEBED

Nettlebed Creamery who make the cheese for our toashies

TON

The Paddock where we pick our rosemary

WANTAGE

wessex Mill

HOME

Home of wessex mill Where we get our flour

Breadsong

BREADSONG

KITTY & AL TAIT

How Baking Changed Our Lives

BLOOMSBURY PUBLISHING

NEW YORK · LONDON · OXFORD · NEW DELHI · SYDNEY

For Albert and Aggie.
And for Katie.

HOW BAKING CHANGED OUR LIVES 6

RECIPES 148

HOW BAKING CHANGED OUR LIVES

KITTY   The very first post I ever put on my Instagram says Breadsong. It's a short film of a row of loaves crackling and hissing as their crusts expand after they've just come out of the oven. If you lean in closely to loaves on the cooling rack – being careful not to singe your ear – it can sound like distant applause. That's the magic of bread.

AL   The story of the Orange Bakery has been chronicled by films and images taken by Kitty that simply capture the joy of baking. I had no idea where we were going when Kitty started to bake bread, but I knew that I had to be alongside her because it was the only thing that made any sense.

This book is about how my then-14-year-old daughter and I came to open a bakery. The people who helped us and the town that made it possible. The drawings are mine, the recipes are mainly Kitty's, but the story is ours.

1
THE BEGINNING

THE TWO QUESTIONS people often ask are *when* and *why*. Even now, I'm not sure that I can answer either. The *when*, I suppose, seems easier because there are a few concrete markers. My parents' golden wedding anniversary party in early spring 2018 stands out. It was the first time in a while that my side of the family had all been together. In the sometimes complicated, nuanced family dynamic Kitty had always occupied an enviously simple slot; she was the funny, chatty one with freckles and red hair who always wore odd socks and made everyone laugh. The change in her had been so gradual that Katie, my wife, and I had failed to realize just how much Kitty had faded into a diminished version of herself. For the wider family, who hadn't seen her for a while, it was stark. Kitty was so subdued, distracted, pale and sad looking that both my mum and sister rang us afterward to check whether she was okay.

Over the weeks that followed, we tried everything to work out what was happening with our youngest child. We wrapped her up as tightly as we could in family. We talked and listened. But the more we tried, the further she seemed to slip away from us until finally, in desperation, Katie took her to see our GP. As Katie asked for help, Kitty sat there mute and found it impossible to explain what was happening to her. The doctor was worried and said he would refer us on for further support. We were at least relieved that we had put something in motion and Kit seemed reassured that she was going to get help. For a while, it all felt better – but like the Phoney War, we had no idea what was to come.

We slunk into our first appointment at the Child and Adolescent Mental Health Services (CAMHS) in Oxford, slightly embarrassed we were wasting their valuable time. However, the trip was a trigger for Kitty. After speaking to the psychologist about how she was really feeling, she could no longer pretend to any vestige of 'normality'. The wafer-thin veneer of putting on a brave face cracked overnight and Kitty became swallowed up by despair and fear. Anxiety gripped her, often out of the blue, and she became unable to cope with even leaving the house. By June, attending school was an impossibility and receded in importance as Kitty was simply struggling to wake up and get dressed each day.

Tracing back, we realized we had noticed changes over some time, for months maybe. While we both still wish that we had acted on these changes sooner, even now we can see why we didn't. Having been a child for a long time, adolescence was starting to rush in. The self-consciousness that Kitty had been blissfully free from now hung heavy. But we had been there before with her older siblings. Parental amnesia blocks out many of the more stressful moments, but we had vague memories that life was pretty challenging for Albert and Aggie at 14 too.

We thought maybe 'self-conscious teen' was a cruel badge that you just had to wear for a while. There were still lots of pluses for Kit – she was popular, doing well at school and we still had her in the box of our 'happy' child. She was the one who literally seemed to bounce through life.

With her huge smile and outrageous laugh, Kitty would bounce into rooms and bounce into our bed each morning. So, she'd stopped bouncing a bit. We thought it would come back.

There was something else that stopped us doing anything about Kitty. That one is a bit harder to explain. We didn't act on our instincts because, as is so often the case, life was complicated. We were juggling the double vortex of A levels with Aggie and GCSEs with Albert and all the baggage that comes with that. Katie was working flat out at her job with the cancer charity Maggie's, beetling down the M40 into London at least four times a week. And I was coming to a crossroads with my career, hoping to step up both the dyslexic work at Oxford University and my role for Now Teach, a charity to get older people into teaching. I'd had a few years of working part time, earning less but being able to be there for the children and keep the house/dogs/schoolwork vaguely ticking over while Katie's workload increased. Financially and personally, we needed to work out what came next. So there was this 'stuff' just going on, all vaguely moving forward in the right direction. It's not that we chose to ignore what was happening right in front of us with Kit; naively, we were waiting for a little bit of space to open up to address it. But soon we had no option.

The *why* is almost impossible to answer and is more for Kitty to say. It's like a pixelated image that takes a while to sharpen into focus and there are details that will probably only become clear a long time in the future. The *why* is what everyone wants to get to the bottom of, as if finding the root of the problem means you can change things at the source or somehow remove it through the power of logic. Surely then everything will be fine.

Everyone wanted to know what the trigger was. There was no single obvious cause, although probably a thousand small ones. Maybe there was some simple DNA that made the situation unavoidable. Social media, for once, wasn't the villain of the piece. Kitty had good friends and there was no sign of bullying. She worked hard at school, our local state secondary that wasn't known for being pressurized academically. Whatever the reason, something short-circuited. It was a bit like the scene in *Apollo 13* where a routine flick of the switch suddenly snowballs into a full-blown disaster.

In the space of a few weeks our lives changed completely. It's very hard to capture what real despair looks like.

It's not exaggerated sadness, rather it's when someone gives up on all the simplest functions – getting up, eating, washing, even sleeping – and it's terrifying to watch. Kitty couldn't see the reason for anything and so one of us needed to be with her the entire time, day and night, to reassure her she was safe. Kitty's mind was so fractured that it was almost impossible to use reason with her. It was upsetting and scary for everyone, but for Kitty most of all. And the weirdest thing was that real life continued to go on around us. People walked down our street, with their dogs on leads and their children in buggies, all enjoying the hot summer sun while behind our front door we struggled to keep Kitty from going under entirely. Katie and I would get to the end of every day and ask each other, 'How did this happen?' After a while we stopped bothering with the big *how* and instead we talked about how we had managed to get through the day.

I WAS CONSCIOUS of Mum and Dad trying to make sense of it all. I knew they felt that they could have somehow prevented it, but they couldn't have. The length of time between feeling okay and not okay was so short that I think nothing would have stopped it. I went from being confident and sure of things to utterly paralyzed with anxiety and unable to even remember who I used to be.

It was like Jenga, pull one block out too fast, too soon, and my whole tower toppled.

I wanted to tell Mum and Dad what was going on, but it was so hard. I just didn't want to be me in any form at all. My mind whirred and whirred until I thought I would do anything to stop it. At the anniversary party, I could hardly talk as I was so sad. I knew that wasn't normal. The cousins, the cake, plates of crisps, family speeches, messing around outside the Town Hall – I couldn't get hold of any of it.

If I had to give a reason – and I have tried so hard to find one – it was partly because I'd completely lost my way with the character I'd created for myself. I felt like a complete imposter, like at the beginning of Shrek when Fiona turns into an ogre at night and has to hide herself away. I was terrified that maybe I wasn't this perfect happy person, maybe I was an ogre and I didn't want people to see that side of me.

As far back as primary school, I always wanted to be the tomboy – the daring one who was a bit cheeky and stood out. I wore odd, fluffy, striped socks pulled up over my calves and handed-down school shorts from my brother Albert. I loved the label of being a bit different, which also meant I didn't need to be the prettiest or have the longest hair (long hair was ALL that mattered at the age of seven). In fact, my hair was a red nest that could house a small family of sparrows and no hairbrush could conquer. I always wanted to take on the roles that no one else did: the spitting camel in the Nativity, always Neville or Ron in the Harry Potter games in the playground, the one that made teachers laugh out loud. I wasn't one of the clever pupils. In fact, I did a fair bit of time in the 'special' group with one boy, Neil. I loved Neil, even though he disappeared every summer term to sell ice cream with his dad on the Isle of Wight and I had to wait patiently for him to come back to school in September.

Primary school was my kingdom and so moving up to Watlington's secondary school wasn't a big deal. Both Aggie and Albert went there and it was only a short walk round the corner from our house. It was scruffy and sat beside the primary school and I loved it. I joined in everything – I was often the smallest and always the one giggling. At parents' evening the teachers would say, 'Kitty never stops smiling.' (I did not have good teeth for that smile – braces were going to play a big part of the next few years.) I was really happy.

I worked hard during those first two years at secondary school. Through sheer determination, I managed to claw my way out of the bottom class. I put my hand up for everything. Mr Rowe, our drama teacher, said I was 'a force of nature' and gave me the part of the granny in the school play. Over five performances, I danced with a Zimmer frame wearing thick black glasses, an orange flowery shirt, a baggy tweed skirt and a hair net. It should have been social suicide, but I loved it. I was not at all self-conscious.

It's so hard to explain, but as I entered year 9, I constantly asked Mum how long education went on for. I panicked that I was trapped in this funnel that might go on for years and, while everyone else seemed to totally get it, I found it harder to understand what the point of all of it was. Slowly, I started to remove myself. I couldn't eat. I couldn't sleep. I wanted to stay at home. I started to have panic attacks, but I didn't want to tell anyone. Dementors moved into my brain with heavy iron suitcases and the weight of them pinned me down.

I remember so little of those early days of summer. Leaving school was almost the easy bit. I just drifted away. There were days and days of feeling lost and incomplete and not wanting to exist at all.

When I could get up, I pulled on the same pair of orange soft cord dungarees.

The sensation of washing my hair was painful to the point of impossibility. I was barely aware of what the rest of the family were doing. Mum slept beside me at night, Dad took me on short walks, Aggie and Albert stayed in the house with me, so I was never on my own, and yet I was lonelier than I thought possible. I wanted to take my brain out, wash it and put it back.

I was aware of Mum and Dad trying to find different ways to help me. Our GP had referred me to CAMHS (although for ages I thought it was called 'Calms') on the outskirts of Oxford. Somehow they managed to get me there twice a week. On every visit, it always seemed to be suffocatingly hot. We would leave the car parked by TK Maxx and cross a square of scorched earth strewn with rubbish – twice we saw a fat rat in the tufts of grass. At the clinic I sat in a small room with two nice women; they would talk to me and I would nod. I was given a prescription for pills – we called them Flo – and lots of 'tools' for coping, including breathing exercises and how to put cold ice under my eyes to stave off panic attacks, but I dreaded each visit. Mum and Dad tried to add in their own therapies at home. Dad painted with me and Mum read aloud Roald Dahl short stories about murders using legs of lamb and babies turning into bees, but my brain stung and I couldn't hold the words in my head. In the end, they stopped trying. The days ticked over.

WE WERE SO completely consumed with the issue of Kitty that we had no stamina to cope with anything else. We put all our energy into looking after her, but it meant we had nothing left to cope with something that shouldn't have been a big issue but became one.

The straw that almost broke the camel's back came with four legs and a short stubby tail – Sibby.

We had made the rather random decision a few months earlier, before we realized Kit was ill, to get another dog. Our elderly, slightly neurotic, but very benign terrier, Sparky, was a perfect family member; affectionate and remarkably well behaved, he would potter along without a lead up to the shops and wait outside patiently. Apart from an embarrassing habit of peeing on other people's picnic baskets at the beach, he was pretty saintly. He even got on with the cats; the mother, Smudge, who we got from a farm, was beautiful but aloof. Her son, Oddie, however, would curl up on the other end of the sofa with Sparky and they both had a penchant for sunbathing. So, we thought, what could go wrong with another terrier?

The answer to that question was *everything*, and we only had ourselves to blame. Sibby was a slightly different model of terrier, but still half-Parson, like Sparky. We ticked every box on the checklist of what not to do; we didn't meet her parents (who were both proper working dogs not given to living inside). We didn't crack on with her training, somehow thinking she might pick up on Sparky's good habits through some kind of osmosis. We never managed to stop her chasing our cats, scrabbling through the house to track them down. As a result, we had this wild dog who dug holes over the garden like a Somme trench-builder, bolted from the front door whenever the smallest chink appeared when a parcel was delivered and would try her utmost to dodge out of her collar and lead while on walks. When she escaped, she was like a heat-seeking missile, disappearing off into the distance. On a good day, this disaster would last 20 minutes. On the worst days, it would be over an hour before we retrieved her, voices hoarse from shouting across the hillside.

So, our hot, scary summer was accompanied by a dog we couldn't control, Oddie who became a ghost cat, occasionally creeping in for food, and Smudge who decided to show her disappointment in our new arrival by peeing on every bed. It would have been easiest – and I think this probably would have been my instinct – to close down completely, retreat into our world, however strange, until Kitty somehow got better. Sometimes I could barely explain the day's events to myself, let alone anyone else. Katie, though, not for the first time, was much braver than me. She chose to be utterly up front with family, friends and neighbors. Talking about it was her way of sorting things out in her own head.

No one could understand how our bubbly, bright Kitty, who they'd seen growing up, could have changed so fast, but they wanted to help. Peter, the gentle, rather buttoned-up man in his seventies who'd moved into the bungalow two doors down, was particularly kind. He'd lost a daughter at an early age and his sympathy and warmth was very meaningful. Lucy and Robin, our earliest friends in Watlington, were a constant, unjudging presence who we felt safe to share the very worst of what we were going through. Others outside our immediate circle were lovely too; teachers, Kitty's friends who would drop notes through our door, sometimes just very random people.

Kit had gone to the local nursery, primary and now secondary school, so we had a whole web of connections. Watlington claims it's the smallest town in England. It has a long, winding high street topped at one end by the seventeenth-century Town Hall and at the other by the War Memorial. It's not a town you would travel to see, but it's a town where families grow up, and so Watlington has a genuine sense of community with compassion and concern. We were to experience that again and again over the next few years.

our street

our house

2
THE FIRST LOAF

DAD MADE BREAD one day. I was sat on the kitchen stool thinking of nothing while Dad mixed flour, water and salt in a bowl to make a dough. It looked gloopy, anemic and sludgy – a bit like how my brain felt. Dad draped the primary school tea towel (the one printed with the faces of my classmates) over the top of the bowl and tucked it away on a shelf. The next day, when I'd finally made it downstairs, Dad had taken the bowl off the shelf and it was sitting back on the kitchen table. I lifted the tea towel to see if the dough looked as unappealing as the night before. It was now like the surface of the moon.

The dough was gently bubbling and as each bubble popped another opened. It was alive.

I WISH I could remember the first time Kitty and I baked a loaf together. In reality, it was just another activity that I was trying out with Kitty that might provide her with some kind of distraction. TV was no good as she couldn't concentrate for anything longer than a few minutes. We'd tried gardening, although after choosing a few flowers and planting them out there wasn't much to do except watch Sibby dig them all up again. We'd experimented with craft, but that proved pretty useless. Sewing briefly lit up a few embers, but our ambitions went way beyond our ability. We painted for a bit and then when that failed, I got a bigger brush and slapped emulsion on a few walls. I was running out of options. Bread baking was pretty far down the list, but I enjoyed it, so we did it.

Bearing in mind how long I had been baking bread, the standard of my loaves was shockingly low. I'd been baking on and off since being a student. I even took a class once, a gift from my siblings for my fortieth birthday, and yet still I seemed to defy Malcolm Gladwell's 10,000 hours maxim. The more effort I put in, the more inconsistent my loaves seemed to be. Dense, doughy and flavorsome, but never things of beauty and rarely presentable, even to the rest of the family.

Bread baking was something I would do on holidays if I found a bit of yeast and space, or on occasional weekends. The class I had taken encouraged working with a very wet dough – although for me, this meant I never got beyond the stage where the dough stuck to our wooden work surface.

However hard I tried, the kitchen looked apocalyptic after 10 minutes of kneading and scraping dough.

The children occasionally shared my enthusiasm when a loaf was fresh out of the oven, but then half-eaten hunks sat forlornly at the bottom of the bread bin, gradually evolving into rocks, easily outranked by something soft, white, sliced and plastic wrapped.

Then someone pointed me in the direction of Jim Lahey's no-knead bread method that involves no kneading and, consequently, very little mess. You simply mix flour, water, salt and a tiny bit of yeast (¼ of a teaspoon at most) together in a bowl and leave it overnight. Initially it looks like wallpaper paste but then the dough starts to ferment and, in the morning, it is a slightly sour, bubbling mass. All you do is shape the dough into a vague ball, put it onto some parchment paper and let it proof before baking in a cast-iron Dutch oven that you shove into your

oven at its top temperature for 30 minutes or so beforehand. Compared to my usual bread cinder blocks, with this method the end product was semi-professional in appearance and tasted quite different to anything I had made before. These loaves went down well with the family and got eaten fast.

It was this no-knead method that I shared with Kitty. I can't tell you what time of day it was, what we'd been doing that morning or how it cropped up in conversation. There was nothing planned about it. I just asked Kitty if she wanted to have a go herself. There was no hallelujah chorus or a blinding flash of light. What I do remember, though, was that she actually looked interested when we pulled the loaf from the oven – and that hadn't happened in a long time. I had no idea just how important that moment was, and I still didn't when Kitty asked to bake that bread again.

I'D NEVER BEEN a good cook in any way at all. I didn't bother to follow the ingredients for a recipe, I just shoved together a whole load of things that I liked. The most basic things went wrong, like my banana bread that sank in the middle and my cupcakes that dried out your whole mouth because I got confused between a teaspoon and a tablespoon when adding the baking soda. I don't come from a family of cooks either. Mum makes two things: 'dogs' dinner', which is mince and rice, and cheesy risotto, which is cheesy risotto. Dad's a much better cook, but his repertoire is very stew-based. Sausage casserole with baked potatoes came around a lot.

But Dad's breadmaking was different. He showed me how he made the dough, proofed it, shaped it and then put it in the Dutch oven to bake.

When he lifted the lid, there was this beautiful crackling, singing loaf that made the hairs on the back of my neck shoot up.

It was alchemy. Something so dull had transformed into something so brilliant. Like the girl who could spin straw into gold, I could do it too. And so I did it again and again and again.

OUR FAMILY REALLY like bread, but there was no way our consumption was going to keep up with Kitty's rate of baking. Two weeks in, when Kitty began experimenting with some whole wheat flour as well as white, we started to face a small mountain of loaves pushing up the lid of our bread bin. It was Katie who suggested asking our neighbors if they wanted a loaf. We live on a one-way street of fifteen houses, all different shapes and sizes, with a mix of families big and small and a few elderly people who live on their own. We knew all of them and so we set off to ask them (or rather beg them) if they might like some fresh bread. Everyone who was at home when we knocked said yes and Kit went home to start preparing the doughs.

The next day we baked five loaves and wrapped them, still warm, in parchment paper and delivered them to our neighbors. They were received with the same kind look that you give to children selling off heavily iced cupcakes outside the school gates to raise money for something. It was a genuine surprise when Juliet, who lived a few doors down, told us that her children had devoured the whole loaf and asked if she could she put in an order for another.

For those first few weeks nothing really changed. Days began very early and we were all mentally and physically exhausted by the evening, often going to sleep when it was still light outside. The sense that we were living in some strange experiment continued. Sibby carried on destroying our sad flower beds. Katie and I played tag being with Kitty, helped by Aggie and Albert.

But there was this small seed of routine.

Kitty would make up a clutch of doughs before bed, then in the morning we would bake, wrap and deliver the loaves up and down the street. Just for a moment – sometimes when she shaped the dough into a ball, when she lifted the lid off the Dutch oven or when she handed over a still-warm wrapped loaf – I would see her smile a real smile. A smile uncluttered by the thoughts crowding her head. A genuine smile of her own rather than a forced one she felt she needed to give.

I STARTED TO live for that small window of time each day when I could bake. The problem was there was only a limited amount I could do. Our oven could only get so hot and it took two hours to cook each loaf. I could make up a lot more dough, but I had nowhere to bake it. I needed more ovens. It was Juliet who offered first. They had just put in an amazing new convection oven that could take four Dutch ovens at a time and reach much higher temperatures than ours. Juliet said I could use their oven any time and I was just to let myself in when I needed to.

A routine was set.

I would wait until they'd finished with their kitchen for the night and then scuttle across the street.

As this was around 9 pm, I would normally have changed into my fleecy pajamas with a coat thrown over the top so I could go straight to sleep afterward. With two old Dutch ovens stacked on top of each other, I would push through their back gate, down their side alley and into their kitchen – saying hello to their dogs, Coco and Boris – then I would quietly slide the Dutch ovens into their oven, trying not to disturb the family if they were watching TV in the next-door room. I repeated the journey as I needed to heat four Dutch ovens in the morning, but I could only carry two at a time. I had to say hello to the dogs all over again though. Back at home, I would mix up the flour, water and salt in a big bucket and then go to bed.

At 7 am the next morning I would scoop all the bubbly dough out of the bucket, lay it on the kitchen table, dust it with flour and roughly shape it into four balls. I would place each ball onto a sheet of parchment paper, which would then be lowered into its own glass bowl and a shower cap stretched over the top. (We started running out of bowls and soon I was using anything vaguely round; we lost our always-empty fruit bowl and once I even used my bicycle helmet.) The dough would then proof for two hours. Meanwhile, Juliet would turn on her oven when she woke up so that the Dutch ovens would get very hot. By the time I went back over with the bowls of proofed dough at 9 am, Juliet and her husband Rick would have left for their garden nursery with the dogs, dropping Iris and Noah off at school on the way.

I would carefully take the hot Dutch ovens out of the oven, lift the lids and lower each dough ball on its paper onto the base.

All the while, I tried hard not to burn my arms on the hot metal, which I did most of the time.

I would go home briefly and then return in 30 minutes to reach into the oven and lift off the lids to release the steam, again trying to avoid scalded skin. But I still wasn't done. The loaves had to finish baking uncovered for another 15 minutes to form a golden brown crust. I spent that time sat on Juliet's work counter, following bakers on Instagram and reading post after post about recipes, tips and experiments.

The bread baked in Juliet's kitchen was so much better than the loaves we pulled from our old oven. The dough sprang up in the higher heat and baked in half the time. The demand for my bread in our street soared and so we bought a whole load more Dutch ovens at the local Sue Ryder charity shop and I asked Charlotte and Phillip two doors down if I could use their oven as well.

Each evening I would go between houses, like a quiet elf in my soft pajamas, carrying Dutch ovens to slide into their ovens.

The next day I would trot between kitchens, lifting and lowering doughs and removing lids, leaving a small trail of flour and parchment paper behind me. By now I was making eight loaves each day. Even with giving out bread along our street, we still had loaves left over. I wanted to find them homes.

We wrote a list of all the people we knew well in Watlington (about three-quarters of the town's population) and dropped a loaf of fresh bread in a brown paper bag on their doorstep. We put a handwritten note inside each bag that had Dad's number on. The bags of bread went everywhere: the hairdresser's, the butcher's, old teachers' houses, the care home at the top of the hill, the fire station, Iggy the postman's house, the homes of friends we knew and houses we simply liked the look of. For a day we heard nothing. We worried that people thought they had just been bread-bombed. Then the texts started to arrive. 'Great loaf. Would love another one. How much do I owe you?' Orders went up to ten loaves a day.

Our subscription service was born.

3
FERGUSON

KATIE WENT BACK TO WORK in September. Albert returned to school. With A levels done and dusted, Aggie headed off to Ghana to work with her cousin Daisy who was living out there. That left Kit and me alone. Katie and I realized there was no way that we could go back to the juggling of jobs and care that had pockmarked the summer. It made far more financial sense for me to be the one at home full time. I had spoken to both Oxford and Now Teach, explaining that I had to stop working for a while. Both organizations had been very sympathetic and supportive, leaving doors ajar, but there was no middle ground.

There really wasn't any way of putting a time frame on Kit's recovery and we knew we just had to commit to her.

Looking back, I wonder why it didn't feel more bewildering; I was fifty, I had a bank balance barely into four figures and I was now unemployed. I can't remember us even talking much about it. If one of us wasn't at home with Kitty there was a strong possibility that she would fall away, so there was really no choice. We added a lump to our mortgage and my career came crashing to a full stop.

I'm not sure initially I was any help to Kitty apart from just being there. I spent a lot of time barreling into verbal cul-de-sacs thinking that maybe I could talk her out of the sadness she was lost in. Endless stretched metaphors and analogies became my tool of choice to try and offer her hope and guidance. Sometimes it felt that they landed but, although she was extraordinarily (and sometimes rather brutally) eloquent in explaining herself, talk as therapy was pretty pointless. Her brain only had the energy and space to transmit not receive.

I remember reading about the power of the amygdala. Located in what is sometimes called our reptilian brain, it is the oldest bit of hardware in our gray matter. It was pretty basic, if powerful, in its functions. The seat of the whole 'fight or flight' response to a perceived fear, the ancient amygdala has the ability to utterly overrule anything reasoned and rational that the much newer, shinier, more sophisticated pre-frontal cortex might be trying to do. Listening and evaluating are all about pre-frontal processing. Kitty, on the other hand, was so busy trying to cope with swirling fears and the possibility of her amygdala hijacking her brain she just couldn't hear. This was deeply frustrating and so, for me as well as Kitty, baking was a respite.

Having mastered Jim Lahey's no-knead technique for the overnight loaf, we were both keen to expand our repertoire. James Morton's *Brilliant Bread* was the book we went to first. James was a Scottish student doctor who had appeared on *The Great British Bake Off*, the one TV program that Kitty was able to watch without her mind wandering away down dark avenues. He had a homespun charm, which matched his Shetland jumpers, and the book was an extension of that; a really eclectic set of recipes that managed to find the balance between ambition and achievability. We tried James's focaccia and his sweet dough, we failed on his English muffins (through no fault of his), we triumphed with his pita breads. But there was a whole section of his book that seemed out of reach to us... that was sourdough. I had tried once or twice in the past to make a sourdough starter and had ended up with scary-looking canning jars full of sinister dark gray liquid separating from murky light gray bases, like one of those glass lighthouses full of sand from Alum Bay. They sat for weeks in the fridge before being thrown away. We bypassed that chapter as it felt too sophisticated.

Inserting the word sourdough in front of anything automatically gives it kudos and an apparent authenticity that promises to make it an 'eating experience'.

Sourdough pizza, sourdough crackers, sourdough breadsticks; these are the high-class, artisan versions of their peers. The prefix sourdough somehow means that it's okay to charge twice as much. And then there's the bread itself. When I was working in Oxford, I'd got into the habit of buying half a sourdough loaf from a deli tucked down a side street near the market. It felt like a passport that allowed me to access all those recipes you'd read in Saturday papers or dishes on gastropub menus; shakshuka, panzanella, perfect poached eggs. It made me feel grown up. And yet there was also something of the Emperor's New Clothes about sourdough. My precious cargo from the Oxford Deli tasted sour enough to be different to 'ordinary' bread, but it was often a bit dry. As supermarkets started stocking sourdough bread, I tried different loaves and came to like it but never loved it. But then there was a moment that summer that made me realize what sourdough was all about.

By late August the monotony of life in Watlington had got to us and we decided to go with Kitty to London for the night to stay with Katie's sister, Alice. Nervously leaving Kit with her cousins in front of a film, Katie and I went out together, just the two of us, for the first time in weeks. We walked to a small restaurant just around the corner. While we were both anticipating the inevitable phone call that would see us scurrying back, we were determined to grab at least an hour together. The place was full of people who felt younger and cooler than we were, but we were oblivious. We abandoned the menu suggestions and instead ordered some bread and cured meat with a bottle of wine, determined to get drunk quite quickly.

Out came a basket of the tastiest bread I've ever eaten; a nearly burnt crust and an interior that was chewy, soft and sour all at the same time.

I asked the waitress where the bread was from. I can't remember what she replied apart from 'sourdough'. So this was what sourdough *could* taste like. I kept a piece back for Kitty, although a few days later I found it crisp and fluff-covered in my jacket pocket. That sourdough was – and remains – my benchmark for good bread.

Over the next few weeks my thoughts returned to the bread I had eaten that night. Eventually, we went back to the chapter on sourdough in James Morton's book, *Brilliant Bread*. We needed to crack this mysterious code. After previous efforts, I didn't even attempt to make a starter. Instead, we researched buying a readymade version and the first one that came up online was from Hobbs House Bakery in Gloucestershire.

The Hobbs House Bakery starter arrived in a neat jar complete with a hand-printed booklet to guide you through the sourdough-making process. The starter was in a much healthier looking state than anything I had created. We began baking with it straightaway.

Our first sourdough loaf was distinctly flatter than our usual overnight mix – more of a Frisbee than a cottage loaf.

However, there was already a much more complex flavor to the bread, which we really liked.

The thing about sourdough is that when it comes to fermenting the dough you've got two elements at work. There's the natural yeast, busily eating the starch in the flour and belching out carbon dioxide to create the rise and bubbles in the bread. And then there's a bacterium (similar to those 'good' bacteria you hear about with yogurt) that gives out lactic acid. It's the latter that puts the 'sour' in sourdough.

We worked on our kneading technique, wondering if this might be the weak spot and why our sourdough loaves were so flat, but it was a slow process. The recipe we were following seemed to use up most of the jar of starter for just a single bake (at that stage, we had no idea that you could easily multiply your starter) and so we were only able to experiment one loaf at a time.

I DIDN'T REALLY get the fuss around sourdough.

What I did get was that sourdough sat at the top of the bread pyramid. I was going to have to master it.

For me, it wasn't the taste of the bread I fell in love with, it was the starters. The first one that came in the mail from Hobbs House Bakery I named Ferguson. He became everything to me and keeping him alive and happy became my job. Ferguson needed ⅓ cup of warm water every morning and the same quantity of flour and then, once he had digested these, half of him had to be tipped away and he needed feeding again. He liked being warm, but not too warm.

I worried about Ferguson alone in the kitchen at night and would get up to check he was still alive, then one night I brought my duvet down to the wide cushioned bench against the wall and slept there. The next night I did the same, and the next night and the next. Knowing I was there for Ferguson made me sleep better and released me from a lot of the thoughts that were somehow trapped in my bedroom – feeling unnecessary and lonely. Being next to Ferguson made me feel the opposite; that I was needed and responsible. The family quietly ignored the fact that I was now sleeping on the kitchen bench and it became as accepted as not going to school or wearing the same outfit every day. It made my brain feel easier and that was all they wanted.

WE WEREN'T BRAVE enough to test our sourdoughs on anyone else yet, so we concentrated on the growing subscriptions for the overnight breads (see pages 152–155). Our range had expanded from the white bread to a whole wheat loaf we rather grandly called pain de campagne and Kitty's Marmite loaf, named the Comfort. This was the first time she had invented something by herself. The Comfort was very simple – an overnight white loaf with a hefty teaspoon of Marmite mixed in with the water – but it was inspired. The saltiness of the Marmite added something quite different to the crumb (what we later learnt bakers call the inside of bread) and the crust, when toasted, came up like Twiglets. It was, in every sense, a really comforting loaf.

Everyone on our subscription list lived within a mile radius and so, after the loaves had cooled down a bit, we would load the bread into the baskets on our bikes and go off delivering. This was a big thing for Kitty (and me, to be honest). Being out in public, interacting with people, I was a bit worried about how it might pan out after our very insular summer, but Kit was amazing.

People were genuinely excited to receive Kitty's bread. The buzz of handing over a warm loaf to a grateful customer lit a spark within her.

THE SUBSCRIPTION SERVICE gave me the confidence to go outside because I needed to know what people thought of my bread. I imagined them eating slices in the morning with butter and preserves and that fueled the pedals on my blue bike with the brakes I had to squeeze really hard. The more I went out, the safer I felt in Watlington. I had a checklist of who I would see in any one early morning delivery round. Bob, who looks after Watlington's streets with his cart and dog Sadie, would shout 'Kitty, Kitty, Kitty' as I passed. I would shout back 'Bob, Bob, Bob.' Maggie on her way to work at the chemist, who had been the Tawny Owl when I was a Brownie, and Darren from the Co-Op with his huge red beard would always wave. I would bike past the small white library, Biggles the hairdresser's, the War Memorial etched with the names of the five Harman brothers, my Uncle Hugh's house with the yellow sun on the front door and Mr Rawstrom's house with the puzzle table in the window. Calnan's the butcher's would be opening and Angela the greengrocer would be setting up in the space under the Town Hall. There was one house where, as I parked my bike outside, a toddler's head would appear at the window and then run round to the front door. When I knocked and he answered, I would pass the warm bag straight to the small brown-haired boy.

He would scamper back to the kitchen with the bread, hiccupping with joy. That felt really good.

The next thing we needed was a name. Dad and I started with 'Breadheads', but then Mum came up with the idea of 'the Orange Bakery' because of the orange soft cord dungarees I always wore, which made me feel safe. Gradually, the dungarees grew more and more encrusted with dough as the

weeks went on, like the barnacle-spattered hull of an old ship, before Mum made me wash them. They were almost like the third member of our team. So, the Orange Bakery we became.

Dad had an old box of alphabet printing stamps. He tied the right letters together with masking tape so we could stamp out the name 'the Orange Bakery' in black ink. Underneath, with a cut potato, I stamped the shape of an orange. For me, this was going back to the level of art I liked – potato printing. We bought some brown paper bags online and we all spent Sunday evenings printing up fifty bags at a go.

Our logo was born.

I loved the overnight loaves, but they weren't enough. I wanted to give Ferguson the audience he deserved, so I knew I had to crack sourdough. I kept working and working at the loaves, but I could not improve on the Frisbee shape. The feeds on Instagram showing those sourdough loaves that I became obsessed by – beautiful, dark and plump – felt way out of our reach. The mothership of them all was a bakery called Tartine. Started by a couple called Chad Robertson and Elisabeth Prueitt (he did the bread; she did the pastries) in San Francisco twenty years ago, their bread was like no one else's. Clearly every baker in the world wanted to be like them. They even had a quote from *Vogue* on the homepage of their website. 'Fresh out of the oven, each loaf has a shell of blistered mahogany and an interior so chewy and preternaturally moist that it shimmers in the light.'

This was the Beyoncé of the bread world.

I bought the first Tartine book (and the second) and then read it over and over.

KITTY OPENED THE Tartine book and showed me these beautiful, dark-crusted loaves that were just on the fringes of being burnt, but then revealed an extraordinary crumb when the loaf was opened up, looking more like a moonscape than a slice of bread. 'That's what I want to do,' Kit said. I thought of our flat brown sourdough loaves and doubted they could ever morph into anything so delicious looking, but Kitty just said, 'We can make bread like this.'

Reading up about these amazing loaves was one thing, but we quickly realized that what we needed to do was to see them in the flesh. Obviously we could not make a trip to California, but perhaps we could do the next best thing – visit professional bakeries that were making something similar to the bread made at Tartine. Kitty soon discovered that there was a clutch of brilliant places in London who aspired to the same kind of loaves as Chad and often had close links – the bakers having worked out of Tartine for a while. The thing was, all these bakeries seemed to be on the other side of the city from us, tucked away in Spitalfields or Hackney. Kit really struggled with being in a single small space for any length of time without her anxiety level going through the roof and so a long car journey was still out of reach. However, Katie noticed a little bakery, October 26, that had set up near Shepherd's Bush in West London. She dropped in one day as she was driving back from work and told us a bit about it. The bakery was a one-handed operation run by a woman called Raluca making a selection of sourdough bread and a few pastries from just a couple of small ovens at the back of the shop. It felt a doable journey time for Kit and so she found the bakery on Instagram and sent a long message, but she wasn't too disheartened when she didn't hear anything back.

We set off for this bakery one Monday morning. Kitty distracted herself on the journey by reading and re-reading an article on my Kindle about Chad Robertson that she had found online in *The New York Times*. She knew every word by heart. We brought with us a loaf of Kitty's Marmite bread, the Comfort, which she had cooked early that morning.

Kitty cradled the loaf on her lap like a small pug.

'Do you think she'll like it?' Kitty asked nervously. 'Yes, she'll love it.'

Raluca was a woman in her mid-thirties, small and slight, her hair tucked up with an elastic band. A selection of dark brown sourdough loaves was stacked onto a wall display and on the counter were cinnamon buns and some Madeleines. Kitty's eye, though, was instantly drawn to the slightly chaotic scene behind. Two small box ovens sat on some wooden pallets. Huge 50-pound flour sacks were piled up beside them and a couple of tall fridges completed the picture. This wasn't some sci-fi spotless kitchen. This was low-fi. Achievable. Replicable.

We waited for the previous customer to leave before introducing ourselves. 'Ah, yes. Kitty, of course,' she said apologetically, 'I'm sorry. I meant to get back to you, I've just been so busy. So, tell me, why do you want to be a baker?' While I can't quite remember what Kitty said, I do remember her tone; the enthusiasm and passion shining through. I felt enormously proud of her being able to capture it so eloquently.

I recall more clearly Raluca's response. 'I used to be in marketing, but when I had my daughter I got into baking and then when I was made redundant I thought, well, why not make it into a business. I knew how to put together a business plan, found a place, bought my ovens and suddenly I had a proper bakery.' She looked around her. I thought at first it was the wistful gaze of someone with a passion fulfilled, but I think it had been a long couple of days because her tone was brutally honest.

'Sometimes I am up at 4 am, sitting on those sacks there waiting for the ovens to warm up and drinking my coffee, and I think what monster have I created? If you want to have nice nails or wear a dress, forget about it. This is a really hard life. By the time I've lifted the flour from the pavement to here, I've carried half a ton. I'm trying to sell bread and at the same time get the next day's loaves started and it's really hard work. I'm sure you're a very good baker and this looks lovely,' she said, holding up our loaf, 'but I don't want to dress it up for you.'

Another customer arrived and we realized that we shouldn't hold her up. (Incredibly she seemed to be doing everything – the baking, the serving, the cleaning – herself.) Generously, she filled a bag with a selection of her bakes and passed it over to Kitty. 'It's been really nice meeting you,' she said, smiling at Kit, 'and good luck.' We waved our goodbyes and walked to the nearby park in silence. We sat down on a bench. I steeled myself to cope with the crushing disappointment that Kitty must have been feeling. Instead of tears in her eyes, what I got was a look of steely determination, a look I was to recognize more and more.

'I don't care about painting my nails or wearing a dress,' Kit said, 'I want to be lifting half a ton and getting up at 4 am. I don't like coffee. I'll work on that. But that's the life I know I could live.'

'That's exactly what I want. I want to be strong.'

4
RUTH THE ROFCO

I CAME BACK from that bakery visit with purpose. I looked at Ferguson. Together we were going to crack sourdough. For that, I needed Chad. Not his books, his Instagram or his articles; I needed him.

After a few quiet hours spent on the computer, I found Chad's home address in San Francisco. (I think if the bakery fails, I'm going into detective work.) A letter is always harder to ignore than an email, so I carefully drafted one. It was written by hand and it basically said,

Your book is the reason I get up every morning. How can I make bread as good as yours? Thank you. Kitty Tait, Aged 14, Watlington, England

But over three pages.

Chad runs a business employing hundreds of people and is probably one of the busiest people in San Francisco. I didn't hear back. I wrote again and this time I put in a hand-drawn picture of one of my failed flat sourdough loaves.

Days passed, which I spent inhaling every word of Chad's books. I took one of my old fluffy school socks, cut it open and used it to practice folding dough his way in any spare moment. Chad's technique is different from any other. It starts with his philosophy that the dough is alive. You treat it with total respect. You don't hammer it or knead it. You don't slap it or pummel it. You fold it and love it.

There is a dominant school of thought that, when it comes to breadmaking, you must show the dough who's boss. When thinking of making bread, you imagine a Frenchman with huge biceps in a small bakery slapping and pummeling the dough. I tried that, but I kept feeling guilty and apologizing to the dough. I loved Chad and his books for his philosophy that the more respect you show the dough, the better the loaf will be.

I've always been a looker-after.

When I was little, I spent a lot of time making sure that all my bears were happy and no one was left in the toy cupboard. I learnt how to make hot chocolate at the age of five and the second anyone in the house was in any way sad, I would emerge with a lukewarm milky cup whether they wanted it or not. I worried about people (and often things) being lonely. I got so worried about Ferguson being on his own that I read up on how to make another starter from a garden apple and called her Muriel. Dad has drawn how in 'Journey of a starter' on page 187.

I practiced Chad's recipes relentlessly and slowly my loaves started to look right. I fed Ferguson and Muriel every morning with a bit of warm water and flour. Once they were both bubbly and happy, I poured two-thirds of each of them into some flour and water, left all the ingredients to get to know each other and then added salt. The salt is like the loud friend at the party, no fun without it but quite disruptive. Salt hates yeast and slows its action down, so it helps to bring it in only after the flour, water and natural yeasts in the starter have had time to mingle. Using Chad's technique, I folded the dough over every hour for four hours until it was plump and gassy, then I tipped it onto the table and cut it into two rounds. This is when the sock practice came through, first flipping the dough onto its back, like a tortoise, then folding the edges into the middle like an envelope. I dusted the round of dough with a bit of flour and then put it in its shell of the bread basket (a banneton). It then went into the fridge.

At first, I didn't get this stage. It felt as though I was being cruel to my warm bubbly dough, but this long chilly sleep gives the dough time to develop a more intense flavor and sourness and the ingredients get a chance to grow into their magic. Being a bit more solid, it also makes it a lot easier to make slits in the top of the dough before baking. The slits allow a loaf to expand as it rises in the oven and prevent what I call 'the bulge' – when the bread doesn't have enough space to expand fully, it can tear open in an unexpected place. A well-placed slit can give a loaf a sort of fin that sticks out and makes the bread look like a well-fed shark.

Not leaving out a single step meant that, when we cut open these loaves, the crumb was totally different. Large and round and a web of gorgeous gluten.

Chad's method of nursing a dough was like looking after a baby. There wasn't really an hour in the day when I wasn't thinking about the needs of my dough. What stage was it at? Did it need to be fed? Was it ready for a nap? Or should it be woken up? All this meant I was completely focused on the breadmaking process. I now had this clear structure and knew I would be constantly needed throughout each day. I had to get up in the morning to feed Ferguson and Muriel. I needed to be there after lunch to turn the dough. I had to be there in the evening to put the dough to bed. I couldn't afford to phase out or lose concentration because the dough needed me.

Dad worried that the new loaves weren't quite ready to go public, but I needed to know if we were at least heading in the right direction. I worked and worked until I had a batch I was really happy with: twenty plump white sourdough loaves with dark brown crusts, sharp fins and a crumb that was like honeycomb. 'We can do this,' I told them as I gently cut each in half and put them in bags alongside the usual loaves going to our subscribers. I added in a note. 'These are my sourdough loaves to see if you like them. Thank you.' I wanted to add more, 'Do you like the crumb? What about the crust? How do you like the sour flavor?' But Dad said that not everyone would be as interested in bread as me.

Waiting to hear what everyone thought of my sourdough was so painful.

Waiting is my least favorite thing as you can't hurry it.

When I heard nothing for an entire day, I panicked that no one had liked the loaves. Then I bumped into (well, pretended to bump into) one of our subscribers, Susan Fotherby, who was coming out of the Co-Op. I tried to ask casually what she had thought of the half loaf. 'I didn't try it, I'm afraid,' she said. 'Will was home and finished the lot.'

It was all going to be okay. I went home to tell Ferguson and Muriel.

WE NOW HAD to add sourdough loaves to the mix as every single subscriber Kitty had sent a half loaf to wanted more. I'd have been happy to potter along with the small number of subscriptions we already had, but every time Kit was approached by someone wanting bread she always said yes.

Kit's night-time flits down the street carrying Dutch ovens were starting to take longer and longer. The logistics each morning of which dough needed to be in which oven and when it needed to come out was totally beyond me. Kit seemed to hang onto it all, but the situation didn't feel sustainable. Katie and I were worried that we were taking advantage of the kindness – let alone the electricity bills – of our neighbors Juliet and Charlotte. We needed to find another way.

Kitty, as always, was one step ahead. She had already started to research an oven called a Rofco. We'd seen them in October 26 in Shepherd's Bush and Kit had been on a quest to find out more about them ever since. A small Belgian company produced these compact box ovens, the biggest of which could take twelve loaves in one go. To us, used to squeezing four loaves into Juliet's oven at a pinch, it felt like the height of industrialization. In my typical way, though, I was full of practical caution.

Our house is an old one. Started in the sixteenth century with one central room and a big chimney, the house has been added to in layers and every builder seems to have been briefed to make no surface level or wall straight. If you were to put a marble on the top floor of the house, it would roll down to the bottom of its own accord. There are odd-shaped doorways, unexpected beams and wide cracks between floorboards. The rooms are freezing in winter with ancient radiators that get only slightly warm at best. The electrics have been patched together over decades – some of the sockets are still those tiny three-pin ones – and the whole house fuses when the heater in the bathroom is switched on. Any expectation that our basic fuse box could take an extra surge of electricity to power an industrial oven seemed not only naive but possibly catastrophic. Also, there was absolutely no space in the kitchen.

What was to follow set a pattern that has repeated itself several times over. My caution was bypassed by Kitty's sheer determination and Katie's optimism that it will all somehow just work out.

At the tail end of October, Aggie, Albert and I set off for a week's holiday in the Scottish Highlands. Kitty and Katie stayed at home with the dogs as the journey was too far for Kit and a big change in location and routine would have been impossible for her to manage. Even though it seemed odd having a split family holiday and we'd never done one before, I desperately needed a break and I was very conscious of both Aggie and Albert needing some time away.

The brutal truth was that, even with the breadmaking helping so much, we were only just coping with the distorted reality we were now in.

Katie and I continued to play tag with caring for Kitty. The needs of the rest of the family had to play second fiddle for a while, which Katie and I felt endlessly guilty about although couldn't avoid. Albert withdrew to his room in semi-hibernation and Aggie, fresh back from Ghana, found herself having to negotiate emotionally choppy waters. It had been really hard for both of them, but Aggie in particular. The younger sister she'd been very close to was changed. Kit found so many things stressful that, incredibly generously, Aggie moved out for a while to her uncle's house to give Kit space. Even though Hugh's was only round the corner and we could go round at any time, it had still been very painful for all of us when she moved out. The trip to Scotland was a chance to catch up with her properly. So, Aggie, Albert and I drove north in a rental car, which felt like a treat in itself after our long line of ancient, decrepit vehicles, although it took us half an hour to work out that it started by pressing a button. The novelty of heated seats got us most of the way to Glasgow.

The white crofter's cottage crouched on its own beside a loch. It had tiny windows, an ancient Aga and thick tweed blankets laid on all of the beds. The water had to be turned on by a tap up the hill behind the cottage and it came out thick brown. There was no WiFi. We went on long cold walks in slanting rain, saw no one and returned to the cottage to eat Hobnobs (plain and milk chocolate) and play cards in the tiny snug in front of the hottest stove in the world. On the last evening, we finally dared ourselves to swim in the loch and it was as cold as it looked. I don't think we talked about anything in particular, but for the first time in a while, it was a week when I didn't feel completely out of control.

We started the journey back home. On the way, flicking through her phone, Aggie stopped on Kitty's latest Instagram post. Kit had started the account when the Orange Bakery was born and it sat surprisingly easy with her. Because it was about bread and baking, she didn't overthink or overplan what she put on Instagram and was always just pleased if anyone liked her posts rather than judging herself by them. This latest one was a short film showing the end of our kitchen where we ate. Or rather a new version of it. Kitty had stripped the wide shelves of recipe books and the usual detritus that gradually builds up and replaced them with bags of flour and other ingredients. The round kitchen table had gone to be replaced by a much longer rectangular fold-up model, which had been in the garden shed and was now covered with floury bannetons. In the corner, where a cupboard had been, was a space

marked out with a square of masking tape and a single word written in capitals on an A4 sheet of paper; 'ROFCO'. I pulled over at a service station and texted Katie, 'Our kitchen?' 'A few tweaks,' she texted back.

When we got home, Aggie and Albert were yet again good humored about the fact that our entire kitchen was now a bakery. Eating together round the kitchen table had been a big part of our family life – even though at times it had been messy and argumentative – and Katie and I had been quietly smug that we had somehow managed to keep the routine going through the difficult teenage years. Like everything else, that had now gone. But the relief that Kit had something to distract her from the bleakness that could still swallow her made a future of eating on our laps in front of the TV doable.

I didn't mind so much about the loss of the kitchen table, but I still wasn't happy about the idea of a Rofco. It felt too permanent, signing up to something that could be and should be more fleeting.

The good news for me was that a Rofco was incredibly hard to get hold of; there was a waiting list as long as a baguette.

The bad news for me was that Kit is not one for waiting. Through her laser-targeted research, she had tracked down and befriended a source – Martin at Beckett's Bakery Engineers – and got her name high up on his list so that when a Rofco became free she could pounce. Kit has always been a saver and she had almost enough from years of birthday, Christmas and now bread money to make the purchase possible. She is also incredibly persuasive and had spent the week I was away talking to Katie about why the Rofco B40 was the patron saint of microbakers everywhere. Worn down, Katie eventually agreed to give Kit the last bit of money she needed. By the time I got back everything was firmly in motion. Martin had located a brand new Rofco, Kit had booked a delivery van and it was to arrive in a week's time. My job was to try and persuade our local electrician, Simon, to rejig our electrics so that I didn't have sleepless nights about the house burning down.

The oven arrived. It looked like a large, square, gray robot with one glass eye.

Katie looked slightly stunned as it was unloaded outside the front door while Kitty glowed beside it. We somehow got it through the narrow corridor, up three steps and round the corner into the kitchen. (Getting things through our house or not is a theme of this book.) 'We've got a proper oven, Dad,' Kitty said, sitting on it and beaming. Her joy wasn't totally matched by mine. Surreptitiously, I checked whether there was a market for second-hand Rofcos in case it was too much of a monster for us.

Part of Kitty's extensive Rofco research (which probably included the eating habits of the engineer who designed it and the manufacturing process of the screws that held it together) had involved tracking down other bakeries who used these ovens. She stumbled on a gem; someone who ran baking classes from her home in Gloucestershire using a Rofco. This was ideal. We'd get to see what the oven looked like in a normal kitchen and learn how to use it from an expert.

Danielle sounded fascinating. After her children had left home, she had decided to turn her breadmaking hobby into something serious. She left her husband at home to look after the cat and took herself off to Normandy where she trained as a professional baker and then worked in a bakery full time. When Danielle returned to her cat and husband, she set up her bakery classes.

The only hitch was the car journey to Gloucestershire. So far, the longest ride Kitty had managed had been to the bakery in West London. Being in the car could make her feel incredibly panicky and we'd had one or two disastrous journeys when Kitty had opened the door and got out (once while we were actually moving, albeit slowly) because she just couldn't bear the confinement. We went into training for the journey by downloading a relaxation app and trying breathing techniques until Kitty admitted she hated them and we stopped. We decided to just go for it.

Danielle told us to bring 10 bannetons of dough to bake, so Kitty sat in the car surrounded by small baskets. We talked bread for an hour and a half as – thank God – we met no traffic. Before we knew it, we were slipping past Bristol and up the Severn Estuary toward Gloucester. We were too early and so I took a side road down toward the canal to stop for a breather for Kit and a Thermos of coffee for me.

We stumbled upon Shipton Mill quite by accident. Sitting opposite us on the canal towpath, there was something distinctly dystopian about the buildings. A huge, white brutalist tower rose up in the center, flanked by long, low Victorian warehouses. Chutes and pipes spurred off the rooftops. The flat, gray industrial scene was in contrast to the brightly painted narrowboats moored to our side of the canal. The strangest thing was the lack of people or movement. You could hear noises – clanking, whirring, the occasional thud – but it looked like a ghost town.

Coffee finished, we got back in the car and headed to Danielle's house. It was her husband who answered the door first, no cat, and he wore the same look of surprise that Danielle did when she came to join him. 'Oh, but it's Tuesday,' she said. I smiled idiotically, trying to compensate for the look of horror that I knew must have been splashed across Kitty's face behind me. 'We're meeting on Thursday,' she finished. 'Oh, but...'

How had I managed to mess this up? I had a daughter who had climbed a huge mountain of fear to be here right now,

I had a back seat full of over-fermenting dough, and I had no idea what I was going to do now.

I tried begging. 'I've obviously been so stupid with my dates,' I said, 'I'm so sorry I don't suppose....?' 'I'm so sorry we're off into Cheltenham to meet someone for lunch. It's impossible,' she answered my half question with a sympathetic look. 'Don't worry at all,' I said, 'Thursday it is. We'll be back.'

I guided Kitty to the car and we inched out of the driveway, up to the main road.

I could feel Kitty about to explode.

I spotted a footpath sign immediately opposite. We lurched across the road, pulled up and she opened up the door and ran through the gate into the fields, tears streaming down her face.

I can't remember what we talked about on that bleak walk. I do remember the soil being that kind of heavy clay that adds a kilogram to the sole of your shoes (which, in my case, were hopelessly inappropriate suede). I also remember Kit's anger, frustration and utter resignation that we were going to have to drive all the way home again and then repeat this journey in 48 hours' time. There wasn't much I could say, but it was heartbreaking to watch. To see those fears so raw and exposed made me realize how amazingly she was doing to live with them most of the time. They were never gone, but baking could muffle them until they were barely audible. Symbolically, we threw the dough into a nearby bin and climbed back into the car.

To be honest, I never meant to go to Bristol, but I missed my turn and it was at that point I had a sudden brainwave. One of the Instagram feeds Kitty most enjoyed was for a bakery tucked under Temple Meads Station called Hart's. 'Let's go there,' I suggested. Kitty nodded.

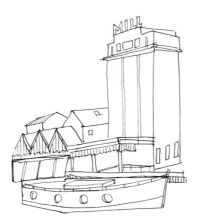

I HATED THAT my resilience was so low, but as soon as Danielle said it was the wrong day, all the demons that had been quiet enough to let me make the journey roared back in again. I can't remember the mud field, just the explosion of anxiety in my head and Dad trying to get me back in the car. I didn't even know we had turned off to Bristol until we were outside the station.

Dad parked the car and sat holding my hand until, eventually, we got out and went to find Hart's Bakery beneath us in the arches. We joined a queue behind parents with double buggies, students wearing bike helmets and smartly dressed commuters checking their watches so they didn't miss the train for their next meeting.

Once inside, the bakery was the coolest thing I'd ever seen in my life.

Long wooden tables filled with people dunking hunks of sourdough bread into soup, eating bacon sandwiches and enjoying slices of cheesecake.

The staff behind the counter had stud piercings and short fringes; one of them was wearing the Lucy & Yak dungarees that I lived in. The best thing, though, was that beyond the counter I could see the bakers pulling loaves of bread from the ovens. There was a low buzz from the bakers and my brain – exhausted from the terrible trip – unfurled a bit. I felt warm and at home. It was all so different. The menu was brimming with completely different flavors and ideas. A fennel and walnut loaf, sausage rolls sprinkled with za'atar, a lasagna pasty. An oozing cheese toastie went past, the sides crispy and slightly burnt.

I wanted desperately to be the other side of the counter, handling the bread with tattooed arms, wearing a stripy top and my hair pulled back by a wide headband.

For the first time ever, I experienced a world I could be totally part of. This was a world in which my anxiety played no part.

WE DID RETURN to Danielle two days later. Kit managed the journey by listening to back-to-back *Desert Island Discs* that featured people she liked the sound of. I think we did two Toms – Hanks and Jones. We discussed what we would choose as our luxury and book. Kitty chose to take Ferguson as her luxury and *Tartine* as her book – no surprises. I went for a lifetime's supply of cheese and *The Tiger Who Came to Tea* as it reminds me of my kitchen growing up. We unloaded our bannetons and Danielle took us through the workings of the Rofco and then, as our loaves baked, made us carrot soup for lunch. She was an incredibly thorough and detailed teacher and we left a lot more confident that we might actually be able to use our new investment.

On our way back we dropped in at Shipton Mill, this time to buy some flour. Once again, there was hardly anyone about but we found a small, square office in the courtyard. A woman in her mid-twenties took our order for a couple of flour sacks and we followed her directions to drive the car up to a warehouse. The plastic curtains flapped. She emerged from the warehouse, a 50-pound sack of flour carried easily on her shoulder.

I knew Kitty was watching the ease with which the woman slung the flour sacks around and how much she wanted to be like that – it was to do with not just strength but also purpose. I could feel Kitty's shoulders going back slightly as she imagined how good those sacks would feel.

I RETURNED HOME and stared at our Rofco, which still looked very clean and shiny but a bit less scary thanks to Danielle. Like I do with everything, I had to look after her and so first I gave her a name. Ruth. When I turned Ruth on and opened the oven door, she smelt of chemicals and brand-new shoes.

I put the first doughs in and stayed to watch them rise through the small porthole. At this point, I was still struggling to watch ten minutes of TV but I could easily watch bread bake for nearly an hour.

Slowly the pale dough transformed into plump golden loaves. When I took them out of the oven, they crackled and hissed happily on the shelf.

By the end of the week, Ruth was dough spattered and loved.

I could now bake 12 loaves in one go and the requests were flying in. Every time I was in the Co-Op – my orange dungarees covered with flour and dried dough on my Converse – I was asked 'Are you the baker girl? How do I get one of your loaves?' It was like being the drug lord of Watlington. I scribbled people's details on scraps of paper and sent them texts with the types of loaves they could order and on which days. There was no way I could keep up with all the extra deliveries on my blue bike, so Dad and I dragged an old white cabinet out of the garage, put it beside our house and coated the inside door with blackboard paint. On the blackboard door, we wrote people's names and which shelf their bread was on so they could pick the loaves up themselves. It was a primitive drive-through. Every time a car stopped and the cabinet door opened, Sparky and Sibby would bark. Sibby would then bark for another twenty minutes, stopping just in time for the next customer.

We called it the Magic Cabinet because quite often people would leave things for us in return. Notes and drawings, boxes of eggs and once a whole bag of something I didn't even recognize – they were quinces. Sometimes Juliet would leave flowers from their garden nursery. You never quite knew what would be there when you opened the door at the end of the day.

5

CHOP MORE WOOD

WHEN I WAS really ill, one of the strategies that Mum and Dad had tried (and to be honest, I think it was more to give themselves a break) was for me to go on short trips with a neighbor called Sarge. Knowing I wasn't well, he came by in his old red truck and offered to take me out on a drive to look at a local swilly hole and some piglets. Mum said, 'Thank you.' Before I could think too hard about it, I stepped up into the passenger seat. Sarge, who was in his sixties, lived near us and knew everything to do with the countryside. He had very strong opinions, including a hatred of planted rows of daffodils and houses with security gates in their driveways, and kept up an endless stream of mutterings about people who didn't know the real ways of the countryside, which I found relaxing to listen to.

Sarge started to take me on outings quite regularly. He told me what witches' brooms are (clumps of twigs growing in a ball in a tree) and showed me how mushrooms grow in a ring, and he also pointed out the houses he felt had been ruined the most by bad planning decisions. Because I only had to listen, it made me feel okay. And Sarge pretended not to notice when I had to sit on my hands to feel safe inside the truck.

On one of these trips, Sarge took me to see some pigs that belonged to his friends Andrew and Eilidh, who lived in a watermill, nearby in Cuxham, that they were doing up. They were unfazed by Sarge turning up with this 14-year-old who was clearly living in a different world and couldn't quite stay in the present.

They showed me their two pigs and Andrew told me about his legendary sausage making. Meanwhile, Eilidh pretended not to hear as she was fond of her snuffly friends.

I didn't see them again until Eilidh got in touch about the sourdough. She'd heard about it and asked for a loaf. I was so proud when she said she loved it. They are both brilliant cooks and run a catering service that dishes up the sort of food that you'd imagine Henry VIII would have eaten – pheasant pies, venison scotch eggs and rhubarb and ginger trifles. Every month, they open the front window of their watermill and people queue up to buy their incredible food: bags of homemade crackling, packets of beetroot-cured salmon, bowls of warm sticky toffee puddings, piles of custard tarts, trays of spiced Eccles cakes. A huge, glorious mixture is passed through the window to customers, which sells out in hours.

Eilidh rang to ask if I would like to sell my sourdough loaves alongside them through the window. 'Yes', I replied.

One Saturday three weeks later, I turned up to the fantastic chaos of their kitchen and watched in awe as they brought steaming trays of wild garlic and asparagus quiches out of their ovens alongside spicy pork pies. My 20 rustic sourdough loaves in their crate looked a bit scared. It was the first time I had sold bread outside the subscription, but it was okay. By 10.30 am, all my bread had gone. Andrew said, 'Well, that was alright then.'

IT WAS ANDREW and Eilidh who encouraged us to think about a Christmas bake. We trusted their opinion when they said our sourdough was really good. Providing we could generate enough loaves and set up the same kind of pre-ordering system they used, they suggested people could come to our door and collect their loaves on Christmas Eve. We would have to get up at 4 am to produce enough dough, but by doing a lot of scheduling on bits of paper, we worked out we could get 60 loaves plus some focaccia and a few baguettes in and out of the oven in a single day.

The orders were easy to get; the hard part was producing that much dough.

It was a lot harder than we thought. At that point, we were still doing all our mixing by hand. Kit and I would stand together, arms plunged into huge buckets, mixing all the water into the flour. By the end our arms ached.

We finished the last bake at 2 pm on Christmas Eve. We looked around. The kitchen was totally destroyed. There was dough in every single nook and cranny – even Sibby had some in her rough black coat – but we had rows and rows of paper bags ready and waiting to be collected. By teatime every bag had gone and more people had dropped by on the off chance – we could have sold it all five times over.

'You know,' said Andrew, as he came by to pick up their loaves as evening drew in, 'maybe you should think about a pop-up. You'll need to get your quality spot on, and that's not easy, but I think you could be onto a winner. I mean, look at this,' he gestured to the empty boxes that littered our front room. 'The demand is there.'

His words stayed with us and acted like a foghorn guiding us through what was, for all sorts of reasons, a hard Christmas. Without the focus of baking – we had persuaded Kitty to take two weeks off – her mind again went haywire. She tried unbelievably hard not to let things get in the way of the holiday, but her anxiety was there and our Christmas and New Year was subdued. Aggie and Albert conceded that we were nowhere near normality and their grace at the loss of the usual customs was almost overwhelming.

CHRISTMAS FELT LIKE something I had to survive and, as January started, all I could think about was getting baking again. And then it happened. Chad Robertson followed me on Instagram. I messaged him immediately.

'Woke up this morning on my mattress by my bread oven to discover you had followed me. I wasn't sure if I was dreaming. Sourdough is all I think about and all I do. It's magic, but only if you give it respect. One day I can work for you and I'm saving all my money to get to California.'

Re-reading this again now, I sound like a bread-mad Cinderella. I wonder if he spent the next month looking nervously at his San Francisco bakery door for a small, red-haired stalker to appear. I followed this up by messaging him five pictures of my bread. Sorry Chad.

Amazingly, two weeks later, a personal message came back. It was cryptic.

'Work hard and take a break to sharpen your axe – then chop more wood faster than anyone else until you need to sharpen the axe again.'

I read Chad's message over and over to decipher what it meant. The bit I understood was 'work hard', but it wasn't until a lot later that I appreciated the bit about sharpening your axe. The overall message was we had to do more.

When I was little, we had a brilliant babysitter called Harriet. She wore bright blue eye shadow and would let us get the art stuff out all over the table and put a mattress on the stairs so we could slide down it. Harriet lived with her family on the High Street. Her dad ran the local pub and her mum (another Katie – there are a lot of them in Watlington) taught Pilates in a small studio beside their house. The studio had low beams and a white painted floor. Pilates Katie was off to Canada for a while to see family and so, while we were talking to her about the possibility of holding a pop-up sale of our bakes, she immediately offered the space. It was the perfect solution.

I started to compile a list. Nutella swirls, soft cinnamon buns, and Scottish pastries called Rowies. (These were our versions of croissants, which we didn't yet feel confident to do, buttery, layered and delicious if not quite as beautiful as their French cousins.) And, of course, bread. Marmite and cheese, potato and chorizo and focaccia with rosemary and sea salt. The first pop-up was in for the end of January. I could make the bread, but I had no idea how to make people come. Brilliantly, my cousin Daisy gave us an idea.

THE CONCEPT OF yarn bombing is a great one. You make lengths of brightly colored knitting and then wrap them around tree trunks or weave them through railings. It is like soft graffiti, catching the eye and entering the subconscious. Then you hit the place with posters using the same colors to advertise whatever it is you are trying to publicize. In Daisy's case, it was a play her university were putting on when she was a student. I'd seen yarn bombing at work in my parents' village as well. Suddenly, one morning, people woke up to find little crocheted flowers tied to their door handles and then at Easter a whole tree blossomed with small knitted eggs. We wondered if we might do the same thing. We already had the color – orange, obviously. Now, we just had to learn how to knit.

Katie's sister-in-law, Lucy, who lives in Edinburgh, sent down a lovely length of orange knitting within days of us talking to her about our yarn bombing campaign. She'd created that in just an hour so, surely, we might be able to rustle up a few meters ourselves. We were hopeless. No amount of YouTube tutorials or one-on-ones from knitters we knew could unlock the magic that is knitting. It was, and remains, a total mystery to me.

We had sourced an endless amount of orange wool, though, in preparation for our prodigious knitting-fest, which sat in a basket on a high shelf away from Sibby whose new obsession was mangling the soft balls. It was Katie who came up with the solution.

Pompoms.

To my rather sad, easily impressed brain, pompoms are also a kind of magic, albeit on a smaller scale to knitting. Somehow lengths of wool wrapped around a couple of rings of cardboard transform into little balls of fluffiness. You can knock one up in five minutes while watching TV. Having made about fifty or so, Kitty put a picture up on Instagram asking for help. Suddenly, we were deluged with beautiful pompoms of every size – but all of them orange – left in the Magic Cabinet.

magic cabinet

NOW WE HAD to put the pompoms up. Mum was nervous about this bit. Did Watlington, who had been so nice to us, really want 500 orange pompoms invading the town? The rest of us overrode her, but we must have been a bit worried as we decided to put them up late one night the week before the pop-up. Me, Albert and Aggie went out with a huge box each and hung them everywhere. Lamp posts, benches, street signs, door knockers, the school gates, outside the public loos, by the bike stands, the iron ring where dogs were tied up outside the Co-Op. We got back at 10 pm and I went to sleep buzzing as Mum nervously twitched the curtains.

The next morning, I went out with Sparky wearing a pompom on his collar. There was the usual cry of 'Kitty, Kitty, Kitty,' from Bob and then he said, 'Are you responsible for these?' I tried to read his face. Bob is the Godfather of Watlington and, with his dog Sadie and his rubbish cart, he rules the streets. 'Yes.' I answered nervously. 'Well better give one to Sadie, then,' he said. I removed Sparky's pompom and put it on Sadie's collar. If Bob was on our side, it was going to be all right. A small heavily wrapped child went past – '45, 46...' – they were counting the pompoms. In fact, everyone was so nice about it and all the shops agreed to put them inside their windows, which led to lots of the houses doing the same. Watlington looked like it had been hit by a tsunami of satsumas.

Dad found a huge wooden wheel – the end of a vast electrical cable round – in a skip and painted it orange like a massive pompom with the words ORANGE BAKERY POP-UP HERE! We rolled it down the High Street and placed it outside the Pilates studio. We were ready. Ish.

Dad had promised to step in and teach some classes for a local school who were desperately short staffed that Friday, so the day before the pop-up I was on my own with the prep. I got the regular subscriptions out the way and had buckets and buckets of bubbling dough waiting to be baked the next day. Mum was at home working in the study and occasionally asked 'Can I help?' This normally meant washing up a few doughy spoons before her phone rang again. An old friend of hers dropped in for a coffee and stayed in the kitchen when Mum had to disappear, ringing phone in hand. 'This is all amazing. Can I help with anything?' 'You could just add the salt to the dough and squish it in,' I said, my hands deep in the trays. She did as I asked, then finished her coffee, gave up on Mum reappearing and left.

Just 20 seconds later, I looked at the white tub she had taken the salt from. It was sugar.

We had never marked either the salt or sugar tub because we automatically knew which was which. I thought I was going to be sick.

I GOT BACK from work at 6 pm and, with Kitty, tried to get the dough back to sour rather than sweet. We made it to bed at midnight only to be up at 4.30 am to start the bakes. I'm not totally sure Kitty went to bed at all, but I didn't ask. We needed all the time available if we were going to bake everything before 10.30 am and give it time to cool.

By 10 am I was panicking as we were never going to have everything ready.

I stood sweating by the oven, but there was nothing I could do to accelerate things. I decided it was better to take the bakes that were ready and set up the room, rather than hang around fretting. I left Kitty to finish off the last loaves and buns. Albert and I loaded up our car to drive everything up to the High Street.

Watlington is at its busiest on a Saturday. People come in from the neighboring villages to get their meat from Calnan's, the butcher's, and their veg from Angela at The Undercroft tucked under the Town Hall. There's normally a plethora of small figures either in pink and blue tutus or football kit ready for Saturday training. As I unloaded all the bakes, I said a few hellos to people I knew, but no one seemed terribly bothered by what I was doing. I brought the last crate in and closed the door behind me. Pretty soon Aggie joined me and we started to lay out the crates, working out the logistics of the 'flow' and where people would pay.

I felt so unsure and unbelievably tired. I imagined us standing in a room packed with bread and no customers.

I'd even rung up a couple of homeless charities in Oxford to ask if they would like to take the leftover bread if we didn't sell it.

Aggie kept having to reassure me. 'It will be alright,' she said, having caught me glancing up at the window for the umpteenth time. I'm not sure what I was looking for because the blinds were fully drawn – even a glimmer of interest would be good. 'People will come.'

At 10.50 am, the door flung open and Kitty and Katie came in carrying the last trays of loaves. 'Is anyone there?' I asked. 'Have a look,' said Kitty, beaming. 'They're actually queuing for our bread.' Through the blind I could just make out the silhouettes of figures standing in a line, like shadow puppets. As we made our final tweaks, I felt flooded with relief that we were at least going to sell some bread.

Four long trestle tables, covered in stripy cloths from Katie's mum, stood against the wall with large wooden crates holding the loaves and buns. We wrote the prices on small chalkboard signs, stuck them on cocktail sticks into fat oranges and placed them in front of each crate. At the end, we placed an orange cast-iron Dutch oven to hold the money next to 200 brown paper bags, hand-printed with our logo. We dressed the room with the last of the spare pompoms and Katie wore the orange scarf knitted by Lucy. As 11 am came round, we opened the doors.

Albert was on the till, Aggie was behind the pastries, Katie was on the bread with Kitty quietly correcting her every time she got the name of the bread wrong. I flitted about fetching bags and marshaling the queue. We hardly looked at each other as everyone who came in wanted to chat. At the end, when the last bun had been sold and we closed the door, I took a photo of us all jumping up in the air. As clearly as I can recall the photo, I remember all of us standing there in a slight daze.

Every last scrap had been sold. It had taken 24 hours to make everything and it had taken 23 minutes to all go.

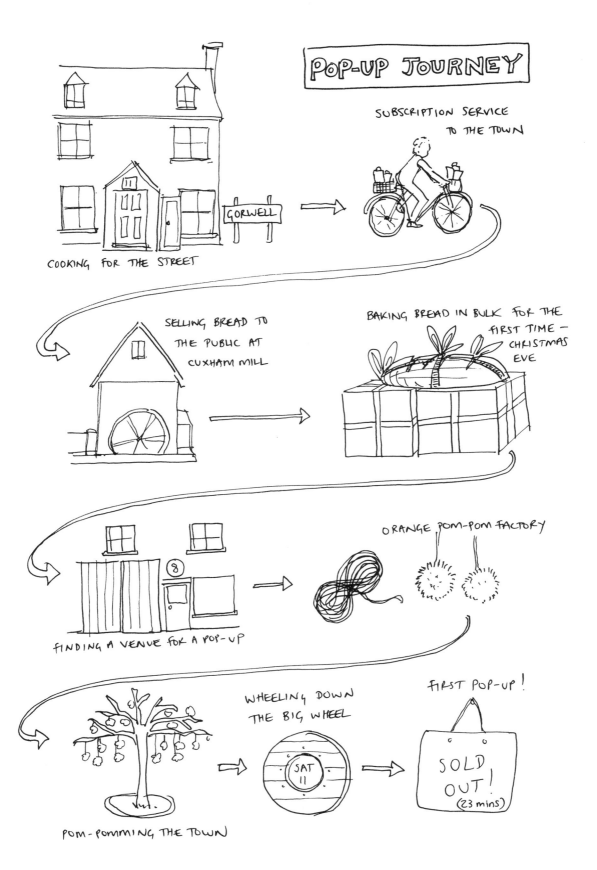

POP-UP JOURNEY

COOKING FOR THE STREET

GORWELL

SUBSCRIPTION SERVICE TO THE TOWN

SELLING BREAD TO THE PUBLIC AT CUXHAM MILL

BAKING BREAD IN BULK FOR THE FIRST TIME — CHRISTMAS EVE

FINDING A VENUE FOR A POP-UP

ORANGE POM-POM FACTORY

POM-POMMING THE TOWN

WHEELING DOWN THE BIG WHEEL

SAT 11

FIRST POP-UP!

SOLD OUT! (23 mins)

6

THE MILK CART OF DOOM

KITTY FINDS IT impossible to keep a secret, so I knew something
was happening in February when she kept asking me which city
I thought would have the best bakeries, but then answering for me,
'Paris?' Then one wet, gray Monday morning I came down to find an
envelope beside my breakfast.

Breakfasts are a really big deal for Kitty and by far her favorite meal.
She prepares for them like a military commander; poached eggs and
bright pink pickle on her favorite sourdough, or a bowl of oatmeal
with banana, toasted pecans, peanut butter and melted chocolate.
All plated up by the time I get downstairs, we sit and eat together.
Normally I scroll through Twitter while Kit flicks through bread posts
on Instagram (it's early and we don't always want to talk).

That morning Kit was watching me. I opened the envelope and inside
were two day-return tickets to Paris on the Eurostar. 'I got them in
the sale,' said Kit. 'I thought we could see it as a research trip.'

My first thought was how on earth was Kitty going to manage at
least six hours on a train in a single day when a two-hour car journey
could send her spinning off miserably, but I couldn't face saying
that when she looked so pleased. I just nodded and weakly said,
'Amazing. When?'

The answer was, as always with Kitty, the following week. We spent
Sunday night with Kitty's godfather, Al, in London – someone who had
been fantastic during the bleakest months, writing Kitty random and
often very funny postcards from his various travels – and got a taxi
to St Pancras at 5 am on the Monday morning. We caught the train
and I slept fitfully on the journey. Whenever I woke, Kitty was staring
fixedly out of the window, even when the view was one of blackness
in the tunnel. 'You're doing great,' I said. She forced out a small smile
and I could hear her rapid breathing.

Sidling into Paris through the rather gray suburbs, however, she suddenly became calmer and focused. Kit showed me the list of bakeries she had painstakingly researched and we opened up the Metro map on my phone to work out which one to visit first.

Du Pain et des Idées stands proudly on the corner of two streets, its old-fashioned painted glass signage fading in the sun. 'Fabrication Traditionnelle' is embroidered on the black awning that hangs over the doorway. It looks very smart and rather stuffy. You walk in expecting neat glass cabinets and carefully stacked loaves, but that's not what you get.

Inside Du Pain et des Idées it's a mess; a lively, tantalizing, glorious chaos.

Bread cools on the racks that are wheeled in and amazing-looking croissants and pastries jostle for position in trays. Two women in tabards speedily slip orders into paper bags and hand over the goods to customers who don't hang around for small talk. It isn't particularly friendly, but it's busy and exciting and there's a buzz. We felt the pressure as the queue of fur-hatted old women and young workmen got shorter – there was no hesitation allowed at the counter. We opted for an almost luminous green pistachio escargot (flaky pastry coiled like a snail's shell) and a quarter chunk of miche (a brown sourdough). We went outside and perched on a couple of concrete bollards. The bread was moist and chewy, if not particularly sour. The escargot, though, was ridiculous; soft croissant dough wrapped around a sweet but still salty pistachio frangipane. It was a good start.

Our next stop was a branch of Poilâne. This is probably the most famous bakery chain in Paris, suppliers of bread to the Élysée Palace, the presidential residence. Poilâne has been making sourdough bread since the 1930s and the current CEO is the third generation of the family. Apollonia Poilâne took up the role aged just 18 after her parents were killed in a helicopter crash. The big selling point of their bread is that it's cooked the traditional way in a huge wood-fired oven. It was brilliantly overpriced. Our mistake was going to a small branch in a smart neighborhood rather than the central one, which was just too far away.

The bread at Poilâne was good, but the atmosphere felt more like a jewellery shop than a bustling bakery.

We tried a couple more bakeries before we struck gold with Ten Belles Bread. Sitting on a side street a few blocks away from the Canal du Midi, the bakery occupies the ground floor of an ugly apartment block – no attempt has been made to dress it up. A supporting wall cuts through the middle of the space; on one side is the bakery and on the other is the counter, leading through to what must have been a courtyard and is now a café seating area. The queue was quite long and so we took a seat in the waiting area where the low shelf was lined with, surprisingly, English books, many of them cookbooks. There was something rather incongruous about finding Delia Smith and Mary Berry jostling for space in this corner of Paris, but then Kitty, researcher supreme, reminded me that the main baker who had set this bakery up, Alice Quilter, was half-English.

A space appeared at the counter. I went for a breakfast brioche, a swirl of buttery dough flecked with bacon and mushroom, while Kitty opted for something sweet, a rye and bittersweet chocolate cookie with sea salt flakes. Then we chose a loaf of dark crusted bread. The loaves were almost black – like a photoshoot for Tartine turned up a notch. Sure enough, Alice had put in some time working with Chad Robertson in California and it showed. We ripped off a hunk of crust and scooped out some of the rich brown crumb. Compared to the Parisian loaves we had tasted so far, this was so much fresher and lighter. 'This,' said Kitty, mouth half-full, 'this is exactly what I want to make. Do you think they would let me have a look behind the counter?' 'I don't know,' I said, rapidly flicking through my internal dictionary of French to see if I had any words capable of asking. It's a very small lexicon and I was about to come up with an excuse not to when the girl clearing our space said in a Mancunian accent, 'Why don't I ask? I'm sure they wouldn't mind.'

It turned out her name was Jess and she had moved to Paris six months earlier. She was an artist who had got a job working at Ten Belles and loved it. Jess was kind enough to ask about the Orange Bakery and then disappeared behind the wall. Poking her head back round, she beckoned to Kit to join her. I went off to re-join Delia and Mary, watching smart Parisians wander in from the street and feeling very British in my flat cap.

Kitty spent a good half an hour in the kitchen and returned with a small armful of goodies. 'Au revoir,' waved the baker who had been her tour guide, 'and come back and work for us one day.' We butted into Jess's conversation with a customer to say thank you. 'A pleasure. And when I'm over next, I'll have to come and visit to get your Comfort loaf. If there's one thing I miss, it's Marmite.'

When we returned home, we actually sent off a Comfort loaf in the post to Jess. It must have been fantastically stale by the time it arrived.

Nonetheless, Jess was very sweet about it and she sent us a picture of it with a poached egg on top.

After eating all our Ten Belles goodies on the Paris version of New York's High Line (an old overland railway track converted into a walkway threading through part of the city), we finished our trip by walking up to Montmartre, something I had never done before. It had been quite a gray, murky day, then as the daylight faded and the lights came on, Paris started to glow. We were both too exhausted and footsore to say much, but I knew the trip had been good for Kitty.

She realized that she could do this and, in turn, that allowed her to fantasize about a future away from home (which mainly seemed to involve living with Jess and riding a Vespa around the Parisian streets).

PARIS MADE ME determined to crack croissant pastry. The only time we'd eaten croissants as a family was when we stayed with Dad's parents and the packet of six from the Co-Op would be warmed in the oven to be placed on the breakfast table, along with grapefruit halves sprinkled with brown sugar. To me they were slightly pointless flaky crescents that Mum dipped in her coffee.

Tasting the escargot with the salty pistachio paste from Du Pain et des Idées turned on every single light in my head.

What I hadn't previously got was that croissant pastry could carry a whole load of other very delicious stuff. Scrolling through different bakery feeds on Instagram, there was one I kept going back to, Pophams in North London. Every picture they posted had me dribbling. Finally, I persuaded Mum to take me there. I woke her at 6 am the following Saturday, so we could be outside as Pophams opened. Mum is not, and has never been, an early riser, which meant not talking and having a coffee ready for her for the car journey to Islington. When we got there, it wasn't open for another half an hour. Mum went off in search of coffee number 2 while I spent the time sat on a bench outside Pophams looking at other bakers' posts on Instagram.

Right from the beginning, there was one baker who just made me laugh. Ducky was from Yorkshire and had first messaged me when I posted asking for advice on which dough scraper to buy. This exchange quickly moved on to a long and detailed discussion on what we most like putting on toast and other people's terrible choices. (Sardines is my worst. Ducky's favorite is peanut butter and honey.) Every time I messaged him, he was in a state of sleep deprivation as he worked so hard. At 17 he had left school to become a baker and the fact that I was only 14 never struck him as odd. His sleep deprivation meant our conversations could become slightly surreal, like how we would go into cheese making if our hands got too wrinkly from kneading dough so the buttermilk would make them softer. Like me, he is obsessed with pastéis de nata (Portuguese custard tarts) and makes the most incredible ones with the juice of blood oranges. That morning, I spent the time sat outside Pophams messaging him about how we were going to set up a pastéis de nata bakery called The Duck and The Cat.

Mum reappeared just as Pophams' doors opened and we were first in. I couldn't decide between the sea salt and rosemary twist, za'atar croissant, pain au chocolat the size of my face or bacon and maple swirl. Mum got them all and we settled down to start eating. I was staring so hard at the bakers that the man behind the counter asked me if I would like to see what they were doing. Before he finished his sentence, I was beside him, beaming. As Mum read the papers, I got a full tour. I met the owner, Ollie Gold, and the head baker, Florin, who had the best-ever tattoos of a spoon, a fork, a spatula and, of course, a croissant. The bakery itself was tiny, but somehow everyone moved smoothly around each other as rack after rack came out of the one oven.

The next week I returned to Pophams with Dad, who wanted to see for himself what I had been talking endlessly about all week. This time I felt like a regular as I was ushered behind the counter to see Florin and talk pastry dough and which tattoo I was going to get when I turned 18. I was there for two hours. The following week Ollie got in touch (I think they were worried I would keep coming back) to say that they'd just upgraded their mixer and the old one was going spare, and did I want it? Within 12 hours I got Dad back in the car and we headed straight to North London. I hugged the mixer the entire way home. It was a gamechanger.

The mixing by hand took hours and had given me the biceps of a mini Dwayne 'The Rock' Johnson.

Getting the mixer meant we could produce double the quantity of dough in half the time without the aching arms. We put the mixer in pride of place beside Ruth the Rofco and I named her Margo.

THE GENEROSITY OF fellow bakers seems to be a trait of the profession. It wasn't just the incredible mixer from Pophams; we had been given so many other things as well. Kit made a return visit to Hart's Bakery in Bristol with Katie and met the owner, Laura. She gave up her time in the middle of the lunchtime rush hour and a few days later sent Kit a whole set of bannetons. Ducky introduced us to Campbell, who owns Rackmaster, a company that makes bakery equipment. After seeing what Kitty was doing, a huge second-hand dough table made from steel and wood turned up. We had to lift it over the garden wall to get it into the kitchen as there was no way of getting it down the corridor. They all believed in Kitty and their validation gave her a tremendous sense that what she was doing, what she was dreaming of doing, was real. The equipment was a huge bonus, enabling us to switch up several gears but, more than anything, these bakers were generous with their time. Despite their busy lives everyone we came across wanted to help and share their expertise. Kate Hamblin was a perfect example.

Kitty was still attending regular appointments at CAMHS. To make them more bearable we would plan something to do afterward that always involved bread. Kitty found out about a bakery in Iffley in Oxford, a short drive from her appointment, and one Friday we went to find a small, very neat shop with old-fashioned lettering above the bay window that read 'Hamblin Bread'.

Kate Hamblin had been running her bakery for a couple of years. It was a deeply impressive operation, even though it was smaller than Hart's Bakery in Bristol or Pophams in North London. Kate pretty much does everything herself. The range of breads is simple but perfect: a country sourdough made with heritage grains, a free-form bake (that isn't shaped in a banneton) called a Stockholm Loaf and a seeded rye. Her commitment to using British grains is strong.

Kate herself is similar to the bakery; quiet, stylish and very calm. Again, her interaction with Kitty was utterly on a level.

Because we lived nearby, Kate immediately offered Kitty a chance to come and work alongside her.

Kitty came back from the sessions buzzing with different techniques, slightly awestruck by Kate's understanding of bread and dough, and more than ever with an appetite simply to learn.

EVERY TIME I visited a bakery, I had so many questions and wanted to find out more. Mum will never be interested in breadmaking and she refuses to understand sourdough beyond eating it, but she was always happy to go on a field trip, and I always had a grateful coffee at the ready. Once she came back from a visit to the dentist with an article, guiltily ripped from the waiting-room magazine, about a bakery called Pump Street in Suffolk, which she liked as it was run by another father and daughter. We could go and have a look, she said.

Two weeks later, the two of us set off for a small Airbnb in Orford, Suffolk, with Sibby and Sparky. I messaged Pump Street ahead of time, but didn't hear back. On the first morning at our bungalow, I got up at 6 am, left Mum asleep and headed off to see if the bakery was open. I took the dogs and walked 15 minutes to the center of the village where Pump Street sat on the corner of a square. What I didn't realize was that they don't bake on site, so the shop was silent and the village deserted. There seemed no point going back so I sat on the bench outside with Sparky and Sibby, like a stakeout, and messaged Ducky for a chat.

At 8 am a woman got out of her car and went to unlock the bakery door. As she turned around, I was right behind her. 'Hello,' she said nervously.

I had practiced what to say and ended up sounding like a clipped robot. 'I'm a baker. Can I see around your ovens?'

Sibby barked at her and pulled on the lead. She stepped back a bit. 'I'm so sorry, we don't bake here, but about half a mile away. I can ring the head baker and ask if you can look around?' For once, Sibby stopped barking and allowed her head to be patted. The women got out her phone. 'That would be amazing. Thank you so much,' I said and headed back to our bungalow to tell Mum.

An hour later, we arrived at a small set of barns on the edge of the village. Eventually, after finding the door, we were met by two bakers who were just coming to the end of their night shift. They were scooping out the fillings for Eccles cakes. The head baker appeared and shook my hand. He had obviously been briefed about this small girl who might appear. He took me upstairs while Mum stayed and chatted to the Eccles cake crew.

At the top of the barns were three mixers all doing different jobs.

A spiral mixer, a hand mixer and a paddle mixer. It was like my room of requirements from Harry Potter.

The head baker showed me how each of them worked and answered my non-stop questions with a lot of patience. Meanwhile, Mum quizzed the girls below about their work-life balance and how they had ended up as bakers and whether they enjoyed it. I think they all felt they had been through a sort of Sherlock Holmes level of investigation, but incredibly the head baker said I could work a shift with them the next morning. Leaving Mum snoozing with the dogs, I was there at 5 am the next day and learnt how to perfect the Eccles cake. Later, we walked by the sea and ate them. The dogs licked the crumbs off our fingers and it all felt so good.

EVERY TIME KITTY went off to see another bakery, she came home brimming with ideas to try out at our pop-ups and her baking just seemed to move up another level. She has an extraordinary ability to understand what flavors go together, how long something needs in the oven and how to take something from ordinary to extraordinary.

Kitty was obsessively learning – both from bakers and from cookbooks – all the time, but I realized that a lot of it was innate and she somehow understood how ingredients could be combined to shine.

Buns appeared flavored with cardamom and orange or fig and walnut. She added miso and sesame seeds or chocolate and walnuts to the dough mix for the bread. She whirled around the kitchen, adding and tasting, folding and whisking like Remy in *Ratatouille* (one of her favorite films). The more she baked, the longer the queues grew.

We did realize, though, that we were going to have to find a new venue for our pop-ups soon. Pilates Katie was coming back from Canada and, totally understandably, was going to need her studio back. In the middle of the High Street sits Watlington Memorial Club. With seven rooms over three floors, there is normally at least one birthday party with balloons in progress and it hums to the sound of band practice or thumps to the sound of judo and Zumba classes. The ground floor has a bar and a large room that always has the faint smell of stale beer, but it was free on Saturday mornings and it was the perfect size.

This time we decided to advertise our new venue with a Miss Marple-style mystery. We potato-printed our orange onto big brown labels and then wrote out the word 'Here?' We put them up in windows throughout Watlington. As always, everyone's tolerance of us was high. The signs went up everywhere, in the estate agent's (not an implausible venue), in the town loos (less likely) and under the small play hut in the paddock by the climbing frame (frankly impossible). As usual, Bob was very understanding of us disturbing the equilibrium of Watlington's tidiness. Finally, the week before the pop-up, we fixed a huge, great painted orange sign to the door of the Memorial Club proudly announcing 'HERE!' along with the time and date.

This time we were joined at our pop-up by Andy, who had asked if he could sell a few of his homemade loaves in aid of a children's home in Ghana he'd always supported. Andy was in his mid-seventies and we knew him well through his daughter, Mandy. She had taught tennis to our three children (and most of the children in the town, for that matter) on the three courts behind the Memorial Club.

Andy was also famous for the fact that he owned a sweater made out of dog hair.

The story was that he used to look after a huge Husky every summer when its owners went away. Whenever he groomed the dog, he was left with massive clumps of hair that he thought was wasteful to throw away. So Andy taught himself how to twist the dog hair into yarn and then, after a few years when he had enough, got someone to knit him a pullover. He didn't wear it on the day of the pop-up, but he did turn up with six small white loaves that he carefully laid out on kitchen towels. They sold almost before anything else, mainly because this was Watlington and everyone knew Mandy and so wanted to support Andy.

THE GREAT THING about the Memorial Club was that we had more space to play with. And there was so much more I wanted to do. I always carried a small notebook with me so that I could scribble down new baking ideas. Each bake led to an idea for another one. Trays of Pillows of Joy (little flumps of sourdough doughnuts dusted with ginger and sugar), Finnish Fannies (a butter brioche with pearl sugar and a brilliant name) and hazelnut and bittersweet chocolate bear claws would disappear almost as soon as I brought them through the door.

The pop-up space was brilliant, the subscriptions were under control, my mind was behaving most of the time.

When we got a call from Soho House, I felt I was flying.

They had heard about us through one of our customers who knew their events manager and asked if we would like to do a pop-up at their Oxfordshire venue in a couple of weeks. After a lot of time spent googling every single thing about Soho House, including all the celebrity guests who had ever stayed there, I was beyond excited, as was Mum who even asked if it might be necessary to stay overnight as it was such an early start. Sadly, it wasn't.

We canceled the Memorial Club for that Saturday. Me, Dad, Aggie and Mum set off for Soho Farmhouse at first light with the car brimming with bread, loads of different pastries, our printed bags and our orange Dutch oven to hold the money we were going to take.

The first problem was our arrival. We hadn't realized that no one can drive into Soho Farmhouse, instead you have to park on the outskirts and get transported in. Already feeling slightly out of our depth, we parked our muddy car up beside a row of four-wheel drives, unloaded everything and were directed toward a line of chauffeur-driven electric milk carts, all painted in pale green with long wooden bench seats. Clutching the crates of bread, buns and bags, we managed to get up the steps into the cart. We sat facing each other, nervously, as we were driven along a short track to a courtyard surrounded by barns. It started to rain.

The day got colder and colder as we set up alongside a handful of artisan stalls mainly selling candles and wooden toys. Gray drizzle pattered on our orange bunting. Families came past, bundled up to their ears against the weather, stopping only to glance at the small petting pen to our left where a sheep was happily lying with her two lambs under a shelter made of hay bales. At one point I wondered if I could get in there with her.

Aggie and I spent a lot of time sneaking into the restaurant loos to try and get warm under the hand dryer and casually looking around to see if we could spot anyone famous. Mum bought a lot of coffee.

Two hours passed and the wind got even sharper. The sheep and her lambs were taken away to somewhere warmer. We were cold and wet. But far worse, we had sold just three loaves and five cinnamon buns, and those I think may have been pity buys. No one wanted to stop and chat or buy anything when there was a warm barn right there with mugs of hot chocolate and beautiful cushions and sheepskin rugs. By lunchtime we gave up. We had to repack everything back into a milk cart, smile at the nice man driving it until we got back to the car, then load it all back in. We drove home quietly.

I felt terrible. We had deserted Watlington for customers who already had a lovely restaurant to go to and just weren't interested in buying bread. It was like the fairytale of The Fisherman and His Wife. Persuaded by his wife, the fisherman asks an enchanted fish for a nicer house to make her happy and yet she keeps wanting more and more, until eventually she realizes that she was happiest in their first house. Or something.

When we got home, I bagged all the breads and put them in the Magic Cabinet and stacked the buns in a covered overflow box. I put a post on my Instagram to say they were there.

Within five minutes Sibby started barking. From upstairs I could see the cabinet door opening and closing.

Within an hour it was all gone, every last crumb. There was a note left in the Magic Cabinet saying, 'Phew! In-laws are here and had promised them your cinnamon buns.'

I really love Watlington.

7

WE GET INTO
NUMBER 10

LIFE WAS NOW moving toward some sort of tentative normality. Kit and I ran the subscription service during the week – experimenting with different loaves, leaving them in the Magic Cabinet to be picked up – and then geared up for the weekly pop-ups at the Memorial Hall each Saturday. Kit's anxiety was far more manageable. She was still being seen by the mental health team in Oxford, but the appointments were further apart.

Whenever she could see a wave of dark thoughts approaching, she could normally sidestep them by concentrating on whatever stage the bread was at. She was able to pack up her duvet in the kitchen and reclaim her bedroom, painting it chalky pink and filling it with green plants. The adrenaline-pumping fear we had lived with for the past few months started to subside and her ear-to-ear smile began to make a regular return. Desperate to hang on to this new normality, we tried to ignore the two large elephants in the room.

The first was Kitty's education. We were nearly a year on from her crashing out of school and for most of that time learning hadn't been any sort of priority – we were just focused on getting her through each day. From the very beginning her school had been great and tried to make things work for us. The headteacher, Mr Hunter, had sent me such an incredibly supportive email about how they were thinking of Kitty and would do anything they could to help her return, that reading it left me gulping. They sent over work packs that mostly sat in a corner. Kit and I tended to drift toward what I knew and she enjoyed, bits of history, the GCSE poetry module, biology and maths. It was a bit of a motley collection, but it was something. One of the first questions people tended to ask, not unexpectedly, was 'Will Kit be doing her GCSEs?' We would mumble some response like 'Yes, she'll do a few,' or 'She'll just take the basics,' but we didn't really have a plan how this was going to happen.

The second elephant we kept avoiding was the fact that I had pretty much stopped working to bake with Kitty and how long that situation was sustainable. Other than the odd bit of teaching, I had given up any regular income and so that meant we were living entirely on Katie's wages. For the time being we could get by; however, we could see university looming for Aggie, and soon after Albert, and it was all just untenable. We were making a bit from the 150 or so loaves we were selling each week, but that was nothing like enough. And it was more than that. Now we were past the crisis months, I wasn't quite sure in what direction I was headed. I felt a bit of a fraud. I hadn't completed a baking course or worked for years in a professional kitchen in France. I was a teacher who was doing a bit of baking to help my daughter and I hadn't signed up anywhere for any of this to be my 'life change'.

It felt like this career change had just happened, rather than being a deliberate decision I had made. And I always seemed to be two steps behind Kitty.

ALL I COULD really think about was bread. How could I improve my loaves? What ingredients would sing together? Walnuts and olives or roasted potato and garlic? Would crisps work in a bake or go soggy? How much za'atar was too much? Why were the miso and sesame loaves always the first to go? Did it matter that the turmeric baguettes made your breadboard slightly yellow? Although I liked it, why was no one else keen on cranberries in focaccia? And if I wasn't thinking about bread, it was baking. Buns with camembert became brilliant with a tiny drop of sriracha, tahini and beetroot made brownies that bit more squidgy and baking the cheese and Marmite swirls for an extra five minutes made the edges brilliantly crunchy while the middles stayed soft.

I also created a new loaf for my brother after he complained that the holes in our sourdough let the butter drop through. Scrolling through Instagram I came across a Japanese technique for making bread called the tangzhong method. You make a roux with flour and water and then add butter and milk to the dough along with the roux. I have no idea what happens next in terms of the science, but the end result is a loaf with a crumb so fluffy and light that it's like eating clouds. There are no holes and this loaf can carry a layer of butter thick enough to see your teeth marks. I called it the Albert.

I was desperate to keep inventing more, trying more and learning more. To disappear entirely inside the world of baking. I wanted to be older so badly, but I was still 14 and Mum and Dad were terrified that I was just going to slip out of the education system entirely. So we kept going. Dad got the work packs sent over by my teachers and we would sit together, with Sparky on the sofa and Sibby gnawing the chair leg, and try out the maths, English and history worksheets. As soon as I started the emptiness would return, although I tried not to show Dad. I went through the motions of ticking the boxes of pronouns and highlighting the pathetic fallacy, but I couldn't make any sense of why it mattered other than it was something that had to be completed. I didn't want Dad to feel bad but the second he felt we had done enough I shot back to the kitchen, scooped some dough out of the buckets and the churning in my stomach would subside.

The only thing that made sense to me was bread, and the only thing I wanted to do more of was bake.

I knew Dad felt unsure as to where we were headed, but I also knew I couldn't do any of it without him. Dad's superpower (and I don't think he even knows this) is that when he gets behind you, he makes everything happen. He was always the one to make sure we had enough flour or fixed the mixer or ordered more bags. Dad is an upside-down swan. All paddling legs on the surface while quietly getting on with it underneath.

I needed to persuade him that the best way forward was forward. That we needed to chop more wood, as Chad said.

And we were about to get the chance.

It was at the end of a Saturday pop-up, as I was bagging up the last four doughnuts, when I saw Mum deep in conversation with a man who looked like Paddington Bear in leathers, clutching a motorbike helmet.

When they finished chatting, he gave Mum a card and walked off holding our last brown sourdough. Mum gestured to me with the flappy hands she does when she gets excited.

'He owns a shop on the High Street. The Rhubarb Tree. Number 10. The one no one goes into. It's going to be up for rent. He wants to know if we'd be interested. Here's his card, he's called Brent.'

We looked across to Dad who was eating the last sausage roll – a few pastry flakes nestled in his beard – and knew that this was going to be a step too far. Without any doubt at all, I knew that it was the way we had to go.

WE WERE NOT ready for a shop. We weren't really coping with Kitty's education as it was, let alone if we had a shop to run too. Plus I had no idea how having a shop even worked. Did you need to be registered? Have a till? Pay tax? Get insurance? Would we ever be able to go away again? Perhaps most pertinently for me, was I signing up to be a full-time baker?

The career path I'd followed might not have been totally conventional or particularly linear, but there was a logic to each step – from mainstream to special needs teaching, dyslexia assessment and coaching other teachers and then finally working with undergraduates at Oxford. There was a thread that tied everything together. Now we were barreling down a route that was completely unknown and my thread felt a bit redundant.

The weekly pop-ups and subscription service could be easily unpicked, but a high-street shop was another level of commitment and it terrified me. The few people we mentioned it too looked mildly skeptical. 'That's a lot to take on,' was the usual response, along with 'But how will Kitty fit it in around schoolwork?' I felt like I was being a really rubbish parent even thinking about it, but the light in Kitty's eyes was firmly switched on.

Kitty operates at her very best when she has total conviction toward something. She knew that the queues at our pop-ups and the amazing comments about our bread and buns meant something. She also knew taking on the shop was the obvious next step. Whatever potential problem I brought up, she had an answer for. Like a ferocious red squirrel working at a nut, Kit eventually made me crack. Katie watched from the sidelines, having realized the second the shop was offered it was going to happen, but let Kit make the case. One of the things that Brent had kindly offered, which helped me sleep at night, was an initial three-month lease – if we utterly failed, we could at least walk away. We had decided we could open four days a week and so somehow we could fit Kit's education around the baking.

The major hurdle I couldn't see a way round was that we just didn't have the money to set up a bakery. And there was a lot to do. The shop currently sold gifts, the kind of thing you might hastily buy for your mum for Mother's Day when you suddenly realized that it was tomorrow. Mugs decorated with birds, 'Spires of Oxford' tea towels, metal dogs as doorsteps, the Queen with a nodding head and a few cards and balloons. Alan, the current shop owner, was gloomy. 'It's not got the footfall. Been in retail a long time, but this one was a mistake.'

Besides Kitty and I never having heard the word footfall before, it wasn't that positive a start. Plus, the shop had harsh strip lighting, the walls were lined with a very practical but ugly shelving system and the floor was covered in peeling tiles. Still, there was a back section to the shop that might just be roomy enough to bake in. We'd do the bulk of the work at home, but we could bake some of the buns and pastries onsite in the mornings to try and clear space in our kitchen at home, but we'd need an oven, a sink and a water supply. On top of the deposit and legal fees, this would add up to way over £5k. I felt almost a sense of relief that the one thing Kitty couldn't do was magic up the money.

It was going to be too much.

'YOU SHOULD THINK about crowdfunding.' We were at Andrew and Eilidh's looking at their new chicks and talking about the shop when Andrew handed me the idea. 'Basically,' he said, 'you tell people about your project and what you need and, if they believe in you, they donate a small amount of money. It's all done online. I think you've got a really good chance.'

Standing beside me, I could feel Dad's shoulders sag a bit.

As soon as we got home, I started researching and found a site called Kickstarter. It was perfect. You posted a description of what you wanted to do and why, set a funding goal and asked backers for small donations in return for rewards. If you didn't meet the target, no money was taken from the possible investors. Lots of foodies seemed to have successfully used Kickstarter. As rewards, we could offer free loaves and a party at the shop to say thank you.

Dad didn't get it. Why should anyone help us to set up a bakery? He wasn't trained, neither was I, and it was all so quick. Maybe we should wait a few years. Over the next month I slowly worked on him. We might not get this opportunity again. It was fairer than the subscription service because anyone could come into a shop and not have to pre-order (this was a good line). We could bake so much more and it meant I could try out all my new recipes (this was quite a good line). The shop was sad and needed a new owner (this was a bad line and didn't work at all). But Dad did like the idea that if we didn't reach the sum we needed to set up then no money was taken from those who pledged, and if we did reach our funding goal then we could offer lots of rewards to everyone for helping us.

Finally he agreed, but I think mainly because he didn't believe it would really work.

I looked at lots of other proposals on Kickstarter and worked out what we needed to do. It was one thing to make an appeal, but we needed people to hear about it. I realized I could use my Instagram. We had now been baking for nearly a year and most weeks I posted a couple of things about what we were doing. New recipes I was trying, Dad and I on our delivery bikes, Sibby eating the orange pompoms, brilliant illustrations of all of us by Aggie and how to make a Cereal Killer bun (using the sweet milk left in the bottom of your breakfast bowl). I had been lucky in gaining followers and they were kind to me. We'd already had a bit of publicity and through that more people who loved baking had found me. It made me feel part of this amazing bread world. My favorite posts were the short, stop-animation films I made with my bakes as different characters. Dad had tried to show me how to do this on his phone the summer before, but I hadn't shown much interest then.

Now I loved these animated films as a way of getting people to understand that bread and buns are basically alive.

The film for our Kickstarter proposal was going to be the ultimate production. The cast. The crew. The music. I drew up a storyboard. It was a simple idea. A real orange jumps out of our kitchen window and rolls away from the house, up the High Street tied to Sibby and then Sparky in a handover, jumps along benches and front doorsteps until it arrives at our new shop where it hops through the letterbox. Dad thought we should just do an interview with some customers, but I swore this would be better.

During a long day of filming, we had to modify the script to take out Sibby after she kept disappearing and being brought back by Bob, the butchers and finally the women from the library. In the end, we had a one-minute film of an orange bouncing from our house to the shop, riding on the back of Sparky (who behaved perfectly, of course) and finally rolling up to the shop window on a skateboard. I posted it on Kickstarter before I went to bed with a bit about what we needed, and put it on my Instagram.

I woke up very early as always and looked at my phone. The film was being shared by bakers from around the country, and even some from around the world. I couldn't believe that everyone from Danish food bloggers to Australian pastry chefs had seen it. And then I saw that Elizabeth Prueitt, the co-founder of Tartine with Chad, had put it on her feed and told her thousands of followers to support me. I flew into Mum and Dad's room, onto their bed, and I think possibly from their reaction I might have been screaming.

THE WAY KITTY had set up our Kickstarter appeal meant that every time someone pledged a donation, I got an email. Soon my phone didn't stop pinging. Donations and messages poured in, from family and friends, from fellow bakers and from our regular Watlington customers, but over half of the pledges were from complete strangers who had been following Kit on Instagram. And then the *i* newspaper picked up the story and printed a picture of Kitty on their front page with the headline 'Flour Girl – the 15-year-old opening her own bakery.' Kit had just shorn all her hair into a close crop of red curls and with her ubiquitous dungarees and a blue headscarf she looked more like someone from the Women's Land Army than a teenage baker, but the effect was startling. Her Instagram followers went through the roof and my phone started pinging even more.

We had originally set a three-week time limit to get to where we needed. It felt like a long shot and a bit of me thought, 'Well, if we don't reach the target the decision will be made for us.' It also gave me time to adapt to the idea of having a bakery and to stop feeling a bit sick every time I passed the shop on the way to the Co-Op. Four days after launching on Kickstarter, we had not only met our target but we had gone way over. Now it all had to happen. Kitty was over the moon. I wanted to feel the same, but the responsibility of what this would mean for her, and me, kept my feelings more muted.

While I went on several long walks with the dogs to try and get used to the idea, Kitty was drawing up an action plan to get into the shop as soon as possible. Brent was due to give us the keys in mid-April when Alan moved out, and Kit was sure we could be in and open by the first week of May. At this point I had given up on the slow-and-steady approach and just started to get all the logistics together. I worked out we would need Simon to do all the electrics – new lights and ovens – and a plumber to put in a big sink. They could both do the last week of April, so we had a week before that to get the shop stripped back and painted. Easter weekend was approaching and we could rope in the family to help.

Brent handed over the keys; Kitty bounced and I tried to look elated. Walking into the shop when it was empty for the first time should have been a moment of utter joy, and I think it probably was for Kitty.

She could imagine painted shelves stacked high with crates of blistered loaves and a counter groaning with amazing buns, doughnuts, cookies, cheese straws and sausage rolls.

I tried really hard to meet her enthusiasm, but looking at the thick vinyl flooring and gray MDF walls I was absolutely overwhelmed. I found myself muttering 'one day at a time' over and over like a recovering addict and trying not to wake Katie up at 3 am to share my nighttime fears that we had bitten off more than we could possibly chew.

We started with the floor and realized within five minutes it was beyond us. In our dreams we had imagined peeling back the vinyl tiles to reveal beautiful wooden floorboards, which we would paint a soft white. In reality we peeled back the tiles to reveal more tiles. And under those tiles, even more tiles. Basically, we had a floor made up of many layers of thick, sticky plastic squares. We stuck back down the corner we had peeled off and decided that no one looked down anyway.

We had better luck painting the walls. We discovered a few loose screws in the shelving and, after a bit of gouging and levering, we pulled away a panel to reveal a lovely stretch of wood tongue and groove. This was more like it. Judging by the windows at the front, the shop was Victorian or at least Edwardian. This paneling looked even older. Our kitchen at home was dark blue so we had decided that was going to be the color of the bakery too as it works well with orange. Over the next two days we all painted and painted until the walls were covered.

We wanted to find a way of thanking all our incredible investors. We got an idea from Southwold Pier. Katie's mum and dad loved Suffolk and over the years we had taken a lot of holidays with them in and around Southwold and along the coast. They were keen walkers and birdwatchers, but when the weather was really horrible we went to the pier. Patience, Katie's mum, collected bags of two-pence coins that she would proudly give to our children and then sit alongside them as they fed them into the coin pusher slot machines. She took it very seriously and no one was allowed to go until every penny had gone. Meanwhile Katie and I walked along the pier and read the names of all the people who obviously loved Southwold so much they had bought a small bronze plaque to have screwed on the top of the railings. The messages were all different and ranged from sad to funny. 'For Tiz, who keeps crabs in the bath.' And 'Old Nan loved a cream tea on the pier.'

We didn't have enough room for plaques but Katie came up with the idea of an orange tree painted on the shop wall. 'You could put the names of each investor in an orange so they could come and see it. I could ask Mad.' Mad was Kitty's godmother and one of Katie's oldest friends. She was also a brilliant artist and illustrator. 'I would love to,' she replied immediately, 'I've never drawn a mural before, but let's see what I can do.'

Mad's mural was extraordinary. She created a small sketch beforehand, but the whole thing was drawn freehand and in one take with a white paint pen. A beautiful tree now occupied one side of the bakery with dozens of painted oranges balanced on its branches. She drew in a large hen for our eggs, bags for our flour, a churn of milk and a huge trug of fruit and veg. Once she was finished, I stood on a rickety stepladder and started the long process of writing all the names into each orange. It took a good couple of hours and a dozen pens, but it was one of the most satisfying tasks I have ever had to do.

To think that each one of these people had donated because they believed we could open a shop made me feel that maybe it was going to be all right.

Even now, whenever I glance at the names, I feel slightly in awe of them. We still get people walking in who we have never met before and who point to a name and reveal that they were investors too.

We had a week to go.

At one of our first pop-ups, we had met a local signwriter called Justin who we asked to do the sign across the shop front. He also came up with the idea of cladding the back wall of the shop with recycled wood from old crates, which looked brilliant. We dropped lights with orange electrical cord across the ceiling and built shelving along one side. For some unknown reason, Kitty spent 24 hours pickling anything she could find so that we had huge glass jars of lurid pink and green vegetables to put on the shelves.

My parents, who were clearing out their shed, arrived with an old slab of oak that Justin made fit in the window as a shelf. My childhood crane went in the window with a loaf attached to the platform and Playmobil workers in hi-viz jackets guarding it. We took stools from our house. There was no overall design idea, other than quite a bit of orange; a lot of it was just things we had and liked. Battered Penguin books, some rusty Ovaltine tins we found at a car boot sale, an old toy dog of Patience's to guard the door and a Victorian picture of a slightly scary-looking girl with a thick, heavy fringe and black boots. And then, like with the Magic Cabinet, people started to drop things by. The charity shop next door, Mercy in Action, gave us some 1950s orange scales. A family of Freds (the Homepride flour man) were left at the door by a friend, Helen.

I painted a wooden crate with the phrase 'We make our bread with just three ingredients – flour, water, salt. Oh, and one more – time.' Katie said if the fourth word had been 'love' she would have left.

With a day to go before the opening, Simon was able to wire in the new Rofco our budget had just stretched to and the plumbing was all in and ready. It was actually going to happen. To be honest, I was probably still in denial but there was too much still to do to really stop and think about it.

IT WAS FINALLY happening and I was so ready. While Dad had been finishing the shop, I was planning the first day's bakes for our big opening. It was going to be the ultimate pop-up. Sourdough of every flavor – fig and walnut, crispy onion and roast potato, cheese and jalapeño pepper – slabs of focaccia and brioche buns stuffed with pesto and chorizo, pistachio and bittersweet chocolate swirls and creamy pastéis de nata... and that was just the start.

We had to be up early. The alarm went off at 4.30 am and Sparky refused to move off my bed.

I zipped into my floury red overalls (the orange dungarees had finally expired), joined Dad in the kitchen and we silently got to work.

Dad fueled by coffee, me by adrenaline. After the first 50 loaves I left Dad to it and went to the shop to start baking the pastries. Walking down the quiet High Street at 6 am, I could see Tom and Kev in Calnan's, the butcher's, and Angela setting up her vegetables in The Undercroft under the Town Hall. I felt a total sense of belonging. I unlocked the shop and got going.

The oven was on a timer and already hot. Dad and I had been working on a new recipe for Eccles cakes, inspired by Pump Street Bakery, and they were the first to go in the oven. A night of resting in the fridge had left them quite moist and, as I tried to shimmy them into the shiny new Rofco, they slipped off the greaseproof paper straight onto the oven shelf. The buttery pastry instantly fused with the stone and smoke poured upward; 10 seconds later the loudest fire alarm I'd ever heard went off.

I switched off the oven and picked up the only thing I could find, one of Dad's many flat caps, jumped on the counter and flapped as hard as I could at the plastic beeper. Nothing. I pressed the button. Nothing. It was so loud. I rang Dad and didn't even talk just held the phone up to the alarm. Four long minutes later his bike appeared at the door and between us we got enough of the smoke out for the alarm to stop.

We went back home, trying not to notice how many lights in the High Street had gone on and still with the alarm ringing in our ears. I was fighting not to cry. We carried all the pastries that needed to be baked back to our kitchen at home, too scared to try the oven in the shop again, and tried not to think about how behind we were.

Amazingly, nothing at home had burnt. Sensing my mood, as always, Dad said, 'We can do this, but we just need to stick together.' Mum, Albert and Aggie appeared and between them started to carry everything down to the shop as Dad and I fought to catch up.

The shop was due to open at 10.30 am. We loaded up the last trays at 10.15 am and ran them down the High Street. Mum had put a thin orange ribbon in front of the door, there was a long queue and everyone was waving at me.

I couldn't work out why the inside of the shop was already full. And then I realized and tried not to cry again.

Dad's entire family had arrived as a surprise and were crammed in the shop. Granny and Buppa, Uncles Paul, Ben and Oli, Aunt Lou and my five cousins. 'We're all here to help.' Jo, who was three, started to pick a raisin out of the nearest Chelsea bun. I went round hugging everyone even though I couldn't see how any actual customers were going to fit in the shop. At that point, Mum's friend Lucy arrived who always helped at the pop-ups. With orange pompoms in her hair, she at once took charge. Within seconds cousins were dispatched to collect the last few things from the house and take Sibby and Sparky for a walk, Granny was to take the money and the uncles were on bagging up. Buppa was in charge of queue control. Aunty Lou went to buy coffees.

We turned the sign to open.

Over the next hour, I think nearly 250 customers passed through our tiny shop. And then it was over. I can't really remember any of it. A blur of noise, chatter, congratulations and Dad and me saying, 'Thank you.'

Our shop was born.

8
BERTHA

WE NOW SEEMED to have a shop. It was open each week from Wednesday to Saturday, giving us Tuesday as prep day and Sunday and Monday supposedly off. Every day started with a queue and every day we sold out. All I can remember of those first few weeks was the breakneck speed we had to work at. Up at 6 am, straight to the kitchen, get the doughs out of the fridge, slide everything into the ovens (we had moved the second Rofco back to our kitchen as it never worked having it in the shop), make the buns, cook the buns, deep-fry the Pillows of Joy, fall over each other, fall over the dogs. Then we loaded up the car and raced as fast as we could to the shop, only to race back again for another run.

The kitchen would be left in chaos and, while I served in the shop, Kitty started all over again prepping for the next day. Aggie and Albert helped whenever they could, Katie loaded and unloaded the dishwasher, scraped the dough off the sink, cupboards and table before heading to work, but basically it was Kitty and me. Kitty was in her element; I less so. We had quadrupled our workload without ever thinking through how we were going to manage.

Kitty is like a Duracell bunny when she is doing something she loves: unstoppable, with enough energy to fuel Didcot power station. I was a 51-year-old man who was more used to sitting in a classroom. By week three my brother Ben came to the rescue. Realizing by my clipped 'We're fine, honestly,' that I really wasn't, he rescheduled his freelance hours in London so he could run the shop every Friday morning. This gave me some breathing space and meant we could concentrate on prepping for Saturday when we baked double the amount. Ben is five years younger than me and is kind and funny. He takes unclehood very seriously and always gives brilliant presents. He looks like me (but without the beard) and his arrival was a lifeline. He came in, reordered the shelves and tried to decipher what everything was.

Labeling was always our Waterloo because, except for the standards – the Watlington (white sourdough), the History Loaf (brown sourdough), the Albert (soft white loaf using the Japanese tangzhong method), cheese straws and cinnamon buns – no two days were ever the same in terms of what we made. The opening of the shop had unleashed a fresh wave of creativity in Kit and new bakes arrived day after day. We still have a drawer full of hastily written labels and flicking through them now is like stumbling on an ancient archaeological hoard. Ingredients tumble out like old coins: blueberry and almond scones; pecan, chocolate and maple syrup swirls; brûlée brioche; fig and goat cheese Danish. Not everything always worked. The 'world cookies' dyed green and blue to represent the earth and sold to support charities backed by Greta tasted amazing, but they looked as if they had been mouldering away for months down the back of a car seat.

The problem was that Kitty often didn't make the same thing more than once or twice. Customers would come in and ask for that 'incredible pastry with raspberries from the week before, please,' and we would have to apologize and say they might come back one day.

Kitty worked and worked to get a bake exactly right, but once it was she then moved on, leaving a dim recollection of something extraordinary.

One man still comes in asking for her marmalade and cheese buns – Kitty swears she never made these, and he swears she did.

While Kitty was creating in the kitchen, I was trying to master the logistics of increasing the amount we baked in order to keep up with the demand of the shop. We bought more bannetons, crates and buckets, but there was a big problem unresolved.

One of the things that often confuses people, when they ask what time we get up in the morning to bake, is that sourdough, for all its complications, means you can get a pretty good night's sleep. The last stage of making sourdough is proofing the dough slowly in the fridge. Despite the low temperature, the dough still rises and, because it does this slowly, it gives the lactic bacilli (the bit that puts the 'sour' in sourdough) more chance to do its work and give the bread that extra depth of flavor. What that means, however, is you need to have a lot of fridge space. We didn't. We had two fridges, one from Katie's mum that still had Snoopy stickers on from when Katie was growing up, and our own fridge. Only by careful stacking could we get all the doughs in their proofing baskets into the fridges. Then the Snoopy fridge, after years of domestic service, started to falter.

We needed a bigger and more professional fridge. A new one was way beyond the funds we had left and so I looked at eBay. Sure enough, a deli in Kidderminster was selling a large double fridge for around £400 (a fraction of the normal price) with just a few hours to go on the clock. Perfect. I put my bid in and won. It was only then I realized that a) Kidderminster was not the nearby Kidlington as I had thought, but a town the far side of Birmingham and a three-hour drive away and b) I had never asked for dimensions. Surely, though, a double fridge was basically the same size as the two fridges we already had.

We booked a man with a van. He showed up with the fridge and a co-driver on a miserable Monday afternoon, the rain whipping on his windscreen. They had clearly had a deeply unpleasant time loading the fridge in the first place, managed to get caught up in a very long tailback somewhere on the M5 and then spent ages sitting in the van outside the locked shop thinking that was where it was going to be delivered to. When I finally looked at my phone and went to find them, they had tried me 15 times. The mood was not a positive one.

They re-parked the van outside our house. 'Where's it going to go then?' the driver asked. 'I'll show you,' I said, walking through the front door. Realizing I was on my own, I turned back around. The driver was looking at the door frame with a scowl on his face. 'Well, it's not getting through there for starters. You'd better have a look at what we've got in here.' He lifted the shuttered back door of the van. There, sitting at an awkward angle due to one of the casters having sheared off, was a huge expanse of dull gray metal, as big as a small room (which, effectively, it was). 'You're right,' I muttered. 'I know I am,' he said helpfully.

My mind was whirring with possible ways in which we could somehow get the fridge into the house, none of which were looking immediately possible. 'Well, it could go in the garage for now,' I suggested. He glanced at our garage door and lit a cigarette. 'Won't fit in there either.'

I sized the fridge up. It wouldn't fit standing up, but perhaps it might on its side? I hauled up the garage door to be greeted by a tidal wave of stuff. Anything and everything that we'd had to move out of the kitchen to make room for the bakery had found its way to the garage, including our kitchen table. I started to haul out the biggest stuff while Kit clambered inside to shift what she could to the back of the garage. The driver and his colleague climbed back into their van to stay out of the rain and watch us through the windows.

Eventually, we managed to carve out a space that might be big enough for the fridge. The men reluctantly climbed out of the van, dragged the fridge to the tailgate lift and then, together, we pushed and scraped it along the pavement to the garage. On a count of three, we managed to lift it over onto its side and then, somehow, hauled and shoved it into the space we had created. To the driver's obvious disappointment, it fitted. There was absolutely no way we were ever going to be able to move it again, but it was off the truck and stashed away.

I felt that moment was our Dunkirk. A small victory snatched from what was, in every other sense, a catastrophic defeat.

I handed over my cash and closed up the garage door. Wet, exhausted, cross, but strangely elated.

Over the next few days, I wondered what on earth to do. Was it best just to relist it? Would anyone want to buy a heavily scratched double fridge that I had probably bust by tipping it onto its side? I measured it up again and again. If we could drag it into the garden, it would go through the wider back door if we took it off its hinges. The question was how to get it there. You can't access our garden except by going through the house. It needed muscles and ingenuity. I felt in short supply of both, still slightly humiliated by my decision-making in the first place.

Yet again we were saved by neighbors. With the constant demands we made on their fridges, ovens and dog-catching abilities, they must by this time have been wondering if living on our street was a good idea. Antony next door said we could use their driveway and take down a panel of fencing to get it into our garden. Jo and Andy opposite said we could borrow their son, Tristram, back from university in America, to help move the iron monster.

We picked a Sunday morning when Katie was out (she hadn't quite clocked the size of the fridge and I wanted to get it in the house before she did). Tristram, Albert, me and Kitty set to work dragging the fridge out of the garage and pushing/pulling it along the pavement and up the bumpy driveway beside Antony's house. We took the fence panel down and managed to haul the fridge through the gap. It was a bit like how the druids must have felt getting a slab of Stonehenge down from the Welsh mountains. We had to use planks of wood as a runway with me as a human sacrifice holding everything up at one end.

Everything that could have worked against us did; the grass was slippy, it began to rain again, and as soon as the fence panel was down Sibby ran away. Leaving long trench marks across our very small lawn, we got the fridge to the back door. Creating a splintered chunk on the door frame, we eventually got it through, dragged it across the wooden floor and into the corner. The wires behind the fridge meant it couldn't sit flush to the wall and obscured half the kitchen window.

I plugged in the fridge and nervously switched it on. Nothing happened for a split second, then it coughed into life and rumbled out an unhealthy growl that never stopped. At this point Katie arrived home to observe silently the now gloomy, half-lit kitchen with a clanking fridge the size of the Titanic in the corner, a destroyed lawn, a wrecked back door and the absence of an escaped dog. It was not a highlight moment in our marriage.

For a while, despite Katie emitting a low growl whenever she looked at her, Bertha worked a treat. She was so big that we didn't just put our doughs in there overnight – she could take trays of pastries pre-made, which cut crucial time off our morning routine and meant we could feel a bit more in control. Then the summer heat came. As we headed into June and July, we had to keep turning Bertha up to keep the doughs cool enough. The colder her temperature the more noise she made, but Bertha's nightly grunting could be heard in our bedroom above the kitchen and that was reassuring. Then one morning, as the alarm went off, I realized that the house was silent.

Bertha had stopped. I opened her doors with trepidation and, with Kitty beside me, looked at the explosion within.

The doughs, now in an insulated unit rather than something cooling them down, had escaped over the top of the bannetons and covered the entire inside of the fridge. Kitty saved the day here. She'd seen a baker faced with a similar problem on Instagram. She pulled out the bannetons that had managed to hold onto their dough and flipped out the spongy mess before remaking the dough into tight balls. It meant they had to proof all over again, but while she did this I started on the pastries.

Although we were an hour late opening up the shop that day, we still managed to salvage over half the breads.

I spent the evening rattling, prodding and turning-off-and-on-again (my entire range of mechanical skills) but Bertha remained resolutely silent. We called up a fridge repair man who came round and did the same before climbing back down the stepladder and sighing. Never a good sign. 'You've got two basic problems,' he said. 'She's old and she's Italian. That means getting parts is a nightmare and, even if we replace the bit I think has broken, there's a strong chance something else will be wrong as well.' 'So...?' I asked, waiting for the 'but'. It never came.

We paid him for the bad news. With Albert's help, I somehow – mainly driven by extreme anger – managed to shove and drag Bertha out of the kitchen, taking another chunk out of the back door and Albert's knuckles, already scarred from getting her in, and sat her on our small lawn. Katie's relief that Bertha was out of the kitchen turned back to irritation that it was going to cost us too much to get her removed. So, for the entire hot summer, she sat on our lawn. A huge redundant fridge squatting on our tiny patch of grass. The plus side was that, like in the book *A Squash and a Squeeze*, our kitchen felt much bigger again.

A lovely customer (thank you, Emma) came to our rescue and lent us her much newer – if much smaller – fridge. We had to go back to making pastries up each morning instead of the night before, but that was doable. Katie's growl was still audible, but only when she went into the garden or looked out of the window. Eventually we paid someone to come and de-gas the fridge and take the motor away, basically leaving us with a large metal box. She (Bertha, not Katie) had to be chopped up using an angle grinder to a size that we could then get into the car and ferry to the landfull. Once I add up the cost of buying Bertha, transporting her, trying to mend her and then having her decommissioned and cut up, not to mention the irritation value for Katie, it probably would have been easier to buy something new. Lesson learned? Hmmm.

ONE OF THE best things about having opened the shop was the chatting. No one came in who didn't want to talk and soon we had a regular set of customers. First, there was Mr Rawstrom. He came every day with a Tupperware box that we filled up with cardamom and orange buns. For a man in his eighties he could eat a lot of buns. Swedish Thomas, who knows his cinnamon buns like the French know their onions, would look at the crate and pick out his chosen dozen. Mother and daughter, Ilona and Daisy, would start by saying that they would share a bun, but then always get one each. Then there was Irish Muriel who came for the soda bread.

Once, having read a recipe suggestion, Dad put molasses in it. Muriel's husband came in, took Dad aside and said, 'I have been eating soda bread for 60 years and let me tell you something'... Dad waited for the huge compliment to come, trying to look casual with his chest puffing up. He finished, 'You NEVER EVER put molasses in a soda bread.' Dad never did it again and is still a little scarred by the encounter.

Tai Chi Nick, with his three boys, started to run a tab as they got through so many pizza slices. Jess was one of my favorite customers, with Joss in a sling on her back and Kit toddling beside her. You'd hear Kit chatting all the way up the High Street until he got inside the shop, when he would go into a silent trance at the pile of chocolate and rye cookies. There were always cyclists in tight Lycra on their bikes who would appear slightly blotchy-faced after having taken on Watlington Hill. They would clack in with their spiked shoes and go straight for the sausage rolls. Dogs were always welcome and licked up crumbs from the shop floor. We introduced sourdough dog biscuits that got a furry cult following.

Different times of day saw different groups. There was always a flurry of activity at 10 am, when the yoga class in the Memorial Club ended and bendy women would appear to load up with Marmite and cheese swirls or fluffy Albert loaves, and again at 12.30 pm, when workers would leave their computers for an hour and get a za'atar and feta puff or the all-day breakfast bun with bacon, egg, tomato and onion. We nicknamed one man Rumpelstiltskin as he once stamped his foot hard when we said we had no Alberts left.

There was something about the shop that meant no one hurried and often total strangers would start chatting to each other.

The bakery was a place that soothed my brain and made me feel safe. I knew what I was doing there, and my anxiety never roared away. It was just a really happy place.

9
GRASS PESTO

THE MORE I baked the more I became obsessed with different ingredients. A lot of these came from some magical shops on the Cowley Road in Oxford – miso, seaweed and smoky black sesame seeds from Seoul Plaza, tahini, roasted red peppers and halva from Maroc Deli. I loved playing around with new flavors and so when a customer mentioned the local wild garlic, I thought it would make perfect pesto for our brioche rolls.

Following the directions we'd been given, Dad and I set off up the Ridgeway clutching an old wooden trug. Past a cottage before the lane turned into a track, we were told there was a good clump on the left. Arriving with Sibby and Sparky, we convinced ourselves that we could smell the garlic before we even saw it. It was a narrow patch of bright green just off the path. Grabbing handfuls, we stuffed them in our bags and set off for home. I rinsed off all the leaves, roasted some walnuts, grated some Parmesan and put everything in the blender.

It looked incredible. Bright frog green. I toasted a slice of an Albert loaf and dolloped it on.

It was disgusting. I had made pesto from grass.

It took Sarge to show me where the best wild garlic could be found. The place he said we had to go to was Pishill just down the road, where he had grown up. (Annoyingly, Pishill is pronounced Pish Hill and not the way you think it should be.) Sarge had grown up in a big house high up on the bank beside the church and further up the hill was a whole bank of wild garlic, small white flowers sitting on clumps of dark green.

'We used to be sent down here to pick up leaves for soup. You only need a few leaves to give enough flavor, but we would come back with huge armfuls. I think, looking back, it was just my mum's way of keeping us busy.

When you get as much wild garlic as this,' he said, waving his arm at the carpet of white flowers, 'it means you're in old woodland. They've probably been picking wild garlic on this spot for a thousand years at least.' 'I bet they picked grass sometimes as well, when they were starting,' I said. 'No,' replied Sarge 'I don't think they did.'

The wild garlic pesto swirls were incredible and they encouraged other people to bring us more ingredients to bake with, which was brilliant.

Susan Fotherby came with rhubarb from her garden, Jo opposite brought bunches of rosemary for our focaccia and Paul (who always read a book on trees while queuing on Saturdays) gave us a whole selection of pears. If the shop was shut, they'd leave things in the Magic Cabinet – I'd open it to find a few bags of muddy beetroot from an allotment or a bunch of hot chilies grown in a greenhouse that gave the miso and sesame bread a bigger kick. Sometimes there was a note saying who it was from and sometimes just a smiley face.

THERE WAS SOMETHING about the way we had set up the bakery with everyone's help that inspired others too. Gradually we were approached by more and more people wondering whether they could sell some of their produce through us. Martin from Clare came by every Saturday with his bucket of beautiful white duck eggs, each one lovingly dated by hand, and a basket of wet walnuts. The Matthews boys – Barnaby, Ollie and Eddie – came by with their mum quite early on. They lived on a farm in a tiny hamlet called Stoke Talmage where each boy had his own beehive. Their honey, as fresh and raw as it gets, was amazing – customers swore that it helped their hay fever, which locally grown honey is meant to do – and so we started using it in our baking as well.

The individually labeled pots showed the boys resplendent in their beekeeper outfits (quite a bespoke market, beekeeper suits for the under-10s).

If I'm honest, before starting the bakery my eco credentials were poor (traveling around in our old diesel car was a shaming reflection).

Now, being able to use these ingredients really matters to both Kitty and me. It just feels right to be using the stuff on our doorstep rather than trying to find the cheapest alternative.

Our eggs come from the free-range farm in the next village where you can scoop up a couple of trays of eggs laid that day and simply leave money in a trust pot. (For ages, we never saw anyone on the farm and Kit and I would imagine the chickens ran it themselves and headed off to a Barbados timeshare in winter.) All our milk comes from the nearby dairy Lacey's and our flour from Wessex Mill in Wantage who only take grain from farms within a fifty-mile radius. This means that quite often the flour we use has come from wheat grown just down the road from us. The fact that the mill is run by another father/daughter combo, Paul and Emily Munsey, means we like it even more.

One of the things that Kitty and I felt most guilty about was what to do with our 'mistake' bread. The loaves that had been forgotten in the oven or sagged in the middle or the Marmite and cheese swirls that were just a bit too crispy. At first, we put them in the food compost bin to be picked up by the refuse collectors once a week. But that always felt a bit sad (and trying to cram it all into small green bins was almost impossible). Then a customer, Henry, mentioned that he had two very large, carb-obsessed pigs in his back garden that the family kept as pets (they were, in fact, vegan). We went to meet Sausage and Beans.

Every Sunday, Kit and I would fill the back of the car with a big flour bag of 'mistake' bread and buns, drive up Britwell Hill and park at the back of Henry's house. At the end of the garden was the neatest pig pen you've ever seen with a homemade shelter piled high with fresh straw. As the car boot opened, there would be a shuffling and then Sausage and Beans emerged. Huge, hairy, black pigs with necks so thick they could only look down. Grumbling and staggering slightly, they would hoover up our offerings and Kit would scratch their backs with a stick. Their appreciation felt much more gratifying than a green food bin.

IT WAS COMING to the end of the summer and we had been open for over three months. It was time for the thank-you party we'd promised our crowdfunders as part of their reward. We picked the second-to-last Sunday in September and asked Kristina at the Parish Council if we could have the paddock, a small park behind the library, for a couple of hours. The easiest thing we could give everyone was slabs of homemade pizza, which we could bake, put in wooden crates and run from the house to the park using Albert and Aggie and a clean wheelbarrow.

Dad and I spent ages devising the best possible pizza toppings. We slow-cooked a tomato sauce that took over 20lb of tomatoes and 24 hours to get rich. Then we tried to create our own mozzarella using Lacey's milk. We watched a YouTube tutorial on repeat. We practiced heating up the whey to near boiling point and plunging our gloved hands into it with a soft ball of curd. A few scaldings later, we decided to leave mozzarella-making to the experts. However, we did learn to make ricotta. No boiling or scalding necessary, just leaving a bag of curds overnight in a muslin bag. We added the ricotta with thinly sliced garlic potatoes and rosemary to the pizza base as a topping and, although I worried it was a bit beige, it tasted amazing.

We were talking about the thank-you party in the shop when Justin, the signwriter, came in with his two-year-old son William to buy their usual cinnamon buns. When we said that we were going to be doing pizza, to go with it Justin suggested could he try making beer from our 'mistake' loaves.

He'd done quite a bit of brewing in the past and had read how you could make beer from stale bread. It sounded brilliant and the next time he came in he showed us the Orange Bakery labels he had designed for the brown vintage-looking bottles the beer could go in. There was just enough time for it to ferment before the party. Ignoring the plaintive looks of Sausage and Beans at their reduced weekly rations (although I didn't feel too bad as these are not thin pigs), we gave Justin a sack of bread and he got to work.

Kickstarter meant we could email an invite to everyone who had funded us. Just a few people came back to say they would be there, but we had no idea how many to expect.

The day of the party came and it was one of those sudden hot September days that takes everyone by surprise. Mum ran back and forth to the paddock with armfuls of our moth-eaten blankets and cushions to lay on the grass and Cousin Daisy turned up to help. As Dad and I shoved pizzas in and out of the ovens, Daisy and Mum set up a long trestle table with the bottles of beer, glasses and a random collection of plates.

By the time Dad and I got to the paddock about a hundred people were sitting on the grass, clutching slabs of pizza and holding Justin's beer bottles or our slightly cloudy homemade elderflower. Aggie and Albert were sitting beside the finally empty wheelbarrow and Mum was doing her flappy hands, telling us to hurry up as the man from the *Henley Standard* was about to turn up to take our photo for the paper.

As we walked up, people started to clap. Dad stood on an upturned bucket, thanked everyone for coming and, as he looked at Mum, started to say that he never thought we would be here and how grateful he was. Then he didn't say anything more. And I realized he couldn't.

Dad got off the bucket and came to stand by me. Mum gave him a beer and the man from the *Henley Standard* took our photo.

10
ULLA BREAD

THAT SEPTEMBER, LIKE the beginning of a new school term, was marked by Kitty making the choice to step away from the NHS mental health team in Oxford. She'd worked out the props she needed – baking and family, dog walks and routine – to keep the panic attacks and sadness at bay and, if they did arrive, she wasn't brought to such shuddering inertia as before. She began to trust that she could feel happy sometimes, as well as how to be kinder to herself. It took us a while to realize it was happening until the signs became clearer and clearer.

First, Kitty's laugh came back. A slightly manic cackle that made her eyes crease up and her body shake.

There's a shot on her Instagram of Kitty leaping into the river that autumn (and it wasn't a warm day). It captures the slightly wild Kitty of old.

The second indicator was noise. Before Kitty had preferred to work in silence, but now music came into her life to throw that into sharp relief. Bowie, Nick Cave and Flaming Lips loomed large on our bakery playlist. And Kitty discovered podcasts. They worked perfectly for her as she could work and listen; TV never had quite the same pull as she couldn't multitask so easily. As she went around the house, her phone tucked into her dungarees, came a disembodied voice talking about Stockholm syndrome or the life of Boudica or the origin of the Mormons. Kit tended to find one subject, become obsessed, dig up every bit of information about it, and then move on. This means that her broad knowledge will always have some basic holes (she would never do well in the general knowledge round of *Mastermind*), but her specialist subjects are pretty wide ranging. I can never see which topic is coming next or how they link together. Sometimes it will be about a business – like the entrepreneur Sarah Blakely who founded Spanx – or just a great storyteller – like the writer Matt Haig on 'How to Fail' – but sometimes Kit would suddenly talk to me about how similar the tulip mania of the 1630s was to the dot.com bubble in the late twentieth century and I was left slightly floundering. She gobbled up knowledge and information as if she was making up for the year she hadn't been able to process anything but bread, and fired questions at me as she worked out how she felt about issues.

That September cemented a change for me as well on two levels. The first was letting go of our guilt about Kitty's education. Both Katie and I realized we had to relinquish the idea of pushing her along some sort of traditional education route as it wasn't going to be right for her. But it was hard as we both worried options were being cut off for her in later life. If she ever went off baking and decided do something else, we were leaving her high and dry without even one qualification and it felt like we shouldn't be allowing her to make such a huge decision at the age of 15. But watching how Kitty was now learning – in fact, devouring information – made us reluctant to channel her back into maths and English GCSEs or even A levels. Besides, she had no interest in doing any of them and so, in the end, we sort of let go the idea of her ever returning to school. It helped that Kitty was our third child and that made us more relaxed. Aggie and Albert had gone through mainstream education, so we weren't trying to make any radical point.

We had to accept that Kitty had chosen a very different route and hope that it was going to work out.

We were also scarred from how very ill she had been and that we still weren't too far away from that cliff edge; there was no way we were going to put her in jeopardy by trying to force a return to a more conventional path.

Our decision was helped enormously by two teachers from Kit's old school, Miss O'Reilly and Dr Hicks. They were both incredibly generous in making time each week to come and talk to Kitty about what she was passionate about – Jackie O'Reilly with English and writing and Jen Hicks on history, especially ancient Greek. It was liberating for Kitty not having to follow a strict curriculum and Jackie and Jen allowed her to go down rabbit holes and simply enjoy the subjects with no end motive. We topped up these studies with a bit of maths, but geared it much more toward the real hurdles of business rather than the abstract ones of geometry and quadratic equations.

In the same way we had to accept the path Kit was on, I had to realize that I was unlikely to go back to teaching. Baking was no longer just a way to help my daughter but actually my new career. I had to jump into it rather than tiptoe round it. During one of my nightly worries about 'should I be doing this?' Katie took over. In a succinct 10-minute speech addressed to me in her pajamas, she went through all the reasons that this lifestyle suited me down to the ground. I enjoyed the hard work of teaching, but I could be quite hard on myself – I often felt I was only as good as my last lesson. I was just as hard on myself as a baker, but I had a lot more chances to redeem myself. If anything, I really enjoyed the fact that we learnt so much from failing. Baking (and running the bakery) satisfied my need to be creative and, despite my doubts, I quite enjoyed the business of it all – the juggling of different demands, pulling everything together in time. At the end of her mini TED Talk, Katie ended with the killer conclusion; it made me happy.

At a supper with friends a couple of week later, they asked Katie and me to witness their wills, which they had just written.

Beside my name, under 'Occupation', I wrote 'Baker' for the first time. And it felt okay.

WHEN MUM OR Dad would tell someone about me being ill, or not going to school, or having depression, they'd often be told 'It's social media, it makes it so hard for them all.' But Instagram was the one thing that always really helped me. My feed was a long string of loaves, bakeries, cooks, recipes, equipment and ingredients and, rather than making me feel small, it made me want more than anything to get well enough to go out and find out more about all of it. There were so many brilliant things happening I didn't want to be stuck with my brain at home. If I tied myself to only the things that made me feel safe, it was going to be so limiting.

Then, in the summer, Instagram did its brilliant thing and through it I got an invite to go to Copenhagen – it was the push I needed to move me on a bit.

A few months before, a Danish journalist called Rasmus had messaged me and said his girlfriend had seen the Orange Bakery on Instagram and could he come and interview me for DR, the Danish equivalent of the BBC. When he came, Rasmus brought with him the softest darkest loaf of rye bread he'd baked the day before, which we ate as we talked. During the interview, munching away, I said how much I wanted to make rye like this, the Nordic way, and then didn't really think about it again. Then one morning in August, my Instagram suddenly buzzed with new followers, all of whom were from Denmark. The DR interview had gone out and the part where I'd said I wanted to learn how to make Nordic rye bread had been included. My messages were full of invites to learn. The message I liked the most was from Nicolas, who was 12 years old. 'My granny Ulla makes the best rye bread of all. We live very near Copenhagen. Why don't you and your dad come and stay with us and she can teach you?'

One of my all-time favorite children's books is *Come Over to My House*, which Mum read over and over to me. In the story a boy with orange hair goes round the world staying in different types of houses. 'Some houses are square, and some houses are round. There are all kinds of houses around to be found.' The boy stays in houseboats and tents and chalets and palaces, all with other children his age, and always seems to have a bath wherever he goes. Visiting Nicolas and Ulla in Copenhagen was *Come Over to My House* come alive and before I could think too hard about it, I just said, 'Yes, we'd love to,' and went to look at flights on EasyJet.

I had to find a way to leave the bakery, the shop and home and still manage. We could go from a Sunday to a Tuesday and still not miss a day of the bakery. Any bit of me that felt sick at the thought of not knowing exactly what would happen when we got there, I pushed down hard.

Three weeks later we arrived at Copenhagen airport to be met by Nicolas's entire family, including Ulla, the famous rye maker. She was tiny with soft, cropped white hair and black glasses, like Tinkerbell at 75, and smiled and nodded at me as we drove through the suburbs to their house. My stomach was cramping with stress, but Dad sat beside me and led a conversation with the boys (who spoke brilliant English) about the differences in crisp flavors between our countries.

We got to their house, which was very white and very square, and went inside. Dad was taken off to see the garden and Ulla firmly took hold of my hand and brought me to the kitchen. I had the sudden feeling that I was going to panic. I could feel my temperature rising and my breath shortening as Dad was nowhere to be seen. Ulla spoke no English, but I think she knew exactly how I was feeling.

She stood beside me with our shoulders touching and pushed my hand gently into a large white bowl of gray rye flour mixed with a starter.

As I put my hands in the familiar mixture, I could feel my breath starting to slow again and my cheeks stopped flaming. Ulla added some seeds and some beer and then held up four fingers on each of her hands with her thumbs tucked in. I thought this was going to be a really special way of mixing something and copied her, but in fact she simply meant we now leave it for eight hours.

It was time for lunch and the family introduced us to the open sandwich. This is like tipping out the entire contents of your fridge onto neat plates and then assembling small towers of food on thin slices of rye bread. There were loads of things I recognized (eggs, cress and ham), things I sort of knew (pickled herring) and then a few complete strangers (Västerbotten Crème, a cream cheese and liver pâté creation that looked like a pink brick). Dad and I copied the family and layered up our bread, then I picked it up and tried to eat it from one end. Dad coughed and I realized that everyone else was using knives and forks. I carefully put the open sandwich back down and caught Ulla's eye who was beaming at me.

Everything the family did was filled with kindness. Nicolas and his brother Frederick took the day off school to show us round Copenhagen. When I asked if the school minded, they said they had been encouraged to 'meet the English bakers'. We started with their local ice-cream shop; it had every flavor you could imagine. I still mind that I chose the key lime pie with whipped meringue when I should have chosen the chocolate and peanut butter. But I'm glad I avoided their recommendation of the black liquorice.

We then went on to the incredible Hart Bageri, which I'd been studying intently on Instagram for months. As I walked in, I recognized all the bakers from my online stalking. Nicolas and Frederick's mum had rung ahead to tell them I was coming and what a massive follower I was, so I ended up the other side of the counter like a fan backstage. I was shown their buckets of bubbly dough and taken upstairs to see their store cupboard of ingredients, where I was really surprised to see pots and pots of Marmite. That's where I met Talia. She had two butter sheets in her hands and talked to me in perfect English (unsurprisingly, as she came from Sussex). She told me about all the bakes and gave me her own creation, the Marmite blondie (hence the pots) – it was incredible and my own version went straight into my menu planning when I got home. Finally, we dropped by to see the Little Mermaid statue, which was surprisingly small.

I'd been really worried about how I would sleep away from home and my own bed, but Dad was sharing the room with me and despite (or perhaps because of) his snoring, it was all right. On the day we left, Ulla prepared a traditional Nordic spread for breakfast. There were bittersweet chocolate thins in a cardboard box and little almond cookies to scatter over a bowl of lemon-spiked buttermilk. The highlight for Ulla was introducing us to Danish oatmeal, Øllebrød. Made with stale rye bread, malt beer, butter and heavy cream, she proudly put it in my bowl with a sprinkle of brown sugar. I noticed Nicolas avoided it and Frederick was trying not to laugh.

It was quite hard to get through – like eating papier-mâché mixed with wallpaper paste – but as Ulla was watching me, I did it. When I'd finished, she clapped her hands with pleasure.

During our time in Copenhagen, Ulla showed me everything I needed to know about rye bread. Making it is a two-day process, but the bread was ready just in time for us to get back to the airport. Its warmth lined my rucksack as we waited for our plane. I don't think the family really understood what their generosity had given me – the confidence to know that leaving my routine didn't have to kickstart a panic attack. I had let go and it had been okay. They had also taught me to make delicious rye bread, which we sold in the shop and called Ullabrød. I had also fallen totally and utterly in love with Copenhagen.

WHILE INSTAGRAM GAVE Kitty a sense of a bigger world she wanted to be a part of, it also gave us brilliant advice. That autumn our loaves started to come out a bit flatter. They still tasted good and none of our customers seemed to notice, but Kitty and I would torture ourselves by comparing them with pictures of our loaves through the summer that seemed bouncier and broader. We went through everything. Our starter seemed to be quite perky. Nothing had changed with our technique. We felt very loyal to our lovely Wessex Mill, but perhaps their home-grown flour just wasn't as robust as the imported wheat from Shipton Mill. We ordered a few large bags from Shipton and went through all the motions, but it didn't seem to make much difference – if anything, it was slightly worse (maybe the loaves picked up on our guilt). We looked at our two Rofcos. We hadn't serviced them since we got them and they were on almost constantly, so maybe they were just losing their oomph. We gave them a thorough cleaning and played around with opening the small windows for longer and putting water in the bottom, but nothing.

As usual, Kitty then took matters into her own hands and sought advice.

Kitty messaged five of her favorite bakers pictures of our flatter sourdough loaves. They all came back with the same answer – you haven't adjusted to winter.

Our dough was simply too cold. Our starter was struggling to kickstart the chilly dough and then we were putting everything into a too-cold fridge. We were still in summer mode, when everything we did was about keeping a lid on the sourdough that was too alive at times. We'd never cooked in bulk as the seasons changed and we needed to get winter ready. We stripped back the starters and used lukewarm water to feed them. We gave everything a bit longer to ferment and let the fridges shift up a couple of degrees. Slowly, our breads came back; if anything, more blooming than before. The relief was enormous. Kit and I gained confidence in the knowledge that we really could bake bread. It also gave us a benchmark. Sourdough is so temperamental (sometimes for reasons only known to itself) and no two days are ever the same, but knowing we could claw our way out of what felt like a disastrous situation was reassuring.

Along with the flatter breads, we had another problem that autumn. That one was a lot harder to solve; Sibby. No matter how much training we did with Sibby, she just totally ran rings around us. We simply weren't up to the job. Our cats were now so traumatized that Smudge never left Aggie's bedroom and she had to have a cat litter tray by her bed. Oddie stayed outside until midnight and then jumped through our bedroom window to lie on my back for an hour for his only form of human contact. If Sibby got even a sniff of one of the cats, she would move like lightning to chase them back to their hiding places. We also couldn't stop her shooting out of the front door the second it was opened. Every time a bakery delivery arrived, Sibby had to be herded into the sitting room and the door shut. Then there were walks. We tried everything to get her to come back to us if we ever let her off the lead. Cooked chicken in my pockets, we would set off and timidly release her. Almost every time Sibby would instantly disappear and the walk would be spent with Sparky happily beside me feeding off the treats while we shouted ourselves hoarse at a small black dot careering around on the hills above us. The only answer was to keep her straining at her collar when we went out, which felt miserable for everyone.

We read all the online advice on dog training; basically, we had a working terrier who, once she got a sniff of a scent, was lost to us. It all came to a head one day in October. Kitty and I were still manning the shop every Wednesday and Thursday while Ben did Fridays. Sometimes Kitty and I would get far enough ahead in finishing the bakes and stocking the shop to take the dogs for a short walk before opening time. That Wednesday in October, we did exactly that. It was a beautiful day; the loaves were plump and the cinnamon buns were piled high in the window. We drove up to Watlington Hill for a quick half-hour dog walk before we opened. Right at the top Sibby, who by now was never off lead, discovered that with a sharp backward twist she could slip out of her new harness. With a glance at Kitty and me, she sprinted for the woods and the badger holes. For once, in a rare moment of disobedience, Sparky decided to follow.

We spent the next 20 minutes crackling through brambles until we heard the muffled sound of barking and realized both dogs had gone deep underground. We were meant to open the shop in 10 minutes. I rang Katie, who was about to go to work, and explained what had happened. She ran down to the shop, clutching her work phone, and grabbed an apron. An hour later, we were still on the hill and neither dog had reappeared. My phone rang. It was Katie. 'Hello, darling,' she said ominously, 'there's someone here to see you in the shop.' 'The dogs are still with the badgers,' I replied, sounding as though I was delivering some World War II resistance code.

Katie mumbled something that sounded broadly like, 'Leave the dogs and get here.'

Then crystal clear, 'The woman from environmental health is here for an inspection.'

Leaving Kit on dog watch, I ran back to the car, drove down the hill and parked outside the shop where there was a queue of about 10 people. Katie was inside, smiling in a slightly forced way as she bagged up the bread and buns. In the corner, clutching a clipboard as she watched Katie, stood a short, flinty-eyed woman who was not smiling.

I was panting, sweaty and my hands were filthy from trying to dig away at the badger hole. She chose not to shake hands. We went into the small back room together and she took a slow look round. I scrubbed my hands in the sink and tried to see the situation through her eyes. It was clean but chaotic. Kitty and I are not natural tidiers and we had piled the shelves high with things that were hard to see were totally necessary in a bakery – a huge thank-you card from Kitty's old primary school where she had gone to talk at assembly, a few maths books from the days of attempting to do schoolwork, jugs of two-pence coins that neither of us knew the origins of, boxes of orange pompoms that we'd used to promote our first pop-up, a picture of Kitty that a customer had painted, the orange scarf and just stuff. I moved everything round a bit and dug out the paperwork, trying to make it look as though it was in the right place. The environmental health lady quietly went through her checklist as I muttered nervously on about the dogs and this not being a normal morning.

After a short lecture on what we could improve, she left.

I raced back up the hill to find that Kitty had managed to lure Sparky out, but Sibby was still nowhere to be seen. I stood one last time by the deepest hole and yelled her name.

Suddenly a filthy, panting bundle shot out and into my arms. 'Oh, Sibby,' I said, scooping her up as she licked my face and then struggled to return to the badgers.

It seemed totally wrong to give up on Sibby, she was just following her hunter instincts after all, and I think we would have stuck by her if it hadn't been for Katie's parents' carer, Jan. Sibby loved Jan, who managed to have total control over her. More and more frequently, she would offer to have Sibby for the day and so through Jan we were given the opportunity to rehome her. A family who Jan knew were looking for a young dog as a companion to their older dog, who also always had to be on a lead. They had a large garden, didn't mind it being dug over and they had fallen completely in love with Sibby. When the day came for her to go, we all felt miserable. On our last walk we bumped into Sam, one of our crowdfunders, and a dog trainer. She was reassuring. 'Sometimes dogs and families just don't match and it's far better to let her go than keep going with something that isn't right for either of you.'

Sibby still makes her presence felt through the gnawed bottoms of every chair leg and the zips that I can't do up because she chewed off the ends. Now, the cats have moved back downstairs and we can open the front door again without the jeopardy of a black streak running off up the road. Sometimes a photo memory will come up on my phone with Sibby in it, her scruffy face tipped to one side, and I feel a pang, but I'm glad she ended up with the right family. I'm pretty sure she's still dreaming of badgers.

11
KRISTIAN AND CHRISTMAS

WITH KITTY IN a better place, family tolerance for the destruction that the bakery brought to our house was running low. Getting through the front door meant navigating flour sacks piled up in the hallway before passing giant pots of Marmite and crates of eggs. Dried dough has a habit of getting everywhere – on the kitchen cabinets, windows, floors, even into our washing. (Something happens to dough in the dryer that makes it go into tiny, hard black balls, which stick to everything. Especially Katie's and Aggie's tights, and that drives them mad.) We still didn't have a kitchen table to eat off. Katie had to nervously dust herself down when leaving the house so she didn't arrive at work with flour smudges on her bottom. Albert avoided the kitchen entirely unless he had to make tea.

Katie put down an ultimatum. We had to find somewhere else to bake.

By Christmas, Katie wanted at the least to have her parents over for lunch, seated at a table and on chairs that weren't sticky from the trays of cinnamon buns balanced on them. We started the search for new premises, but it soon became clear that we couldn't afford much more expenditure on top of the shop rent and anywhere that we could afford felt grim and cold. The prospect of Kitty and me working in an airless container on an industrial estate in the middle of nowhere at 6 am each morning felt distinctly unappealing. It was Kitty who came up with a solution. During one of her rabbit-hole information exercises, she had briefly become obsessed with tiny homes and how to build them. We had a gap to the side of the house, where the bins sat, that was concreted over and her idea was to build a shed on this space to bake in. I started to investigate what structures we could easily buy online, but then Kitty met first Charlie, then Kristian and, as usual, the decision kind of made itself.

CHARLIE CAME INTO the shop one day and asked to work some shifts. He was a student at Cardiff University but had trained as a baker for a year before changing track. Because all breadmaking follows broadly the same technique, you can help out at any bakery and get a breadmaking hit. That's one of the brilliant things about bakeries. His dad, Henry, owned Sausage and Beans, our waste-disposal pigs. Charlie helped us sometimes when he was home from uni and told us about his friend, Kristian, who was currently working on a building site in nearby Thame, but who also made incredible treehouses out of old bits of wood. Boom. We could build a recycled bakery.

Charlie gave me Kristian's number. Before Dad could ask too many questions, I got him to come round and look at the space.

As I fed Kristian chocolate brioche, he drew out what he thought could work for the bakery.

Kristian always had a pencil behind one ear, a buzz cut and a beard along with a brilliant tattoo of a red kite, the birds that constantly hover above Watlington. He told me about all the offcuts he had hoarded at his home, which included a lot of old doors. By the following week, he had started the build. Working in furious bursts in between his Thame shifts, the structure began to take shape. It was brilliant. He was brilliant.

A friend of Mum's had inherited an old farm with outbuildings piled high with windows and timber. She let Kristian and Dad ferret around and pile up his Land Rover with whatever they could find. Within six weeks the bakery was built. It was made of up reclaimed doors (two of them still had keys in) to make the sides with a corrugated iron roof. A sliding door (that had been part of a cattle shed) divided up the storeroom, a decked veranda made of planks from a closed-down pub led into the garden and half of a wheelbarrow made up the step to get inside. Dad and I painted green the bits that needed painting and our bakery was nearly ready – we just needed to get the ovens in.

By this point, I had realized that my beloved Rofcos were never going to be able to keep up with the growing demand of the shop. We really needed to move to a proper, grown-up 'deck oven' that could take 20 loaves at a time. I pored over pictures of them. Huge metal rectangles with long shelves and levers that opened their doors. I measured one up. It would fit. If we got one, we could really start to fly. I just had to convince Dad.

I REALLY DIDN'T want to get a bigger oven. This was one of the rare times that Kitty and I properly argued. My point was why did everything have to happen so fast? It was too expensive, too big, and we didn't really need it. As the parent, I'm not quite sure why I don't win these arguments. I think that it's because, when it comes to the bakery, Kit and I act as business partners and not father and daughter. Her motto is 'Ready, fire, aim,' – yes, that way round – while I am more cautious and want to think through all the angles. Kit is also like a seasoned barrister when it comes to arguing her case. This time Kit managed to override me because she had a plan that took away my main concern: cost. Even though it still left a logistical nightmare.

Back in the spring, when we were setting up the shop, Kitty had asked Ducky who she could talk to about second-hand bakery equipment.

Ducky had said to get hold of Mr Beam, who sounded like a baking superhero.

Kitty found Mr Beam on Instagram and messaged him. He replied that he would be in our area over the following week and could come to see us. His name was, in fact, Andrew Nightingale, but the family business was called Mr Beam and they had huge expertise in setting up bakeries. Alongside that, they were also extremely generous – they believe in helping new businesses early on so they can get on their feet.

Andrew sat in the garden with us and talked about all the different projects he had worked on and who it might be worth us getting in touch with. Toward the end of our conversation, he casually remarked that he had a couple of old deck ovens sitting in the back of his workshop that he would be really happy to give us should we ever expand in the future. I think I just nodded and smiled, thinking the Rofcos would do us forever, and filed the offer away under 'ridiculously generous, but impossible'. Of course, Kitty hadn't forgotten this conversation and, with the new bakery built, she got straight back in contact with Mr Beam to ask if we might still have one of the ovens. His answer was a very lovely 'yes' and so finally, after a lot of persuasion by Kit, I conceded.

Our house had just about survived the electrical demands of a Rofco, but a deck oven was a whole different beast that needed three-phase electricity – a phrase that would come to haunt me.

Broadly, domestic homes are run on single-phase electricity for the usual lights and heating, but if you are using a high 'load' of electricity and it has to be at a constant rate, you need three-phase power. That involved an entirely new power system, which didn't sit well within an old house. Cue a lot of people arriving, sucking their teeth, looking at where the new oven was to go and sadly shaking their heads. It felt as if we were pitching a new moon landing.

Every suggestion seemed to involve drilling through beams or digging up floors. What's more, our electricity supplier, SSE, couldn't see how it would work in tandem with our domestic power supply. Irritatingly, I couldn't now let the idea of a deck oven go, having been sold the dream by Kitty, realizing its potential and having been offered one for free.

After two weeks on the phone with SSE there was a breakthrough, like cracking a code. A new person asked a simple question. 'Is the bakery building separate from the house?' 'Yes, it is,' I answered. 'Then it can have its own separate supply of electricity.' That was it. We had done it. The cables would still need to come through the house, but not through our domestic fuse box. Simon, our problem-solving electrician, devised a route the cable could follow – from the street, through the wall by the front door, into the kitchen, across to the back door and then out to the bakery. In a flurry of activity, suddenly it all happened.

Pavements were dug up. A special meter box was installed.

A cable as thick as a python was snaked through the house. We were rigged up.

Kitty rang Mr Beam and the following week Andrew's brother arrived with two helpers, who brilliantly worked out how to bring the massive deck oven through the small, winding corners of the house and into the bakery. After our complete failure to go this route with the fridge earlier in the year, they made it look easy. They set the decks as Kitty supplied them with crispy cheese and fried onion toasties and tea. The ovens went on and their glow filled our homemade bakery. Katie totally ignored the fact that there was now a fat cable running straight through the house because she was getting her kitchen back in time for Christmas.

LAST CHRISTMAS I'D felt so horrible that I wanted it all to pass as fast as possible, but now my life felt very different. I had the new bakery, which I loved, and I had the shop, which I also loved. I wanted to embrace every single bit of it. I was in good company because Mum, who isn't particularly sentimental about many things (she is the only person I know who doesn't really like dolphins), goes above and way beyond in December. And this year, after an enforced break the Christmas before and with her newly restored kitchen, she was back with a vengeance.

First, there is the annual finding and hanging of the woollen sock advent calendar. Knitted by a neighbor when we were little, it comprises 24 small red and green socks tied to a length of rope that is slung over the banisters. They are then filled with penny chews to be eaten on each day of December. The socks survived well for the first few years, but then a family of mice obviously found them and now most of the toes are nibbled away and the sweets fall straight through. The advent calendar lasted long enough to become tradition and so it still has to come out, even if most of the socks are now held together with staples.

The Christmas tree can only be bought after the 19th December and only from a particular farm at the end of a long, muddy drive where a mournful elderly farmer has a small collection of firs. Mum feels this is less commercial. What it normally means is, by the time we get there, one small sad tree is left, which we haul away. Somehow, Mum feels we have saved it.

Then the tree decorations emerge. Mum has a story to tell about each one. The robin that Aggie made out of plastic beads, the beheaded angel, the decorations passed down from Granny, including some glass balls that her father (my great-grandfather) was meant to have hand blown, and then the pièce de résistance, the silver bird for the top of the tree. This was made by Mum when she was four and is basically a lump of tin foil with a button eye and some pink feathers randomly stuck on.

When we were younger, we would try and argue for something that actually looked nice, but now we sit silently as it is placed reverently on the thinning top branch. Finally, and this bit brings catastrophizing Dad out in a cold sweat, real candles are clipped to the branches of the tree ready to be lit when the needles have had a chance to get tinder dry in front of the fire.

This happens on Christmas Eve. Mum lights the tree candles and then we all sit on the stairs outside the sitting room in pitch dark and sing 'Silent Night' in German. (We sing quite fast because Dad worries that the whole tree is smouldering next door and none of us speak German anyway, so it's pretty incomprehensible.) Then we get to go in and open our presents. I know – on Christmas EVE. Mum has a tiny bit of German on her side of the family and they do it there, too. It doesn't end there. We have raclette for supper (because it's good to line your stomach with cheese the day before you have the biggest meal of your life) and are forced to go to bed early because Mum is not going to wait that long before dropping large, red stockings (again mouse-eaten, same cupboard) on our beds.

By Christmas Day, it's all calmed down a bit. The stockings are opened in Mum and Dad's bed and always have a satsuma and a walnut in the toe. When we were little, we spent Christmas with Mum's parents who also did all the same rituals including stockings in their bed, which included Dad as well. He says he is still traumatized by spending Christmas Day morning in bed with his mother-in-law.

Then follows the traditional muddy walk with our neighbors, the Shaws, and a complicated game of betting on what words will crop up in the Queen's speech.

The one thing that Dad insists on is the biggest, fattest turkey you've ever seen. None of that messing around with goose or ham, even though every year we all say how dry turkey is.

As I say, there are a lot of traditions at Christmas.

THIS WAS THE year I discovered that Kit has inherited every last bit of DNA from Katie's Christmas gene. Personally, I'm a bit bah-humbug about the whole thing (other than the turkey's fatness) and suggested we might put up a few sprigs of holly in the bakery and think about some mince pies. Kit had other ideas. By early December, the shop looked like a scene from *Elf* and I had given up on any semblance of control.

Watlington comes into its own in December. Lights festoon the High Street, linking chains of mini Christmas trees, and Bob hauls up the biggest spruce you've ever seen by the Town Hall.

At Angela's, boxes of chestnuts and parsnips sit alongside great stalks of Brussels sprouts and her helpers are dragooned into elf hats. The Co-Op window is entirely bricked up by a display of Quality Street and Roses and even the chemist breaks open the cotton wool to make a scene for Father Christmas riding over small hills of compression stockings.

Kitty had invested in so many fairy lights they gave the bakery a Tardis-like glow. We bought a box of oranges from Angela and punctured them all (and our fingers) with hundreds of cloves before balancing them in precarious pyramids on the shelves. An assortment of Playmobil characters acted out the Nativity scene in the window and hundreds of cut-out paper snowflakes hung from the ceiling. From the lighting shop we bought an Austrian wooden scene of two cable cars passing on a mountain, which I painted with the words 'orange' and 'bakery'.

Again, the donations came in. Little stars made from dried orange peel and copper wire from Helen (who gave us the original Homepride flour men) and a massive green wreath made by Juliet almost covered the whole door.

And then there were the bakes. With the new deck oven up and ready, Kitty went into overdrive. Mini panettones with chocolate chips and orange zest topped with almond crackling, doughnuts stuffed with a segment of Terry's Milk Chocolate Orange Ball, sticky toffee brownies, bacon and pecan swirls, drunken Eccles cakes made with brandy-soaked dried fruit and mince pie croissants swirls jostled for position on the counter. On the shelves our usual bakes were joined by our Christmas dinner sandwich with turkey, stuffing, cranberry sauce and Brussels sprout slaw and a Stilton and red onion chutney plaited bread.

By Christmas Eve, the High Street was heaving. Our queue matched the butcher's on the other side, where everyone waited to pick up their pre-ordered turkey. The whole family were helping in the shop and by lunchtime every crumb had been sold. Katie went home with Aggie and Albert to start getting the house ready for her parents' arrival the next day (and to get the stairs hoovered for the German singing that night). Only then I realized that the one thing I had kept reminding myself to do every evening for the past two weeks I had never actually done.

I hadn't ordered the turkey.

I saw the butcher's every day and clocked the boxes and boxes of free-range birds arriving, but for some reason I had never actually put our name down. I went over, mouthed apologies to the queue, and grabbed Tom by the arm. 'Is there any slight chance you might have a turkey left over?' 'No,' said Tom, 'they're all named and paid for.' He looked sad for me. I ran to the Co-Op – not one bird remained. I went home and informed the house. Katie, who was in the middle of wrapping up presents for stockings (I'd long ago lost the argument that Father Christmas doesn't wrap), was unperturbed as it's not one of her keystone traditions – if we didn't have raclette cheese, it would be different – but it was Albert who looked the most stunned, like I'd announced we'd decided not to do presents.

There wasn't time to look elsewhere for a turkey because Katie and I had offered to do mulled wine for the carol concert that evening outside the Town Hall and we still had to cook it up alongside baking a mountain of cheese straws. The carol concert is led by Watlington's brass band and in previous years had taken place by the War Memorial. It was always packed, but slightly lethal, as people spilled off the pavement into the road while the local bus tried to inch its way past. This year Bob had led a movement to stop traffic for an hour on the High Street and move the band to under the Town Hall. There had also been an aggressive advertising campaign with every lamppost in the town wrapped in a carol concert poster along with the banner that there would be a 'special' visitor on the night.

It was a cold, clear evening. As we set up outside the bakery with a huge urn of mulled wine and piles of cheese and paprika swirls, more and more people turned up. Bob had told me to make enough for around 300 people, but by 6 pm at least double that were crowded around the Town Hall. The mulled wine was drained in what felt like minutes as the Christmas spirit hit and carols were yodeled out. I ran to the Co-Op to get more red wine and took it back home to heat up. Aggie and Albert carried the pans of mulled wine along the High Street and poured them into the urn as Kitty and Katie doled it out. By 7 pm we were all exhausted and, as the last refrain of 'five gold rings' came to a loud and raucous halt, the distant sound of bells could be heard.

Around the corner came a pony and trap carrying Father Christmas. In a slightly surreal moment, it became clear the driver was the famous actor who lives in the town. He was looking distinctly uneasy. The pony, understandably, was unused to a crowd that a police horse at a football match might be unnerved by. The huge cheer that went up when Father Christmas stood up didn't help. As the actor clutched the reins, there was clearly a moment when the whole sleigh could have carved straight through the middle of the families with small children in mittens perched on their shoulders. Somehow, they managed to stop. Father Christmas quickly did some present dispersal and ho-ho-ho'd before the pony decided it was time to head on. It was a stunt Tom Cruise would have thought twice about doing himself.

We packed up the sticky urn, wiped down the table and headed home.

My phone pinged and it was a message from Tom the butcher. 'In ur cupboard,' it read.

We got to the front door and there on the bottom shelf of the Magic Cabinet was a slightly squashed, large white box. Scrawled on it were the words 'not picked up'.

It was a turkey.

12
DODO

SOMETHING ELSE NEW appeared that December, as well as the bakery shed – our van. When we first opened the shop, we didn't really think through how we would get the buns and bread from our house, up the High Street and into Number 10. It is only a four-minute walk but the distance is too far to carry everything by hand. We tried out a few things. A second-hand green trolley with slightly wonky wheels that was just too big for the pavement had to be pushed along the road, but we still had to do the journey about five times. After a long morning baking, it was backbreaking. We reverted to loading up our old car with precariously balanced crates.

After a few collisions, when the Danish pastries met the Marmite and cheese swirls, we realized we needed to get a proper bakery van.

I had just started to google different models when an ad popped up on the sidebar for a bizarre-looking bubble of a van that I had only seen a handful of times. The S-Cargo (say it a few times, you'll hear the word play) was built in small numbers by Nissan back in the late eighties and early nineties. The chassis was from a very basic existing car, but Nissan handed the design for the bodywork over to an LA-based, Japanese tattoo artist (as you would). He came up with a small range of bizarre, retro-looking vehicles including the S-Cargo. The factory only made about 8,000 of these vans, but that was enough for it to make it into *Business Week*'s official list of the 50 ugliest vehicles of past 50 years (it came in at number 13). The van in the pop-up ad was currently languishing in a haulage yard in Birmingham. Albert and I arranged a time to go and have a look at it.

It had an engine about as powerful as a hairdryer, made an apologetic beep when reversed, had a huge, curved windshield that seemed to touch the sky and was utterly comical to drive and to look at; in other words, it was perfect.

Once the van was delivered, we got Justin to paint a big orange on the side with our logo. Kristian designed some wooden shelving to go in the back, which we could slot all the bread and bun crates into. Kitty ran a competition on her Instagram for a name and, after stiff competition from Margo the Escargot and Anne Embarrassment (thank you, Eilidh), Dodo was chosen. She is brilliant, turning heads wherever she goes (which is always very slowly). She makes Kit and me feel very grown up and professional and yet at the same time as though we're in an episode of *Noddy* every time we drive her up the High Street.

We took a short break at the beginning of January and with it the chance to get a slightly better system going. Our daily menu was now so full that to get everything ready and on the counter, and do the serving ourselves, meant we were constantly running behind. Our days were finishing later and later. We had Ben one day a week, but we needed more help.

The answer was 'Shop Katie' (not to be confused with Pilates Katie or even Wife Katie, as I will now be calling her). Shop Katie and her family were one of our first subscribers and whenever we handed her a fresh loaf, she would lift it up and breathe it in. Back in the seventies, her parents had run a grocery shop that sold fresh bread – it took her straight back to childhood. Shop Katie agreed to do two mornings a week and is possibly the calmest, most unflustered but deeply bread-knowledgeable helper you could have. At 9 am every morning I would stack up the van and race (slowly) in the S-Cargo down the road to the shop. Shop Katie (and the queue) would be waiting as I unloaded the breads and buns before heading back for the next load. This often meant that Shop Katie had to guess at what some of the bakes were as I didn't have time to fully brief her. She was brilliant at working out ingredients and knew exactly how Kitty's mind worked. Once she spotted orange peel in a bun, she knew cardamom would be involved as well.

Shop Katie was also a brilliant double act with Ben who arrived at 8 am every Friday from London on the Oxford Tube (confusingly a bus). Shop Katie would sometimes come in when Ben was there and we would hear them quietly conferring about new systems of labeling or pricing – systems that would have made more sense than our usual chaos, but we never quite managed it and their tolerance levels remained thankfully high. Ben had his own set of loyal customers who he would take time to listen to and who we think started coming especially on a Friday to see him. On the occasions Ben couldn't make it, I would stand in and find myself apologizing for his absence. Friday lunches started to become an event in themselves. Ben would finish at the shop and Wife Katie would normally be working from home, so the four of us would sit at the kitchen table and have soup and finish up the bread. We'd pretend that we were doing a Saturday paper interview where people always seemed to sit and have lunch in sunny rooms with white sofas in the background and a bunch of flowers on the table. Ben would then retire to the distinctly non-white sofa, light the fire and, after his dawn start from London, snooze off as he watched Netflix along with Sparky, always delighted the fire was lit so early.

THE NEW BAKERY made me feel like the shop, safe and cocooned. When you went into it and shut the door you were enveloped in the smell of dough and yeast and Marmite and chocolate. Like the shop, it soon filled up with random items. On a shelf, fat gold letters spell out the word CRUST and a knitted figure of Dad in a flat cap and braces that arrived through the post sits beside a bowl of the small railway figurines I put in my short films. There are a lot of pictures of oranges (by children and adults) that we've been given as presents – drawn, painted and lino prints. On the wall by the window is an old black and white photo of a wedding that is one of Dad's favorites. Neither of us knows where it comes from, but the bride looks so unhappy we want to spirit her away.

Dad and I do a sort-of bakery dance in this small space, moving around each other between the huge table in the middle and the oven, the mixer and the store cupboard.

I missed being in the shop on weekday mornings and talking to everyone who came in, but it meant I could experiment more. Channeling Chad again, I was ready to chop more wood. First, I decided we should branch out into cheese toasties. I called in Dad as he is the expert here – cheese, after Sparky and Mum, is the love of his life. Cue a deep dive into the world of the perfect toastie. Together we hunted down the most melting, oozing, cheese-packed feeds on Instagram we could find. Then we planned out a toastie crawl in London.

Taking the Oxford Tube early one Sunday, Dad and I got on Boris Bikes at Victoria and set off for Borough Market. By the time we got back on the bus at 5 pm, we could hardly get up the four steps to greet the driver.

We had eaten five cheese toasties, taken notes on all of them and – other than not wanting to eat another one for a while – we knew what we wanted the Orange Bakery toastie to be.

First, there was the cheese itself. One of my favorite place names ever is a nearby village called Nettlebed. It always makes me think of *Grimms' Fairy Tales*. When I was younger and my friends were collecting the *Rainbow Magic Jewel Fairies* books, I made Mum read me all the *Grimms' Fairy Tales*. They are about as far removed from unicorns and pixies as anything could be. I think I liked the Grimms' stories because often the female characters in them are allowed to be clever and strong, sometimes even brutal, like Gretel who pushes the witch into the oven and the mother goat who rescues her kids by cutting open the wolf's stomach. My absolute favorite though, which Mum read to me again and again, was the tale of 'The Six Swans'. The princess must rescue her six brothers (who had been turned into swans by their evil stepmother) and save herself by sewing shirts made from nettles. Whenever we drove through Nettlebed, I would think of the story and how the youngest brother still had a swan's wing in place of one arm because the princess didn't have time to finish the final shirt. So, when Dad mentioned Nettlebed had a famous creamery and we should talk to them about their cheese, I liked the sound of it immediately.

We met Rose on a very cold February morning, and she told us how they had farmed Guernsey cows for two generations. She had decided to make the milk into three sorts of cheese, which were all named after nearby villages. She thought the Highmoor would be perfect for our toasties and was happy to give us offcuts.

Over the next week, we experimented every day with toasties for lunch. We realized that we already had the perfect bread for toasties in our Albert loaf: classic loaf-tin size, no holes in the crumb for cheese to drop out of and, as it already had milk and butter baked into it, the outside went brown and crispy when toasted. The Highmoor cheese was too rich on its own, so we mixed it with some mild cheddar for extra ooze and then a highly secret (not really) mixture of scallions, mustard, and a drop of sriracha. We invested in a huge toastie machine and rolled it out at the bakery one Friday. First lesson learnt was that you have to put greaseproof paper in the machine or the fire alarm goes off. Second

lesson learnt was that the toasties take too long to put together on site and so we have to have them all made up in advance, otherwise the queue gets even longer. But the third and final lesson was that everyone loves our cheese toasties.

Next up for experimentation was cookies. I had mastered some favorites (chocolate halva tahini and stem gingersnap) but wanted to take them a step further. The true cookie master (apart from the Cookie Monster) is Christina Tosi of Milk Bar. I stalked her on Instagram and scoured her cookbooks for ideas. What she gave me was the confidence to pick something I loved and turn it into a cookie. For me, it had to be Snickers.

Dad, Mum and I always work together in the shop every Saturday. Once we are closed and cleaned up, Dad goes to Tom the butcher and exchanges a couple of loaves for some sausages, brings them home, puts them in the frying pan, cuts up an Albert loaf, slathers the slices with ketchup, mayonnaise and mustard, adds in a few roasted tomatoes with the sausages and then wolfs down the perfect sausage sandwich. That is always followed by a Snickers bar before he pulls his flat cap over his eyes and takes a 20-minute nap either on the bed in the kitchen (everyone should have a bed in their kitchen) or on the porch outside the bakery in a very ratty old armchair.

Even though we have spent the morning selling Nutella swirls and salted caramel-filled doughnuts, by this point in the day Dad just wants a Snickers and a snooze.

For him, I decided to make a deconstructed 'Snickers' cookie with chocolate, peanuts and a Rolo. It's now one of our bestsellers (although Dad still sticks to his shop-bought Snickers).

Thanks to Christina, I also got a lot braver with spices, soaking raisins in a mixture of Earl Grey tea and garam masala so the Chelsea buns had a lovely smoky taste. Za'atar went into brioche buns and a sprinkle of cardamom edged its way onto the morning buns. And my loaves, which were now so bouncy and content, could happily take other flavors.

I developed the Rosie, a loaf made with cider, sharp cheddar and walnuts, after watching *Cider with Rosie* over Christmas, and the Vincent made with sunflower seeds, honey and severed ears – or that was what Dad kept saying until he realized that no one was buying the Vincent and his ear joke was working against the poor loaf. Once he dropped that line, it became more popular.

Dad's patter in the shop on a Saturday became mine and Mum's own version of bingo.

It was a complicated game that changed weekly, but broadly you scored one point when Dad said, 'Dogs are very welcome, they are the shop Hoover', two points if he said, 'Anything from the shelf of temptation?' and five points if he mentioned, 'The locusts have been,' when customers came late and saw empty shelves. My personal best was a total of 30 points.

It was also around this time I came up with one of my all-time favorite bakes – the Happy Loaf. CBD oil was getting big and Tai Chi Nick had set up a business in the village called Raised Spirit, selling jars of CBD oil mixed with flavors like coconut and cocoa. He had given us some to sell in the bakery as well as a few jars to try at home. One morning we ran out of time to make up the usual doughnuts, so that meant we had a whole tub of enriched dough going to waste. I transferred the dough to a tin, slathered it in caramel and baked it, then spotting Nick's CBD oil with chocolate, I heated that up and brushed it over the top. It went on the shop counter that morning. And then the next morning. And the next. Fat, thick slices of treacly doughnut-based deliciousness with a sprinkling of CBD joy. The Happy Loaf.

Finally, as February got colder and colder, we thought it would be nice to offer a free small cup of hot coffee. We didn't want to compete with The Granary Café down the road where they served lattes, flat whites and hot chocolates, so we wanted something simple. The answer came from our 80-year-old neighbor Ginny. Ginny lived on her own and was a constant presence on the High Street, pushing her walker and stopping to chat. Her son Nick lived in Poland with his wife and daughter (little Ginny), but came over every few months to stay with Granny Ginny. He always came into the bakery. He had created a coffee business back in Warsaw and offered to create our own blend of the Orange Bakery coffee beans. He even sent us a Moccamaster drip-filter coffee machine that we set up in the corner of the shop. Soon the smell of fresh coffee hit our waiting customers along with the comforting aroma of bread. We only offered black coffee as we were never organized enough to get milk in the morning, but doling out a quick, free caffeine hit to our customers made us feel slightly less guilty about the cold queue.

Being able to source everything for the bakery within such a small radius made Dad and me feel more and more grateful that Watlington was our home.

One weekend Dad took an old wall cabinet and painted it blue with the words on top 'Proud to Shop Local'. The doors opened to show Playmobil people carefully chosen to represent everyone we got ingredients from; Angela and Tom and Rose were lined up along with an egg from Pyrton and a small bottle of milk (actually white paint and water because the real thing would have gone off very quickly) to represent the nearby Lacey's dairy. The cabinet sat in the window.

Going in to deliver a last batch of cinnamon buns to Shop Katie one morning, I saw she'd moved the fake milk bottle to the counter. As I picked it up and went to put it back in the cabinet, Shop Katie said, 'Oh yes, I had to use that as someone wanted a white coffee.' 'But it's paint and water...'

For the first time ever, Shop Katie appeared flustered as she looked down the High Street and tried to spot anyone retching over a cup of coffee. We never found out who it was.

13
MAN THE BARRICADES

SHOPPING LOCAL WAS about to become more important than we could ever have imagined. It was Ben who acted like a canary in the mine about the arrival of COVID-19. He worked freelance for a big insurance company where they suddenly announced that they were cutting back on staff as they could no longer conduct house visits in London. Ben came to help us in the shop full time, but soon the virus was everywhere. The first full coronavirus lockdown was announced.

At this point, Watlington came into its own, as if it had been waiting for this moment. It was a historical glimpse of how the Home Front would have worked. All the shops on the High Street got together to plan out who could deliver what to whoever might be isolating. Every street was given a warden to look after anyone on their own and there was a surreal moment when we got a visit from a member of the Parish Council asking what our baking capacity might be if the town was 'cut off' for a while. Albert went from working flat-out for his A levels on a Friday to a sudden juddering halt and no school or exams on the Monday. I went to Bristol to pick up Aggie from her halls of residence, leaving most of her things behind in her room with no idea when she might return. Wife Katie disappeared entirely into a world of Zoom calls and barely seemed to move from the computer as her charity, Maggie's, attempted to support the thousands of people with cancer who were now isolating.

There was a constant low-level thrum of anxiety and panic. Kitty and I responded to it by making more and more bread.

It felt like that was our responsibility. We had everything we needed; the flour from Wessex Mill kept coming, our starters pretty much fed themselves and all the other ingredients were on our doorstep, from eggs to milk. The shop is so tiny that we decided to sell from the doorway, like Andrew and Eilidh did from their kitchen window, so we could keep social distancing. We wheeled up an old hospital trolley from home that we had kept wool blankets on. It acted as a barricade across the door (more *Carry On Matron* than *Les Misérables*) and was perfect as a makeshift counter. We could even use our payment machine through the glass of the side window, so we felt safe and our customers did too.

The atmosphere in the shop changed completely. Before the shop was always packed and the chatter rate inside was deafening. Now only one person could come to the sheltered doorway at a time and it became like a confessional: a short murmur about the latest pandemic news, then an agreement over how lucky we were with the weather, a bread order (with at least one bun for morale) and then a careful move away with a nod to the person behind. Shop Katie understood entirely that we felt it was unsafe for her to continue serving and we all felt teary when she worked her last shift.

Those first few weeks of lockdown are now a bit of a blur. There was a strange atmosphere of paranoia in the High Street and across the town.

Normally alive with old ladies and their small dogs, children on scooters and teenagers on bikes, the town became like the scene in *Chitty Chitty Bang Bang* when everyone slams their shutters closed as the Child Catcher arrives.

If you saw someone in the street, you would move into the road in an exaggerated fashion and even saying hello would sometimes seem too intimate. Moving around the Co-Op became an exercise in logistics as they experimented with various complicated one-way systems using tins of soups as traffic barriers.

We settled into a rhythm only made possible by Aggie and Albert being at home. First Albert took over the deliveries to those isolating. He managed somehow to decipher the scrawled notes I had written down on scraps of paper and shoved in a drawer and transferred them into a large black diary so he could see who needed what on each day. Every morning he skimmed off what was needed and loaded up his ancient red Polo to start his deliveries. Aggie was looking after Ginny, who like so many others couldn't leave her house. Ginny would ring her at 9 am on the dot and give a short list of what she needed from the

Co-Op along with her copy of *The Times* and Aggie would deliver it to her door and check she was okay. Every morning, without fail, Ginny would open the door as Aggie knocked and say something positive like 'That's a lovely shirt you're wearing.' It made Aggie's day.

Aggie would then spend the morning serving in the shop while Kitty and I baked and baked and baked.

It was Aggie who spotted the trend. First it was customers coming in asking if we sold flour – she was always happy to siphon off a small bag. Then we started to get requests for sourdough starter. Instagram had exploded with pictures of bread and every time Kit posted a recipe it got a brilliant reaction. We gave out pot after pot of our starter, but soon realized that we just didn't have enough. Then Kitty being Kitty spotted the potential of creating dehydrated starter packs. She spread some starter on greaseproof paper and left it out in the sun to dry before she used our tiny coffee grinder (stopping every 10 minutes when it overheated) to crush the flakes into powder. She then poured these precious granules into little brown envelopes and Aggie sold them from the counter. Alongside these Kitty started putting together 'Magic Bread Mixes' – flour mixed with the dehydrated starter so anyone could create their own loaf. We hardly had time to put them out on the shelves before they sold.

I FOUND THE queues building up outside the bakery each day incredibly stressful. There had always been a trail of customers stretching down the road, but now with social distancing and everyone at home the queue snaked down past the Memorial Club.

Saturdays were the busiest as everyone had worked out that you could get everything you needed for the week in Watlington. Sometimes the whole High Street felt like one long queue. Strings of people outside the Co-Op and the butcher's almost had to dance around each other and it could take up to an hour in the bakery queue before you got to the confessional booth and could claim your loaf.

Seeing everyone waiting patiently to get into the bakery made my feeding instinct kick in.

One Saturday I made up a whole load of soft brioche puffs with a melted chocolate button inside and put each one in a brown paper bag. Dad attached a leather strap to a wooden tray that I could hang round my neck. With the small brown bags lined up in the tray, I went down the queue, handing out the chocolate puffs to make the wait a bit better. I did it again the next week with some mini doughnuts coated with ginger sugar. Now it's a Saturday ritual, and everyone knows it's coming. There's one little boy called Toby who does a small jig as I come down the street and claps his hand over his mouth with excitement as he gets his bag. It makes me feel very lucky and less guilty that everyone is patiently waiting.

Feeding everyone became a big part of lockdown for me. Looking back, I'm not quite sure why Dad and I felt we had to double our production, but at the time we didn't even question it. We went from the bakery being open from Wednesday to Saturday to adding on Monday and Tuesday. That meant Sunday became our prep day and we didn't have a day off.

I became so utterly focused on making the bread that when we hit August and took our first break since March, I realized I was slightly broken.

Adrenaline had been keeping me going, so when we stopped to take two weeks off, my body dipped and the exhaustion hit. My energy to bounce went and that then sent my mind spiraling off. It was terrifying that those feelings could return so quickly. I was too exhausted to bake, my body was shattered, but when I tried to listen to it and stay in bed my mind cracked.

I couldn't concentrate on anything. I felt panicked and breathless. I was exhausted, but I couldn't sleep.

I needed to work out how to balance my absolute need for the routine of bread and baking against my body's need to rest. I found stopping baking so painful that it was easier to keep carrying on, but that meant eventually I just went under. It was Mum who helped me toward the answer by doing a lot of lying on my bed with me. Understanding that looking after myself would mean I could carry on was fundamental. Mum couldn't tell me how to do that but she kept listening so I could try and work it out myself (I think some of the time she had a quick nap as well). I haven't got any clever answers here as I only know how my brain works (or am trying to work it out).

Baking is everything, it gives me a sense of being but I also know that it's not safe to completely rely on it and I need other things alongside it.

I haven't got a perfect list, but there are things that help. Podcasts about brilliant people, learning Danish (mainly to fulfill my fantasy of living in Copenhagen and working at Hart Bageri) and eating dumplings in the bath watching *Kung Fu Panda* are all good. But it's something I'm constantly working on.

14
THE SCOUTS

KITTY SLIPPING BACKWARD caught me totally unawares. I was so used to her being beside me – chirruping away as we did our dance around the bakery, usually to The Proclaimers, tipping out dough, shaping the loaves, filling the fridge and then the oven – that I had totally failed to see she was faltering.

When we finally stopped for a break in August and it became clear how exhausted Kitty was, I felt terrible.

For five solid months we had got up at 6 am (5 am on a Saturday) and worked till evening to bake bread and buns that sold out every day. The more Kitty did, the more she wanted to do, and I loved doing it beside her. But I felt I had utterly failed as a parent to protect my 16-year-old daughter when, as we hit our break, Kitty virtually collapsed.

It made me question what we were doing and why, and if I was some sort of Bill Sykes character making money out of small child labor. As usual, it was Katie who brought me out of my wallowing guilt with her pragmatism, and Kitty who then reinforced it.

Katie pointed out that the bakery had been Kit's path to recovery – without it we would never have got out of the first box. We had helped make it happen, but it had to be up to Kitty to then manage how she made sure that her baking wasn't all-consuming. Feeling guilty that we hadn't somehow 'stopped her' from crashing was disempowering for her. We couldn't always be responsible for how she felt or in fact think it was up to us to make her feel 'better' or, even worse, 'happy'. Kitty put it even more succinctly.

Kitty was the Formula 1 racing driver and we were her pit crew. If she drove off the track going too fast, it was her fault. We could help keep the car running, but she was behind the wheel.

I returned to my station in the pit and considered our race tactics. I totally understood where Kitty and Katie were coming from, but I also realized that we did need to implement some changes. The first of these was working hours. With the bakery just a door away from our home kitchen, it was very easy to keep popping in to finish off something, or start something else, or tidy up or simply double-check everything was all right. We had got a whole lot more efficient, but as soon as Kit and I freed up some time, we tended to fill it by baking more. We had to learn how to shut down the day and draw a line under the week.

The second issue was space. Kitty and I fitted brilliantly in the tiny bakery shed, breathing in when we passed each other, one going high, the other low when passing with trays. But it was tight. As soon as anyone else came in, the dance became a muted jig because you just couldn't move. We really needed to have another baker because that was going to be the only way to liberate Kitty. At that moment, the bakery was her everything, but there was a danger it might set her back once she was ready to steer her own course. Already she was researching 'stages' she could do – a sort of unpaid internship where you work briefly in another bakery to learn techniques – but she would only be able to go when we (I) could cope without her. In two years, the bakery had become a proper business and important source of income for the family, so we could never afford to close it down even just for a few days.

The answer was obvious; even though we had only been in our newly built bakery for a year and both loved it, we had to find somewhere else to bake. Somewhere we could close the door at the end of the day and somewhere big enough that we could take on one or maybe two extra people and so keep growing. Reluctantly, we started to look at options.

First, we talked to John, our local farmer, an extremely generous man with a quiet manner. Every year he hosted a family thanksgiving service in his barn with the tractors neatly lined up outside, hay bales for the congregation and an array of animals looking on in pens, including one year an enormous bull with such massive testicles it was difficult to concentrate on singing 'All creatures great and small'. While talking to John, he suggested we look at the huge, corrugated shed that sat beside his farm shop. They had power, water, lovely high ceilings and no bulls. We got quite far with measuring up before we discovered that, like most farm buildings of that age, the roof contained asbestos. Perfect for sheltering a combine harvester, but less good for food production. We did look at building a sealed bakery within the shed, but even Kit conceded that it had got quite complicated.

Next up was a purpose-built space at the local industrial park, which we had considered before. It was only a few miles away, reasonably priced and impeccably clean, but it made both Kitty and me feel a bit sad.

We knew we didn't want to work somewhere that felt so sterile and airless. Kitty was convinced the bread wouldn't like it either.

We kept thinking and looking, our radius getting wider and wider. Then, like every cliché, we realized what we'd been looking for had been hiding in plain sight.

We had arrived in Watlington from Shepherd's Bush in London 13 years ago when our three children were aged three, five and seven. To ingratiate herself as a newcomer, Katie had made the children join everything on offer. Kitty attempted ballet lessons in the Memorial Club (very short lived), Aggie did Irish dancing in the school hall and we signed Albert up for Beavers (the group that precedes Cubs) in the old Scout Hut tucked behind the High Street. Every week he would trudge off to a session with the group leaders, Otter and Badger, a kindly middle-aged couple who took Beavers very seriously. He would come home with notes saying things like 'Next week, please dress your Beaver warmly,' and 'Beavers should now be able to tie their own shoelaces.'

Albert lasted a term before handing back his Beavers badge and taking up tennis with Mandy (already mentioned as the daughter of Andy with the dog-hair jumper). Albert loved tennis from day one, partly because there were no uniforms, group activities or tying knots involved. Walking with him to Mandy's lessons, I would pass the Scout Hut beside the tennis courts where the Beavers were busy with these activities and hear the murmurs of Otter and Badger as they tried to suppress 14 small boys who mainly wanted to set fire to things. And then the hut went quiet. Otter and Badger retired. The pack was moved to the new sports pavilion, where they had the whole of the Rec to run around rather than a small car park. The old Scout Hut settled back on its haunches and, with no activity inside, it started to look a bit sad. Ivy crept its way through the windows and more and more slates came off the roof.

The Scout Hut belonged to the Memorial Club, which runs as a charity, and had happily bumbled along until some new members were made trustees and decided that the hut could be revived. One of these trustees was Sarah, who runs brutal (to my eyes) fitness boot camps at the Rec and is a brilliant force of nature. It was Sarah who suggested to us that it could make the perfect bakery.

Kit and I went to have a look. As the door swung open, it felt as if the Beavers had only just left the building. It still smelt of small boy and there was a pile of old flags on the floor alongside a huge wooden board with different examples of knots stuck to it.

The window frames were splintered and rotten, the false ceiling was sagging alarmingly and there was harsh strip lighting. We know the pattern here. My heart slightly sunk at the amount of work it would take to make it function. Kit went straight home and drew up how it might be our dream bakery with a walk-in fridge, two sinks, massive work tables and a three-decker oven.

The Memorial Club were brilliant. After a lot of toing and froing, they offered to put up the money for a basic refurbishment if we signed up for a long lease. As well as fixing the roof, replacing the windows and, crucially, getting it all through planning, they would also organize the installation of three-phase electricity (my nemesis). We would then need to fit it up to be a proper bakery.

It felt like a massive and terrifying step.

We would have to almost double our income to make back the money spent on the rent for the Scout Hut and the shop. It would also mean we were tied into the bakery for at least five years and a fair amount of debt. But if we didn't do it, we could never grow any bigger and release Kitty to concentrate more on what she was brilliant at – the creativity of baking – and less on the sheer daily grind of producing bread. We said yes and signed the lease.

BY THIS TIME, I had got through a lot of noodles in the bath and had moved onto *Kung Fu Panda 3* (disappointing). As autumn appeared, I realized I was feeling okay-ish again. This was a relief as there was no way Dad could do everything on his own and, although he never said it, I knew that a bit of him must be thinking 'Am I really going into this with a teenager who at times has to lie on the bakery floor or put her face in the fridge to fight back an anxiety attack?' These horrible brain hijacks were never caused by the fear of what we were taking on, that was the only thing that kept me going, more by a horrible cold swamp of loneliness – a loneliness that didn't really make sense as I knew I was surrounded by people who loved me, but was still just there.

For the last two years, my main company had been family and customers. They were all I could fit in around the bakery. Aggie and Albert made me laugh more than anyone else I knew, but friendships with my age group seemed far removed from what I was doing and I didn't look for them.

I sometimes felt that I had a surfeit of love – love for my loaves and the family – but there was more left over and I didn't know where to put it.

It was Sparky who gave me the idea. Sparky loves Dad above all others and Dad speaks to Sparky in a voice that carries more emotion than the end of a Richard Curtis film. Sparky likes the rest of us, but he quite probably dreams about scenarios where he could give up his life for Dad or rescue him from a flooded stream or an angry bull. I knew that persuading the family to take on another dog when Sibby had been such an unqualified disaster was going to be hard, but I did my research carefully. A dog that was small but not too small, that was a herder not a hunter (and therefore wouldn't go down badger holes), that would appeal to Mum's deep and abiding love of the Queen (no other royal members) and came from Wales where we had always spent our best holidays. The arrow pointed one way – a Corgi.

I spent a month going down the rabbit hole of Corgi research. The differences between a Cardigan Corgi and Pembroke Corgi (long tail or short), how to train them, groom them and where to find one. I put together a short PowerPoint of key facts about Corgis, illustrated by the best pictures I could find and with a written pledge that I would carry out all puppy duties. Mum and Dad were still unsure. Bringing in a puppy seemed to add another layer of chaos when they felt we were still bobbing along with our heads only just above water.

Plus, they felt terrible that we had to give away Sibby and that we would look as if we never learnt from any mistake. I kept on and finally persuaded Mum to drive with me to Wales to meet a Corgi breeder so that she could ask more questions. We turned up to a cul-de-sac in the middle of Swansea, went through a front door and were met by a pen of fluff. Seven Corgi puppies were piled up on top of each other as their mum slept exhaustedly on the family sofa.

I sat in the pen. One of the fluff bundles peeled off, staggered over, and collapsed into my lap. Mum knew the cause was lost.

A month later we were back in Swansea and Scout belonged to me. Named after the girl in *To Kill a Mockingbird* she takes all the love I can give. She is utterly confident in being the strangest looking dog you can find. She is fox colored with huge ears, massive paws, short legs, a bushy tail the same length as her and an inability to get up the two stairs to the kitchen without tripping up. She talks constantly, although rarely barks. It's a mixture of yowls and groans and she lies on the end of my bed presenting her tummy to rub. She is fiercely loyal and obsessed with carrying long sticks. Now bakery bingo is replaced with Scout bingo when out on walks. She invariably draws comments. Two points for 'Is that a Corgi?,' five points for 'My granny used to have one of those,' seven points for 'Is the Queen nearby?,' and the rare shout of a small child 'It's a fox! It's a fox!' gets the full ten points. Scout assumes she's important, and head held high she trots past her admirers while Sparky almost shrugs his bushy eyebrows behind her. Scout is mine and she is very special.

THE TWO SCOUTS – the dog and the hut – became a big part of our lives and, with Kitty firmly beside me, I started to marshal the brilliant team of locals, who always seemed to make things happen for us, to start work on making a building into a bakery.

Kristian clad the walls and Joe installed the plumbing and there was the usual hiccup with the electricity when it was discovered that the big wooden pole at the end of the lane was rotten and would need to be replaced, but even that passed remarkably smoothly. We invested everything we had in a walk-in fridge the size of a small mortuary and a new oven from the ever-wonderful Mr Beam. Kitty and I again picked up brushes and painted everything we could white. Somehow, we got Campbell's dough table out of the bakery shed (it had to go over the garden wall again) and Albert and I trundled it noisily up the street with Kitty sitting on it clutching Scout, as resplendent as the Queen.

Within six weeks we were just about ready. Now all we needed was to find another baker.

In my mind I had the kind of person we wanted lined up; an experienced baker able to take our amateur enthusiasm up a few notches – in other words, someone who knew how a proper bakery worked rather than our guesswork. Not an easy find, but now we had the bakery set up, not impossible. Perhaps we could put the word out on Instagram?

I talked to Kit.

'Oh, I've already found her.'

'Sorry?'

'I've already found the perfect person.'

'Is she experienced?'

'Well, she's a really good baker.'

'Bread?'

'Occasionally.'

'So, she's an occasional bread baker?'

'Yes, but she makes brilliant stuff and most importantly, look, she does a great bakery dance.'

Kit showed me an Instagram video of someone dancing around her kitchen, a broom for a guitar, with exactly the same expression as Kitty when she is excited about a new bake. Her feed was full of incredible cakes and buns she had made including one with Marmite and cheese, which swung it for me.

'I like her,' I said.

Kitty messaged her and asked straight out if she would think about working for us. It was very Kitty; we hadn't yet met her, but it was a gut instinct.

It wasn't part of Karishma's game plan as she was thinking about moving to the West Country with her boyfriend, Sean, but we arranged a Zoom chat anyway and she was every bit as funny and lovely and knowledgeable as she was in her videos. We gave her all the time she wanted to think about it while Kit and I kept our fingers crossed. She lived about half an hour away in Reading, just around the corner from where my dad had been a GP all his life. I convinced myself there had to be some kind of serendipity about it.

Karishma came to meet us and to see the Scout Hut. She and Kitty talked non-stop. The next day she said yes.

Having Karishma in the bakery has been a joy. She has shared her knowledge of all things sweet with us while, in turn, she has learnt how to perfect her loaves. She crosses over between the two of us, listening to my long rambles on growing up with eighties politics and music whilst endlessly playing 'Would you rather?' with Kitty on subjects like 'Would you rather live without gluten or without dairy?' She has added to our breakfast repertoire with cheesy fried eggs and we all troop back home for lunch in the middle of the day, where Katie is usually waiting once she discovers that Karishma has brought some of her mum's amazing curries with her.

What having both the Scout Hut and Karishma has meant, though, is the freedom for both Kitty and me to look slightly outside the world we have created. Kitty is now 17 and her sights are firmly on the future. Now her low points are few and far between, with dungarees and bucket hat on, she disappears to London on the Oxford Tube most weeks to work at different bakeries from Kew to Bermondsey. Once again, this extraordinary community of bakers have opened their doors and she has bounced right in.

Kitty comes back from other bakeries alight and buzzing with new ideas and techniques, which I soak up from her like a needy sponge.

For me, it has meant a bit more time to come to terms with everything that has happened. Writing this book has been very cathartic for all the hard work of squeezing it in around the shop and baking and life generally. Recounting the past few years has made Katie and me revisit some of the times when it would have been easier to shut ourselves away and instead acknowledge how deeply scared we were at the beginning that we might lose Kitty. It has also made us realize just how much help and support we have been given – from other bakers, from family and friends, from the generous crowdfunders, and from Watlington itself.

Aggie and Albert have been through, first, having a sister who almost disappeared, to putting up with their home becoming a bakery while they tried to negotiate their own lives through different lockdowns. They were forgiving and kind and quietly resilient.

I could not have foreseen that, at the age of 50, I would change careers and become a baker – and I am deeply grateful that I am. I wish that Kitty could have bypassed some of the grimmest bits of this story, but I also know that we wouldn't have done any of this if it hadn't at first been driven by desperation. I also know that the part of Kitty's brain that makes life difficult for her is also probably the same bit that gives her extraordinary drive and determination and a way of seeing life differently. Virtually all the recipes in this book have been created by her alone and she understands ingredients and taste in a unique way.

Cooking intuitively and unimpeded by having to do things conventionally, she constantly surprises me. I have absolutely no idea what comes next other than that baking will be at the heart of it.

AND NOW IT'S TIME for the outside world and I finally feel so ready. Thank you Layla's, The Snapery Bakery, Sourdough Sophia and Rye by the Water, who were the first four places I went to do a stage. I know that by the time this book comes out there will have been many others.

I look back on that accidental trip to Hart's Bakery in Bristol at the beginning, when I could hardly speak and wanted so badly to be a part of that world, and now I am. I am. I pull hot loaves out of different ovens, I mix and shape dough and I learn from other bakers who have been doing this for years. I stand in vast walk-in fridges nibbling at varieties of chocolate I've never heard of. I wear the baker's uniform – hello Crocs and socks – and headbands and dungarees.

I talk the dough talk and my heart almost leaves my body when a bakery takes on one of my recipes.

I go to bed at 8 pm and get up at 5 am. I look after myself. I can get low and tired and sad, but it passes and I come home to be met at the door by Scout, a tennis ball deposited firmly at my feet.

I unpack my green rucksack holding new loaves and buns to show Dad. I head to the Scout Hut to see Karishma and share why we must put whole peanuts in our next cookies. I love standing behind the counter in the bakery and seeing people pulled between the new rhubarb and custard brioche or the chocolate, hazelnut and orange swirls and then taking both.

I look back at that 14-year-old who could not make any sense of why she existed and I want to show her where she is now.

THE END

RECIPES

One of the hardest things about writing this book was deciding which recipes would make it into *Breadsong*. The bakery is full of tins and tins of labels from over two years of Kitty's experiments, many of which were never captured in any way. Sometimes Kitty might post a bake on Instagram, but virtually everything she does is from memory. So, first choosing and then codifying her recipes felt like a mammoth task.

Kitty bakes mainly by instinct and yet now we had to pin down recipe quantities and techniques. Step forward Kitty's godparents, Julia and Al. When we asked them to take on the role 17 years ago they didn't know that, alongside renouncing the devil, they would also have to become recipe testers. Julia and Al are the perfect combination. Julia is a brilliant cook, neat and precise, and able to offer suggestions for making things work even better. Al is – in his own words – 'a deeply novice baker' who is happy to have a go.

We started by sending Julia and Al three recipes each week, then we would nervously wait for their feedback. They took the role seriously, passing back detailed comments and photos that Kit and I would pore over, excited to discover which of our ideas worked and making adjustments when things didn't. Al's pastéis de nata (see page 256) were a triumph and his focaccia (see page 159) looked better than ours. He created a street WhatsApp group for taste testers; soon it became a highly sought-after role with neighbors clamoring to join. Julia's love of Marmite is famed, so our Marmite and cheese escargots (see page 267) went on repeat. Overcoming her fear of puff pastry, she perfected cheese straws (see page 253) and sent photos accompanied by lots of exclamation marks and a smiley face.

We wanted our recipes to really unpick some of the fear around different doughs and pastries, and the feedback from Julia and Al was that for them the recipes did just that. We hope they do the same for you too.

Notes on measuring ingredients
· Flour, sugar and cocoa cup measures are spooned and leveled
· Brown sugar measurements are firmly packed
· Other non-liquid cup measurements are loosely packed
· We have given measurements in cups and in metric weight but please use only one set of measurements.

BREAD

MIRACLE OVERNIGHT WHITE LOAF

This was the first bread recipe I learnt to bake, and how the simple ingredients transform into a loaf still feels like magic. All you need to make a loaf twice as tasty as anything on the supermarket shelf, with a crunchy crust and pillowy crumb, is a Dutch oven with a lid and an oven that can get up to 450°F. At the beginning our oven could only reach 350°F, so even if yours is lacking oomph then your breadmaking is not doomed. If you make only a single recipe from this entire book, this one will probably give you the biggest thrill. It's truly a miracle.

MAKES 1 LOAF

- 4 cups (500g) bread flour, plus extra for dusting
- 1¼ teaspoons (10g) fine sea salt
- 1 teaspoon (3g or ½×¼-ounce envelope) instant dried yeast
- 1⅓ cups (330g) lukewarm water

1. Sift the flour into a large mixing bowl and add the salt and yeast. Stir everything together using either a sturdy spoon or – my personal favorite – your hands. Bit by bit, gently mix in the lukewarm water until a shaggy dough forms. We call this the Scooby dough in homage to Scooby-Doo.

2. Place a damp kitchen towel or shower cap over the rim of the bowl and leave in a cozy (draft-free) place to proof for 12–16 hours, overnight is best. Like the fairy godmother turns a pumpkin into a carriage, time transforms your scrappy, dull dough into a bubbly, live creature of its own (although, I think I'd prefer the pumpkin over the carriage).

3. Once your dough has risen and is bubbling away, tip it out onto a lightly floured work surface. Remember it's alive, so the greater respect you show the dough with gentle handling, the more it will reward you and the better your loaf will come out. Gently shape the dough into a ball (a well-floured plastic dough scraper really helps here), making sure there is a light coating of flour all over.

4. Place the shaped dough on a sheet of parchment paper, cover with a damp kitchen towel and set aside in a warm, cozy place to rest for 1 hour.

5. Halfway through the resting time, preheat the oven to 450°F (or as high as it will go). Put a large Dutch oven with a lid and a heatproof handle into the hot oven for 30 minutes to heat up.

6. Once the Dutch oven is good and hot, carefully take it out of the oven and lift off the lid. Uncover the dough and, using

the parchment paper, lift and then lower the dough into the heated Dutch oven. Using a sharp knife, razor blade or scissors, score the top of the dough with slashes in any pattern you like – one long slash, a cross, a square or even a smiley face. You might want to invest in a baker's lame for this (basically a razor blade in a stick and dirt cheap but, alongside your dough scraper, a good friend).

7. Pour a couple of tablespoons of water inside the Dutch oven around the dough, replace the lid and put the dish back in the hot oven. Bake for 30 minutes with the lid on. Remove the lid to reveal your magnificent loaf and then continue to bake uncovered for a further 10 minutes to get a nice, golden crust or 15 minutes if you like your loaf a bit darker. I do.

8. Place the loaf on a wire rack and leave to cool for at least 30 minutes. This is the hardest part, but it's also the most important as the bread keeps cooking after you take it out of the oven. If you listen carefully, you might even hear the loaf sing: this is the 'breadsong'. Just don't scorch your ear...

You've just made bread. No mess (though I always find a way). No kneading. Just magic. And a little fermentation.

VARIATIONS

▶ **Pain de Campagne**
Swap 2 cups (250g) of the bread flour for whole wheat flour. This results in an earthy loaf that makes you feel you've been working in a field all day.

Serving suggestion: With a slab of salted butter and some chunky country pâté.

▶ **Seeded Rye**
Swap ¾ cup (100g) of the bread flour for rye flour and add ¾ cup (100g) toasted seeds of your choice. My favorite combo is pumpkin, sunflower and flaxseed. This makes a dense loaf with a nice, roasted nuttiness. But be warned, working with rye is like handling wet concrete. When your hands get all sticky from the dough, use a bit more flour to wipe them clean. Sounds weird, but it's so much better than scraping off dough under a running tap.

Serving suggestion: Cut thinly, toasted and spread with a scraping of horseradish sauce, some smoked salmon and a couple of thinly sliced cornichons.

▶ **The Comfort**
Add 1 or 2 tablespoons of Marmite or other yeast extract, dissolving it in the 1⅓ cups (330g) of warm water before mixing it into the dry ingredients. This is my favorite loaf. I started making this bread at a time when every day seemed like a war zone, full of panic attacks, extreme lows and constant blasts of exhausting mental shrapnel. Every night I looked forward to mixing the dough, that I'd bake in the morning. Everything about this loaf makes me feel safe. Its sweet, slightly charred smell, its savory crust, its squishy, soft, more-ish center. Whenever I knew the day ahead would be hard, I'd make this loaf.

Serving suggestion: If I had my way, I'd be very happy eating The Comfort loaf with cheese all day, every day.

▶ overleaf, clockwise from top left: Seeded Rye, The Comfort, Pain de Campagne, Overnight Focaccia

OVERNIGHT FOCACCIA

Miracle dough is like Mystique in *X-Men*. Just when you think it's one thing, it can suddenly transform into something else entirely. Like this bubbly rosemary focaccia.

MAKES 1 LOAF

- 1 quantity of Miracle Overnight White Loaf dough (see page 153)
- a good glug of cold-pressed rapeseed oil or olive oil
- a handful of rosemary needles
- a good pinch of flaky sea salt

1. Follow steps 1 and 2 of the Miracle Overnight White Loaf recipe on page 153. In the morning, transfer your bubbly dough into a well-oiled piece of parchment paper lining a smallish rectangular roasting pan (6×8 inches/15×20cm), spread it evenly to a thickness of 2 inches (5cm) and rub a little of the oil over its belly. You can use olive oil, but we prefer to use an amazing oil made from locally grown rapeseed, which we love. Leave in a warm place to proof for 2 hours. You could cover it if you want, but the oily surface should stop a skin forming.

2. Preheat the oven to 425°F.

3. Drizzle a little more oil over the top of the dough and then, using your fingertips like a masseur, gently dimple the surface. (You can mutter 'relax, relax' at this point.) Sprinkle over some rosemary needles and flaky sea salt.

4. Bake in the hot oven for 20–25 minutes or until crisp and golden. As soon as the focaccia is out of the oven, brush it with more oil. Lift the focaccia out of the pan and leave on a wire rack to cool for 10 minutes.

   Serving suggestion: Doused (or drowned) in a little pot of olive oil mixed with balsamic vinegar or sliced laterally and filled for slab sandwiches (we like mozzarella, tomato, avocado and a bit of salami in ours).

CHALLAH

We first came across challah watching *Friday Night Dinner* on TV,
a brilliant British sitcom about a Jewish family in North London. It's
the brioche-like plaited bread that's made for the Sabbath meal.
Less rich than normal brioche, challah is wonderful toasted and
even better soaked in egg and fried in butter to make French toast.

MAKES 1 LOAF

- 4 cups (500g) bread flour
- 1¼ teaspoons (10g) fine sea salt
- 2 teaspoons (7g or a whole ¼-ounce envelope) instant dried yeast
- ¾ cup (170g) water
- 1 tablespoon plus 1 teaspoon (45g) cold-pressed rapeseed oil (or sunflower oil)
- 2-4 tablespoons honey (at least 2 spoonfuls, but you need to experiment to find out how sweet you like your challah)
- 2 eggs
- 3 tablespoons (50g) soft unsalted butter
- 1 egg lightly beaten with 1 tablespoon milk, for the egg wash
- a handful of poppy seeds (optional)

1. Sift the flour into a large mixing bowl and add the salt and yeast. In a separate bowl, mix together the water, oil and honey. If you're using creamed honey, you might find it easier to use hot water for mixing with the oil – just let the oil mixture cool a little before pressing ahead. Crack the eggs into the oil mixture and stir everything together.

2. Make a small well in the center of the flour and pour in the wet ingredients. Knead either by hand for 5 minutes or in a stand mixer fitted with the dough hook for 3 minutes. Keep kneading the dough while gradually adding the butter, a generous dollop at a time, until you're left with a smooth, elastic dough. This will take 9–10 minutes by hand and 5–6 minutes in the mixer.

3. Transfer the dough to a well-oiled bowl, cover with a kitchen towel or shower cap and leave in a warm place to proof for 1–2 hours or until the dough has doubled in size.

4. Once your dough is puffy and plump, tip it out onto a lightly floured work surface and divide it into three equal pieces. Roll each piece into a 16 inch- (40cm) long strand, roughly 1 inch (2–3cm) thick (equal length is more important than equal thickness here). Lay the three strands of dough side by side on a sheet of parchment paper and pinch together the ends that are furthest away from you.

5. Braiding a challah is just like braiding hair. Lift the strand on the right at the top and take it over the middle strand, so that the right strand becomes the middle strand. Next, lift the left strand and take it over the middle strand so that the left strand now becomes the middle strand. Repeat these steps until you have braided the entire length of the strands to shape the whole challah. Pinch the strands together at the bottom and tuck them under the braid to neaten it up.

6. Lift the paper carrying the challah and place it on a baking sheet, cover with a damp kitchen towel or oiled sheet of plastic wrap and leave in a warm place to proof for 1 hour.

7. Preheat the oven to 400°F.

8. Before you put the challah in the oven, brush it all over with the egg wash. You can always sprinkle a few poppy seeds over as well. Bake in the hot oven for 30–35 minutes until golden brown. Leave on a wire rack to cool for 20–30 minutes before serving.

Serving suggestion: To make French toast, whisk together 2 eggs and a bit of milk in a shallow dish. Cut two slices of challah and soak them in the egg mixture for 2 minutes on each side. Heat 1 tablespoon of butter in a non-stick frying pan and fry the soaked challah slices until crisp and brown on each side. Serve with crispy fried bacon and drizzled with maple syrup.

BIGA BREAD

A biga is made by pre-fermenting a certain amount of dough overnight. Just like the no-knead bread method on pages 153–4, you don't need to do anything more than mix all the ingredients together. In the morning your biga should have grown bigger and have a nice, puffy skin and a whiff of alcohol. This means the fermentation process has started. All you do next is mix in a bit more flour, water and yeast. The gluten strands in this new dough need to be strengthened. You can help with this by stretching and folding the dough several times during the following few hours before shaping and proofing the bread. It is very much the same process used to make sourdough, and the finished bread is pretty close to sourdough too (why we call it cheat's sourdough). There's a rich, nutty butteriness to the loaf that comes from the dough having a bit of time to develop some flavor. The added bonus is because you're using commercial yeast (but not very much) it will be pretty consistent. So, if you don't feel ready for the world of sourdough starters and all the feeding they require, this is your perfect halfway house. The quantity I've given here is for two loaves because one is never enough in our family. If you don't need that much bread, you can bake half of the dough into a loaf and use the other half to make pizzas or flatbreads.

MAKES 2 LOAVES
OR 1 LOAF AND
4-6 PIZZA BASES

FOR THE BIGA
- 6⅓ cups (800g) bread flour, plus extra for dusting
- ½ teaspoon (roughly 2g) instant dried yeast
- 2⅓ cups (550g) cold tap water (you don't want to speed the yeast up by using warm water as a slower ferment is of the essence here)

FOR THE NEXT DAY
- 1⅔ cups (200g) bread flour
- 2½ teaspoons (20g) fine sea salt
- ½ teaspoon (roughly 2g) instant dried yeast
- ¾ cup (200g) lukewarm water (not cold, this time)

1. The night before, place the ingredients for the biga in a bowl and fully mix everything together. Leave overnight at room temperature, covered with a kitchen towel.

2. The next morning the biga will be bigger (we never get tired of that joke). Add in the extra flour, salt, yeast and water. Mix it all up again thoroughly with your hands, or you can use a stand mixer fitted with a dough hook.

3. Once combined, you then need to fold the dough every 30 minutes to strengthen that gluten. Wet your hands with some water. Imagine the ball of dough in the bowl is a clock face and then, beginning at 12 o'clock, grab a handful of dough and stretch it out before folding it back into the middle of the ball. Turn the bowl through 90 degrees, so you are now at 3 o'clock. Repeat the grabbing, stretching and folding. Continue this process twice more at 6 o'clock and 9 o'clock. Then repeat these four folds again. You can also scoop the whole ball of dough up from the middle using both hands – like lifting a small sleeping puppy – let it stretch and then fold it down on itself (although don't do this with any actual puppies). You'll soon feel the gluten in the dough becoming much stronger and your ball will go from shaggy

OUR   BREAD   IS

MADE   WITH   JUST

3   INGREDIENTS

FLOUR, WATER, SALT

OH, AND ONE MORE,

TIME

to quite tight and firm. This is the gluten doing its work. You want to squeeze in at least three rounds of folds during the first 2 hours, but then let the dough be for the last hour.

4. After 3 hours, scoop the dough out onto a lightly floured work surface. Divide it into two equal pieces with a dough scraper. If you are going to make pizzas, chop one half of the dough into smaller pieces.

5. Gently shape the dough you are using to make bread into a neat round. Place the shaped dough on a floured sheet of parchment paper and then back into a bowl. Alternatively, put the dough into a well-floured banneton. If you want to make a sandwich loaf, you can plop it straight into a well-oiled loaf pan. Leave to proof in a warm place.

6. This loaf only takes 1 hour to proof so halfway through the resting time, preheat the oven to 475°F (or as high as it will go). Put a large Dutch oven with a lid and heatproof handle into the hot oven for 30 minutes to heat up.

7. Just like you do for the Miracle Overnight White Loaf on page 153, carefully take the Dutch oven from the oven and lift off the lid. Lower the parchment paper carrying the dough into the Dutch oven and put the lid back on. If you only have one Dutch oven and you're making two loaves, put the second ball of dough in the fridge while you are baking the first. Remember to give the Dutch oven enough time to get really hot again for baking loaf number two. If using the loaf pan, just slide it straight into the oven.

8. Bake the loaf with the lid on for 30 minutes and then uncovered for a further 20 minutes. Baking it for slightly longer with the lid off gives the loaf a good crust, which is a perfect crunch with the buttery crumb. The loaf pan should take about 40 minutes to bake, longer if you want a darker crust.

VARIATION

After you've divided the dough into two and shaped one half into a loaf, roll what's left into 4 or 6 balls (or how many suits) and let them rest in the fridge with a kitchen towel draped over the top. They'll sit there happily for a few days until you're ready to cook pizzas. To make the bases, simply flatten out the dough to your preferred thickness. Smother the bases in your favorite ingredients and cook them at the highest temperature your oven gets to. Everyone talks about how the toppings make a pizza, but once you've tried this dough, you'll start to think it's all about the base.

1. Biga Bread → page 162   2. The Comfort Loaf → page 155
3. The bakery dance (that's my hair, not Dad's beard)

FIVE GO TO BILLYCOCK HILL   ENID BLYTON

FIVE GO TO MYSTERY MOOR   ENID BLYTON

FIVE GO ADVENTURING AGAIN   ENID BLYTON   HODDER & STOUGHTON

WHAT KATY DID   SUSAN COOLIDGE   WARNE

SODA BREAD

This is just about the quickest bread you can bake. The best soda bread in the world is made in Ireland and this loaf feels like you're being hugged by a Galway granny. At its most basic, you just need all-purpose flour and baking soda. The baking soda pretty much starts doing its work as soon as you have mixed it with anything liquid, so speed is important. There's no kneading required and it can be a bit messy, but it still amazes me that something so tasty can come from something so fast. Buttermilk is great to use, and you can also create your own by adding a tablespoon of lemon juice to whole milk.

MAKES 1 LOAF

- 2 cups (250g) all-purpose flour
- 2 cups (250g) whole wheat flour
- ½ cup (50g) oats (any type works — old-fashioned, quick-cooking etc.)
- 1 teaspoon baking soda
- 1¼ teaspoons (10g) fine sea salt
- 1 tablespoon sesame seeds (optional)
- 1¾ cups (420g) buttermilk (or 1¾ cups/420g whole milk and 1 tablespoon lemon juice whisked together and left to curdle slightly for 5 minutes)
- 1 tablespoon molasses (optional, but really lovely despite what Muriel's husband says on page 93)

1. Preheat the oven to 400°F and line a baking sheet with parchment paper.

2. Sift both the flours into a large mixing bowl and then add the oats, baking soda, salt and sesame seeds (if using). Make a small well in the center and pour in the buttermilk and molasses (if using). Stir until there are no visible patches of dry flour, but don't overmix. Don't worry if your dough resembles a wet sandcastle at this point.

3. Scoop your dough out onto a lightly floured work surface and shape into a round. It's a sticky dough so you may want to coat your hands in flour or use a well-dusted dough scraper. Transfer the shaped dough onto the lined baking sheet. Using a sharp knife, cut the traditional deep cross into the loaf (this is to keep bad spirits away, and you never want these in your kitchen). So that the loaf keeps the cross shape while baking, cut deep to within 2 inches (5cm) of the base.

4. Bake in the hot oven for 40–45 minutes. Transfer to a wire rack and leave to cool for 30 minutes before slicing.

Serving suggestion: With cheese, cheese, and a bit more cheese.

GUINNESS SODA BREAD

At the bakery, we make a loaf with malted grains that have been soaked in Guinness for 24 hours to give them a lovely sour juiciness. This bread definitely needs some molasses or blackstrap, but if you're struggling to find either, honey will be fine too – you just need something sweet to balance the bitterness of the Guinness.

MAKES 1 LOAF

- 2 cups (250g) all-purpose flour
- 2 cups (250g) whole wheat flour
- ½ cup (50g) oats (old-fashioned are best)
- 1 teaspoon baking soda
- 1¼ teaspoons (10g) fine sea salt
- 3 tablespoons (40g) soft unsalted butter
- ¾ cup (200g) buttermilk (or ¾ cup/200g whole milk and 1 teaspoon lemon juice whisked together and left to curdle slightly for 5 minutes)
- ⅔ cup (150g) Guinness or other dark stout
- 3 tablespoons (60g) molasses or blackstrap molasses (or use dark honey)

1. Preheat the oven to 400°F and line a baking sheet with parchment paper.

2. Sift both the flours into a large mixing bowl. Add the oats, baking soda and salt and then rub in the butter. Make a small well in the center of the flour mixture and pour in the buttermilk, Guinness and molasses. Stir until there are no visible patches of dry flour, but don't overmix otherwise the dough becomes stodgy and the bread doesn't rise.

3. Scoop your dough out onto a lightly floured work surface and shape into a round. It's a sticky dough so you may want to coat your hands in flour or use a well-dusted dough scraper. Transfer the shaped dough onto the lined baking sheet. Using a sharp knife, cut the traditional deep cross cut into the loaf to within 2 inches (5cm) of the base.

4. Bake in the hot oven for 55–60 minutes or until hollow when tapped. Transfer to a wire rack and leave to cool for 30 minutes before slicing up.

Serving suggestion: This is a great bread for dipping into soup, especially something comforting and beige like leek and potato.

PITA BREADS

I'm obsessed by eggs. Everything about them is brilliant: their shape, their colors, the fact that they're eaten around the world and there are so many recipes to choose from. I'll add an egg to pretty much anything, so when I came across the recipe for sabich (basically a pita bread stuffed with tahini, hummus, fried eggplant and as many eggs as you can possibly squeeze in) I was virtually packing my bags for Tel Aviv, the home of the best sabich in the world. First, I had to master a good, reliable pita bread recipe. This is it.

MAKES 8 PITA BREADS

- 3²/₃ cups (450g) bread flour
- ½ cup (50g) whole wheat flour
- 1½ teaspoons (12g) fine sea salt
- 2 teaspoons (7g or a whole ¼-ounce envelope) instant dried yeast or ¼ cup (50g) sourdough starter (see page 190)
- 1¼ cups (300g) lukewarm water
- 1 tablespoon (10g) olive oil

1. In a large mixing bowl, combine all the ingredients. Knead either by hand for 10 minutes or in a stand mixer fitted with a dough hook for 5–6 minutes, until you have a smooth, shiny dough. Transfer the dough to a lightly oiled bowl, cover with a kitchen towel or shower cap and leave in a cozy place to proof for 1 hour if using instant dried yeast. If using sourdough starter, leave the dough to proof for 3 hours and fold the dough on each hour using the same clockface folds as outlined on page 162.

2. Tip your dough onto a lightly floured work surface and cut it into eight equal chunks, each weighing around 3¾ ounces (100g). Shape each chunk into a round and then leave to rest for 30 minutes. This gives the dough a chance to relax.

3. Preheat the oven to 450°F and place a baking sheet or baking stone in the oven to heat up.

4. Roll out each ball of dough into an oblong or oval shape that is roughly ½ inch (1cm) thick, or even thinner if you can. Slide onto your hot baking sheet or stone. You can try using a well-floured piece of plywood or even a well-floured sheet of stiff card.

5. Bake in the hot oven for 6 minutes or until the pita breads balloon up and are beautifully plump. Cover with a cloth while they cool slightly, then slice open and eat while hot.

Serving suggestion: Fill with fresh hummus, fried eggplant slices (sprinkled with a bit of za'atar if you can find it), some cornichons, and then sliced eggs (soft boiled so that the yolk has just hardened) – lots and lots of them. PS. For perfect soft-boiled eggs, bring a pan of water to a boil, lower in the eggs and boil them for 6 minutes. Immediately plunge the eggs into cold water for 1 minute and then peel.

BREADSTICKS

These are great for bread-on-the-go. The sweet version makes
a perfect travel snack and is brilliant for breaking up and dunking
into black coffee (Dad) or peanut butter (me). The savory breadsticks
are perfect for picnics, either on their own or dipped into hummus
or pesto.

MAKES 5 BREADSTICKS

- 4 cups (500g) bread flour, plus extra for dusting
- 1¼ teaspoons (10g) fine sea salt
- 1⅓ cups (320g) lukewarm water
- 2 teaspoons (7g or a whole ¼-ounce envelope) instant dried yeast
- ¼ cup (50g) sourdough starter (see page 190, if you have some but don't worry if not, it's just to add a bit of extra flavor)
- any extra flavorings (see variations opposite)
- semolina, for dusting
- flaky sea salt

1. Line two baking sheets with parchment paper.

2. Sift the flour and salt into a large mixing bowl. Make a small well in the flour and pour in the water, yeast and sourdough starter, if using. Knead into a smooth dough either by hand or in a stand mixer fitted with a dough hook. This takes around 7–8 minutes by hand and 4–5 minutes in a mixer. Let the dough rest for 5 minutes.

3. If you're staying plain, then don't worry about this stage, but if you're adding in any extras (see variations opposite) then knead them into the dough for 2 minutes by hand or 1 minute in the mixer.

4. Transfer the dough to a lightly oiled bowl and put a damp kitchen towel or plastic bag over the top. Leave in a cozy area to proof for 1 hour or place in the fridge overnight (this slower proofing at a colder temperature gives the bread time to develop a much deeper flavor).

5. Tip out the dough onto a work surface lightly dusted with flour and semolina, then divide it into five equal pieces, each weighing around 6½ ounces (180g). Roll each piece into a long sausage, then take an end in each hand and twist like a cheese straw. Dust with more semolina. Transfer onto the lined baking sheets and leave to proof for 1 hour.

6. Preheat the oven to 425°F.

7. Slide a roasting pan filled with water into the bottom of the oven to create a nice, steamy atmosphere.

8. If you're making the breadsticks with dark chocolate, sprinkle over a few coarse sea salt flakes. Bake in the hot oven for 15–20 minutes or until golden. Leave to cool on the pans for 10 minutes (both are delicious eaten when still warm and spread with salted butter, if actually you decide to go nowhere).

VARIATIONS

▶ **Cheese and Olive**
Add 1 cup (100g) grated cheese (we like the nuttiness of Colby, but any hard cheese works), ½ cup (100g) chopped black or green olives and 3 tablespoons (25g) diced jalapeños (great if you enjoy a kick).

▶ **Bittersweet Chocolate, Hazelnut and Sea Salt**
Add ¼ cup (50g) bittersweet chocolate chips, ½ cup (50g) roughly chopped roasted hazelnuts and 2 tablespoons honey or maple syrup, then sprinkle the sticks with flaky sea salt just before baking.

BAGUETTES

It always feels like baguettes should be the easiest bread to
master, but actually there are a lot of different stages so don't
worry if they take a while to perfect. Remember, most baguettes
are churned out in factories to look perfectly identical, so don't
be too harsh on your mis-shapes as they will still taste great.
This recipe makes five loaves, which is perfect for a big picnic.
If that's too many, you can always freeze some after baking or give
some away. Alternatively, just halve the quantities given below.

MAKES 5 BAGUETTES

- 5²/₃ cups (700g) all-purpose flour, plus extra for dusting
- 2½ cups (300g) bread flour
- 4 teaspoons (14g or 2 whole ¼-ounce envelopes) instant dried yeast
- 3 teaspoons (25g) fine sea salt
- 1 quantity of poolish (see below, optional, but worth giving a go for flavor)
- 2 cups (500g) lukewarm water
- semolina, for dusting

FOR THE POOLISH

- ⅓ cup plus 1 tablespoon (50g) bread flour
- 3 tablespoons plus 1 teaspoon (50g) lukewarm water
- smidgen of a teaspoon (1g) instant dried yeast

1. First, make the poolish. A poolish is a bit like a poor-man's sourdough starter. It adds a slightly fermented quality to the loaf. Not essential, but it definitely adds something special. Mix together the flour, water and yeast in a bowl, cover and leave to proof for at least 4 hours or, even better, overnight.

2. When you're ready to make your baguettes, combine both the flours, yeast, salt and water in a bowl and add the poolish as well. Knead the dough either by hand for 10 minutes or in a stand mixer fitted with a dough hook for 6–7 minutes. This is a stiffer dough than many of the others in the book. Leave to proof for 1 hour or so until the dough has doubled in size.

3. Tip your dough out onto a lightly floured work surface and cut into five equal pieces. Press each piece down with the palms of your hands to make a rough rectangle. Fold the rectangle into three in the same way you would fold a letter into three to get it into one of those annoyingly narrow envelopes. Leave the dough for 5 minutes to relax a bit.

4. Meanwhile, get out your largest baking sheet – or two sheets, if necessary – and line it with parchment paper. Dust the paper with flour so that it is well coated.

5. Once the dough has relaxed, with the fat strip of dough sitting lengthways, take the shorter edge furthest away from you and fold it into the middle of the dough, pressing down with your fingers at the center seam. Repeat this action to make a tight roll. You should be able to do this at least twice or perhaps three times.

6. Place your palms flat in the middle of the folded dough and, applying a light, even pressure and moving your hands outward from the middle to the ends, roll out the baguettes to your preferred length (but no longer than the baking sheet) and thickness.

7. Dust the baguettes with semolina (or regular flour, if you don't have any semolina). Gently lift them onto the well-floured, lined baking sheet, spacing them well apart. Leave to proof for at least 1 hour.

8. Preheat the oven to 425°F. Slide a roasting pan filled with water into the bottom of the oven to create steam.

9. Using a baker's lame or sharp knife, make several long slits on a slight diagonal down the length of the loaf. Bake for 20–25 minutes or until golden but darker on top. Let cool for 15 minutes then cut open and slather with salted butter.

BIALYS

The awesome thing about Instagram is seeing what other bakeries are making all around the world. One of our favorites is Northern Rye in Newcastle (North East England) because, just like us, they started out with only a couple of little Rofco ovens. When they posted their bialys, we were intrigued – we'd never seen anything like them before. A bialy looks like the lovechild of a bagel and a pizza. It turns out that bialys are something that was made by Ashkenazi Jews in Białystok (hence the name) in Poland – Dad loves finding out these bits of history. Traditionally it's filled with slow-cooked onions and poppy seeds (which is delicious) but it's perfect for filling with whatever you want (see below for a few ideas). The recipe is based on the simple no-knead method we use for our Miracle Overnight White Loaf (see page 153). It's a very basic bread, but you do need to make up the dough the night before.

(see page 153)

MAKES 8 BIALYS

- 4 cups (500g) white bread flour, plus extra for dusting
- 1¼ teaspoons (10g) fine sea salt
- 1 teaspoon (5g) granulated sugar
- 1 teaspoon (3g or ½×¼-ounce envelope) instant dried yeast
- 1⅓ cups (320g) lukewarm water
- filling of your choice (see below)

1. Place all the ingredients in a bowl and mix together until just combined. Cover the bowl with a kitchen towel or shower cap and leave overnight somewhere not too hot and not too cold – the Goldilocks sweet spot.

2. The next morning, scoop out the dough onto a lightly floured work surface. Chop up the dough into 8 equal pieces and then roll each piece into a ball. Place the balls on a baking sheet lined with well-floured parchment paper. Leave to proof for 1 hour or until the balls have doubled in size.

3. Preheat the oven to 425°F.

4. Poke a deep indentation in each ball and then use two fingers from each hand to stretch the crater out as if you were a small mole digging. Fill the cavity with your chosen filling.

5. Bake in the hot oven for 12–15 minutes. Put on a wire rack and leave to cool for 10 minutes. You can either eat them as they are or cut them open so that they are the ultimate in pimped-up rolls.

FILLING SUGGESTIONS

▶ Caramelized onions and poppy seeds (this is the traditional choice)
▶ Pesto, chorizo slices, a couple of olives, any cheese of your choice
▶ Olive tapenade, sun-dried tomatoes, slivers of Parmesan
▶ A fat blob of camembert and any chutney (Dad's favorite)

FATAYERS

We first came across these flatbreads at an epic cafe called Za'atar Bakehouse on the Cowley Road in Oxford, run by Mahmoud. He is passionate about bread and the whole eating experience, and you get to see his team of bakers creating, assembling and baking your meal in a huge, ferociously hot, domed oven. We're using a dry frying pan instead, which gives a great result, but you might want to open your windows because it can get a bit smoky.

MAKES 6 FLATBREADS

- 2 cups (250g) bread flour, plus extra for dusting
- 2 cups (250g) all-purpose flour
- 1¼ teaspoons (10g) fine sea salt
- 2 teaspoons (7g or a whole ¼-ounce envelope) instant dried yeast
- 1 tablespoon honey
- ¼ cup (50g) good olive or cold-pressed rapeseed oil
- 1 cup (250g) lukewarm water
- ¼ cup (50g) sourdough starter (see page 190, optional, great for extra flavor, but not essential)
- any flavored oil, for brushing (see opposite)

1. Sift both the flours and salt into a large mixing bowl. In a separate bowl, whisk together the yeast, honey, oil and water. Make a small well in the flour and add the wet ingredients, including the sourdough starter, if using. Mix together until there are no visible patches of dry flour.

2. Scoop out the dough onto a lightly floured work surface. Knead either by hand for 7–8 minutes or in a stand mixer fitted with a dough hook for 4–5 minutes or until your dough is smooth and glossy. Place the dough in a bowl, drape a damp kitchen towel over the top and leave to proof for 1 hour. If you have added sourdough starter, proof for 2 hours with a couple of folds during that time.

3. Once the dough has almost doubled in size, knock back your dough and knead it around, pushing all the gas out of it. Now put it in the fridge for 12–16 hours – this gives it a much richer depth of flavor and makes the dough a bit easier to work with. If you need to, you can use the dough straightaway.

4. Divide the dough into 6 equal pieces and roll each piece into a thin oval. Fresh dough can be quite elastic so you may want to do an initial roll and then come back to the dough after 5 minutes to finish them off. This gives the gluten a chance to relax and makes it easier to work with.

5 .   Heat up a frying pan until it starts to smoke (open up your windows). Once hot, place a rolled-out flatbread into the frying pan (you might fit a couple in, depending on the size of your pan). Cook for 3–4 minutes on one side and then, using a spatula or a fork, flip the flatbread over and brush any flavored oil onto the cooked side. Once golden on both sides, brush the flatbreads down once more with the flavored oil and eat while still hot from the pan.

VARIATIONS

Make a flavored oil by combining a couple of tablespoons of olive oil or cold-pressed rapeseed oil and any of these flavor combinations in a small bowl or glass. Brush the flatbreads with the oil while still warm.

▶   Smoked paprika and finely chopped garlic
▶   Honey and za'atar
▶   Rosemary needles, flaky sea salt and crushed red pepper flakes

Serving suggestion: Fill with homemade hummus and baba ganoush, the dip made from burnt eggplants and tahini.

BAGELS

Bagels are another food, like crumpets, that we've got used to buying from stores in plastic wrappers printed with the American flag. Absolutely fine, but when you eat the real thing, you suddenly realize what you've been missing. We like to leave the bagel dough in the fridge overnight because it makes them much easier to handle for the boiling bit and then you've got them for breakfast. But you can make these bagels up on the same day, if you're short on time.

MAKES 8 BAGELS

- 4 cups (500g) white bread flour, plus extra for dusting
- 2 teaspoons (7g or a whole ¼-ounce envelope) instant dried yeast
- 1¼ teaspoons (10g) fine sea salt
- 1½ tablespoons (30g) light brown sugar
- 1 tablespoon plus 1 teaspoon (24g) molasses or malt syrup (honey is fine to use, too, if you can't find the other two)
- 1¼ cups (300g) lukewarm water
- 5 teaspoons baking soda, for boiling
- egg white, for brushing (save the yolk for a carbonara sauce or to make homemade mayo, if you're brave)
- poppy seeds or sesame seeds, for sprinkling

1. Mix all the dry ingredients together and add the liquids. Give everything a good stir to combine. Knead by hand for 6–8 minutes or in a stand mixer fitted with a dough hook for 4 minutes. It is quite a stiff dough, but it should come together nicely and be quite smooth. Drop the dough into a lightly oiled bowl, cover with a damp kitchen towel and leave to proof for 1 hour or until doubled in size.

2. Scoop out the dough onto a lightly floured surface. Using a dough scraper, chop the dough into 8 pieces – each one should be around 3½–4 ounces (100–110g).

3. Roll each piece into a tight ball. Using a finger, poke through each ball to make a hole. Then, using your thumb and forefinger pincered together, gradually make this hole bigger by pulling open the hole. Transfer each bagel onto a baking sheet lined with an oiled sheet of parchment paper.

4. At this point, we put the bagels straight in the fridge to proof slowly overnight so they are ready to bake for breakfast. Otherwise, they only take about 40 minutes to proof.

5. Preheat the oven to 450°F.

6. Fill your biggest saucepan with water and bring to a boil. Add the baking soda to the boiling water (this helps give the dough its distinctive chewiness).

7. Working in batches, boil the bagels for 30 seconds on each side, then drain and plop them back on a baking sheet. Once all the bagels have been boiled, brush them all over with the egg white and sprinkle with either poppy or sesame seeds.

8. Bake in the hot oven for 15–20 minutes depending on how dark you like your bagels.

FILLING SUGGESTIONS

▶ Cream cheese, smoked salmon, cornichons and crispy fried onions

▶ Bacon and fried egg (a bib is essential for this one)

▶ Ham, Emmental, avocado and thinly sliced tomatoes

ange

kery

BREADS

TARTINE £3

MICHE £3

ALBERT £3

★ SPECIAL £3

PASTRIES

CINNAMON BUN £1.50

HOUSE COOKIE £1

PAIN AU CHOCLATE £1.50

CHEESE TWIST £1

ECCLE ROLL £1

★SPECIALS

TOAST

HOMEMADE BUTTER £3
WITH CHOICE OF
SPREADS ON HOUSE
SOURDOUGH

J T Brant, Orford Suffolk
Smokehouse & Fishmonger

FRY'S CHOCOLATE

cheese twist

TODAY'S SPECIAL
BREAD

TODAY'S
PAS

SOURDOUGH BREAD

Sourdough can be seen as this intimidating and cruel beast, superior to anything and everything else. Making sourdough bread is often lumped into the same category as running a marathon or learning another language. The truth, however, is that it's actually pretty tolerant and kind. All it wants is a little love and respect. Making sourdough is not rocket science; you learn by making mistakes, correcting them and then making more mistakes. You may feel like you've failed when your sourdough loaf comes out flat and 48 hours of work gets thrown in the bin, but that's okay. Sourdough isn't going anywhere. Just take your time, but know that it's all worth it because the moment you pull a plump, golden loaf from the oven, you'll be floating on a soft, bready cloud. For me, sourdough is one of the biggest loves of my life, but you don't need to master or even like it to be a good bread baker. Come to this section only when you want to and not because you feel you should. But if you do fancy it, hopefully the following pages will help turn sourdough from a puzzling Rubik's cube to a nice game of snap.

JOURNEY OF A STARTER IN ⑦ DAYS

Tiny wild yeast microbes

Grate the skin + flesh of one apple

Add 4 cups bread flour and 1½ cups water

Tepid

Mix and pour into a 2-quart jar

1 2 3 leave for 3 days

bubbles

discard half

add 2 cups flour + ¾ cup water (called the FEED)

⑦ 4 5 leave for 2 days → discard half + feed → 6 leave for 1 day → 7 READY

BAKING WITH A STARTER

Making bread is magic, and the starter is your wand. Without an alive starter to make it rise, your bread may resemble a cinder block; good for constructing a garden wall, less good for eating. I've always had a very Hufflepuff approach to challenges – if I try hard enough and put in the hours, I'll finally overcome them. But sourdough is different. It's a mystical, enigmatic creature. It's like a griffin; it needs respect.

The starter is alive; it eats, it breathes, it sleeps, and it can live for centuries. Sourdough starters have been passed down from generation to generation. It's needy and demanding, wanting love and constant feeding (I'm very similar) but with a little time, your starter can become a best friend, helping you create loaf upon loaf of beautiful, soft, pillowy sourdough. It just requires you to be more of a Ravenclaw; give it time, give it respect and watch it carefully.

CONJURING YOUR STARTER

Attempting to create a starter from scratch can often lead to jars and jars of putrid smelling grayish gloop. I bought my first starter online (just google one) and I still have him today. I named him Ferguson. The site said he was fifty-one, which means that someone had kept him alive for half a century (apparently there are some starters being used in San Francisco that can be dated back to the Gold Rush). After a couple weeks of caring for Ferguson, I felt he looked lonely (mid-life crisis) and I needed to find him a friend. This time I decided to make him one.

Sourdough purists manage to make a starter from just flour and water, using the natural wild yeast within the flour. I tried and failed quite a few times before reading about this trick of using the peel and flesh of an apple to kickstart the fermentation process. On the outside of apples (and green grapes too) there are a lot of wild yeast microbes. The fruit needs to have been grown organically for the simple reason that pesticides can kill off the natural yeast.

For the same reason, using either filtered or boiled water (then cooled, of course) also helps. Once you've got your starter going, it doesn't matter so much about the water, but you need to be a bit kind at the beginning of its life.

I plucked a grubby apple from the tree in our garden, washed it down and grated its skin into a canning jar. Then I stirred in equal amounts of water and bread flour until I was left with a pale, thick blob that resembled wallpaper adhesive. I screwed the lid on top (but not too tight as a little air flow is needed) and placed it in a warm, cozy area next to Ferguson who, by this point, was getting excitable. And the wait began...

It felt like months, years, decades, but I had to wait for three days before unscrewing the lid. Expecting to peer in on a lively party of bubbly acidic matter, my heart sank as only one solitary, apologetic bubble rose to the surface of the liquid. My stubbornness kicked in and I resolved not to give up. I discarded half of the starter and added more flour and water to what remained, mixing well with a fork. I screwed the lid back on and left it for two more days.

This time, I gave myself a little pep talk before lifting the lid, so I wouldn't be too disappointed. As I opened the jar, I was greeted by the same bubble, but this time it wasn't alone. Some buddies had joined in. The starter smelt mildly acidic and was definitely alive.

It was time to name my new starter. I decided on Muriel because Ferguson needs a bit of gender balancing from time to time.

DAY 1

- 1 tablespoon grated organic apple or pear (use the peel and flesh, but not the core)
- 4 cups (500g) bread flour, whole wheat flour or rye flour
- 1½ cups (360g) lukewarm water

Weigh a 2-quart canning jar or clip-top jar. This will help later on when you are taking out and adding stuff to the mixture. Mix the grated apple or pear with the flour (white is fine, but a bit of whole wheat or rye is great) and lukewarm water. Press the mixture down a bit with the back of a teaspoon and put the lid on loosely. Draw a mark on the glass against the level of the mixture with a Sharpie, or slip a rubber band over the jar and match it to the level. This will let you see if those magic microbes have started to do their stuff and the starter has grown. Leave the jar in a warm place – it doesn't need to be a light space, just cozy, so a linen cupboard or a windowsill above a radiator is good. Now wait three days...

DAY 4

- 2 cups (250g) bread flour, whole wheat flour or rye flour
- ¾ cup (170g) lukewarm water

Open up the jar – the starter should now have the acidic tang of apple cider vinegar, have risen a bit and have a few bubbles visible on the surface. Squash the mixture down again with the back of a spoon. You now need to get rid of half of it. You can either be strict and weigh out half the mixture (remember to subtract the weight of the jar) or be a bit more slap-dash (like me) and simply do it roughly by eye. Once you've scooped out half the starter, add the flour and lukewarm water to the jar and mix up thoroughly. Put the lid on. Shift your marker, whatever it is. Leave it to sit for another 2 days.

DAY 6

- 2 cups (250g) bread flour, whole wheat flour or rye flour
- ¾ cup (170g) lukewarm water, plus another 2-3 tablespoons (30-40g)

Everything should be nice and bubbly by now and risen even higher than the first three days. If the starter has a layer of gray liquid on top, don't be disheartened – just give the mixture a good stir. Next, tip out half the starter again and feed with the flour and lukewarm water. Once you've stirred this in, see if you need a little more water (2–3 tablespoons or 30–40g) to make the mixture a bit less stodgy. It wants to be smooth, but not too runny. Leave it again for another day before using it in any bakes.

FEEDING AND STORING YOUR STARTER

Basically, all those little microbes in wild yeast live to eat and burp. They break down the starch in flour into sugar, which is what they thrive on, but then they'll pop out carbon dioxide farts to create bubbles. If you leave a starter for too long without replenishing the flour and water, the microbes will run out of food unless you store it properly. So, all you need to do is either keep feeding your starter (the first option) or suppress its appetite (the second option).

For the first option, feeding, all you do is tip out a bit more than half the existing starter (this is known as the sourdough discard and we've got some recipes for using this up on pages 211–213) and add more flour and water until you've got a thick paste again. We add slightly more flour than water – roughly 60% flour to 40% water – but you'll soon get a feel for the right kind of consistency (remember wallpaper adhesive).

If you're a regular baker, by which I mean every or every other day, keep your starter at room temperature and feed it every time you use it.

If you're likely to bake just once a week, the best thing to do is keep your starter in the fridge – this is the second option. The colder temperature slows down the rate at which the microbes feed. You will need to bring the starter up to room temperature before baking with it, so take it out of the fridge the night before, tip out around half and feed it with fresh flour and water. By the next morning, the starter should be happy and raring to go.

If you're not planning to bake within the next two weeks, put your starter in the freezer and it will last for years in its frozen state. When you're ready to bake bread again, take it out of the freezer and leave it to thaw, then discard half and top up with fresh flour and water.

The Watlington

OUR ULTIMATE SOURDOUGH BREAD

This is our No 1 dough and makes an insane white sourdough, which we call 'The Watlington'. In the shop, these loaves sell out in a click of the fingers. This dough is the perfect base for folding in different flavors.

MAKES 1 LOAF

FOR FEEDING THE STARTER
• ¾ cup (90g) bread flour
• ¼ cup (60g) lukewarm water

FOR THE BREAD
• 1½ cups (350g) lukewarm water
• ½ cup (120g) sourdough starter (see page 190)
• 3⅔ cups (450g) bread flour, plus extra for dusting
• ⅓ cup (50g) whole wheat flour
• 1¼ teaspoons (10g) fine sea salt dissolved in 2 tablespoons warm water

1. The night before, feed your starter. Discard all but a few tablespoons, feed with ¾ cup (90g) bread flour and ¼ cup (60g) lukewarm water, then put the lid back on.

2. For the bread, grab a mixing bowl or tub, preferably clear glass or plastic so you can see the bubbles as the fermentation develops. Pour the lukewarm water into the bowl followed by the bubbly sourdough starter, then stir to disperse. Using a sturdy spoon, mix in both flours until you are left with a shaggy, scrappy, Scooby dough. Place a damp kitchen towel over the bowl and leave in a cozy area for at least 30 minutes.

3. Once your ingredients have had a time to mingle, add the salt dissolved in warm water by gently indenting the dough with your fingertips and pouring the salt water over the top. Squish and squeeze the dough between your fingers until all the salt water has been incorporated. Put the damp kitchen towel over the bowl again and rest for 1 hour. This process goes by the posh name of 'ending the autolyze', which automatically makes you feel like a professional baker.

4. Next, give your dough one set of stretches and folds. Just like we described for the Biga Bread (see page 162), wet your hands with some water. Imagine the ball of dough in the bowl is a clock face. Starting at 12 o'clock, grab a handful of dough and stretch it out before folding it back onto itself. Turn the bowl through 90 degrees, so you are now at 3 o'clock. Repeat the grabbing, stretching and folding. Repeat this a couple more times, working around to 6 o'clock and 9 o'clock. Leave a damp kitchen towel draped over the top of the bowl. You need to repeat this process two more times over the following 3 hours. You don't have to be too religious about the timings, but working three sets of folds spread across 3 hours is great. This is called the long or bulk fermentation. It's when the dough does a lot of its own work, breaking everything down, including the gluten. Your stretches and folds are just helping the process along.

5. About 30–45 minutes after the last set of stretches and folds, scoop your bubbly dough onto a lightly floured work surface. Using floured hands or a dough scraper, give your loaf its first shape. Everyone has their own way of shaping dough. Our method is to repeat the steps of the long or bulk fermentation. Pull out hunks of dough around the clock face and then flip the whole thing over like a turtle. Next, slide the dough scraper into the gap between the dough and the work surface at the 3 o'clock position and then drag it back to 12 o'clock, gently pulling the dough up and toward you. You should find that the skin of the dough soon starts to tighten and take on a smoother shape. Feel free to repeat this a couple more times until the dough takes on more of a ball shape. After this mini workout, let the dough rest for 30 minutes – this is called bench rest. Remember, bread is awesomely forgiving and so if you forget a set of stretches and folds or don't have time for the bench rest, your bread will survive and may even give you more interesting results.

6. Shape your dough into a round or oblong depending on what you are baking the loaf in. Gently lift and lower the shaped dough into a loaf pan (seam side down), floured banneton or even bowl lined with a floured lint-free kitchen towel (both seam side up). Everyone has a different method, so it's up to you. Place a damp kitchen towel or shower cap over the top of the dough to stop a skin from forming. If you're baking the loaf the following day, put it in the fridge until morning. Despite the cold temperature, the dough will still proof. This extra proofing time gives the bread a greater depth of flavor and it means warm bread for breakfast. Otherwise, place it in a warm, cozy place for 2 hours to proof more quickly.

7. Once your loaf has nearly proofed, preheat the oven to its highest temperature (450°F, if it can reach that, although when we started baking bread our elderly oven could only get to 350°F). If using a large Dutch oven, place it in the oven for 30 minutes to heat up. If you've put it into a loaf pan, skip this part and go straight to stage 8.

8. If baking your bread in a loaf pan, place the pan straight into the oven and slide a roasting pan filled with water underneath to create steam. (There is no need to score the top of the loaf, but if you want to, a single slit down the middle can give a nice fin.) Bake the loaf for 40 minutes or until it sounds hollow when you knock the pan underneath with your knuckles. If you have used a banneton or a bowl lined with a kitchen towel to shape the loaf, turn out your

1. Making 'clockface' folds   2. Shaping dough into a ball
3. Placing dough in a banneton   4. Dad at work making loaves

dough onto a sheet of parchment paper and score the top with a baker's lame or sharp knife. Carefully take the hot Dutch oven out of the oven, remove the lid and lower the parchment paper carrying the dough into the pot. Pour a tablespoon of water into the pot around the dough and quickly replace the lid. Bake the loaf for 30 minutes before removing the lid (the moment of truth) and then continue to bake for a further 10 minutes to get a nice golden crust or 15 minutes if you like your bread a little blackened (my preference). Once baked, place the bread on a wire rack and let the loaf cool for at least 30 minutes before eating.

VARIATIONS ON THE SOURDOUGH THEME

Once you feel confident with the method for making sourdough, it's very easy to start exploring what happens when different flours are used or extra ingredients are added. For the latter, we tend to add ingredients at the first turn stage – in other words, at least 30 minutes after mixing the basic ingredients up.

▶ **Whole Wheat Bread**
Follow the recipe for Our Ultimate Sourdough Bread but change the proportions of the two flours – instead of 3⅔ cups (450g) use 1⅔ cups (200g) bread flour and instead of ⅓ cup (50g) use 2⅓ cups (300g) whole wheat flour.

Serving suggestion: This bread is fantastic with good sausages (warm or cold) and a slick of Dijon mustard.

▶ **Oatmeal Bread**
In a medium saucepan over a low heat, warm up ¾ cup (75g) quick-cooking oats and 7 tablespoons (100g) water until thick and creamy. Spread the oatmeal mixture over a sheet of parchment paper or a greased baking sheet and set aside to cool with a kitchen towel placed over the top. Follow the recipe for Our Ultimate Sourdough Bread but change the proportions of the two flours – instead of 2⅔ cups (450g) use 2 cups (250g) bread flour and instead of ⅓ cup (50g) use 2 cups (250g) whole wheat flour. On the first stretch and fold, scrape the oatmeal from the pan and spread it on the top of your dough. Fold the layer of oatmeal into the dough, scrunching it between your fingers to break everything up. When shaping your loaf, roll the dough in a bowl of oats before placing it in your banneton, bowl or loaf pan.

Serving suggestion: This bread has an almost creamy texture and is brilliant spread with jam, preserves or honey.

SOURDOUGH FOCACCIA

Yes, we already have a focaccia recipe in this book, but this sourdough starter one takes it up to a whole new level. One of our bakery trails very early on took us to the brilliant Dusty Knuckle in Dalston, East London. It's an oasis of calm and cool and their focaccia is like crispy clouds, all bubbles and salted crunch. This is our homage. We only make this on Fridays and we have some customers who now call this Focaccia Day instead – move over Freya or whoever it was who gave Friday its original name; your time is up.

MAKES 1 LOAF

- 1½ cups (350g) lukewarm water
- ½ cup (120g) sourdough starter (see page 190)
- 1 quantity of poolish (see below)
- 3 tablespoons plus 1 teaspoon (50g) olive or cold-pressed rapeseed oil, plus an extra 2 tablespoons
- 4 cups (500g) bread flour
- 1¼ teaspoon (10g) fine sea salt
- your choice of toppings (see below)

FOR THE POOLISH

- ⅓ cup plus 1 tablespoon (50g) bread flour
- 3 tablespoons plus 1 teaspoon (50g) lukewarm water
- smidgen of a teaspoon (1g) instant dried yeast

1. When feeding your starter the night before, make a poolish. This is basically a turbocharge for your focaccia and adds yet another layer of flavor. Stir together the flour, water and yeast, put a cover over the top and leave overnight.

2. Follow the recipe for Our Ultimate Sourdough Bread on page 193, adding the poolish and oil at the same time as the sourdough starter. Make the stretches and folds as usual over the following 3 hours.

3. Instead of bench resting the dough, grab a medium baking sheet lined with parchment paper and drizzled with oil. Tip in your dough and flatten it out to the edges of the pan – it should be about 1 inch (2–3cm) thick. Drizzle over more oil (yes, I'm slightly obsessed) and leave to proof for 1 hour.

4. Preheat the oven to 425°F.

5. Using your fingertips, gently dimple the dough and then scatter over your chosen toppings. Bake in the hot oven for 30–35 minutes and then leave to cool for 30 minutes before eating.

TOPPING SUGGESTIONS
▶ Rosemary needles and flaky sea salt
▶ Confit or roasted garlic, thinly sliced potatoes and onions
▶ Sun-dried tomatoes, chorizo slices and olives
▶ Goat cheese, peach, thyme sprigs and crushed red pepper flakes (if you're feeling brave)

1. Sourdough Focaccia → page 198   2. The Albert → page 203
3. Cider with Rosie → page 200   4. Miso and Toasted Sesame Sourdough → page 201

CIDER WITH ROSIE

← PICTURED
ON PAGE 199

Adding a splash of hard cider to a dough, alongside the water, adds a really lovely tang to the bread. Essentially, what we've created here is pretty much a ploughman's loaf without the chutney.

MAKES 1 LOAF

- ¾ cup (200g) lukewarm water
- ⅔ cup (150g) hard cider
- ½ cup (120g) sourdough starter (see page 190)
- 2¾ cups (350g) bread flour
- 1¼ cups (150g) whole wheat flour
- 1¼ teaspoons (10g) fine sea salt
- ½ cup (50g) walnuts, roughly chopped
- ½ cup (50g) grated strong cheese
- 1 apple, cored and grated (you can also go for thin slices on a mandolin)

1. Using the ingredients given here, follow the recipe for Our Ultimate Sourdough Bread on page 193, but add the hard cider at the same time as the water.

2. On your first set of stretches and folds, add the chopped walnuts, grated cheese and grated apple. Make sure all these extra ingredients are evenly distributed throughout the dough.

3. Shape, proof and bake the dough just as you would for Our Ultimate Sourdough Bread, following the instructions on pages 194–197.

Serving suggestion: Enjoy in a classic British ploughman's lunch with cheese and chutney, naturally.

MISO AND TOASTED SESAME SOURDOUGH

← PICTURED
ON PAGE 199

This was one of our Cowley Road (in Oxford) experiments. We found a fantastic Korean supermarket that stocks everything from octopus balls to seaweed chips. They also sell blocks of red miso, a fermented soya bean paste. Miso, like Marmite, adds a very different, subtle saltiness to bread (which is why we drop the amount of salt added) and the combination with toasted sesame seeds is epic.

- 1½ cups (350g) lukewarm water
- ½ cup (120g) sourdough starter (see page 190)
- 3¼ cups (400g) bread flour
- ¾ cup (100g) whole wheat flour
- 1 teaspoon (8g) fine sea salt
- 1 heaping tablespoon red miso paste
- ⅓ cup (50g) sesame seeds (you can toast these in a dry pan or the oven if you want an extra depth of flavor), plus extra in a bowl for rolling

1. Using the ingredients given here, follow the recipe for Our Ultimate Sourdough Bread on page 193.

2. On your first set of stretches and folds, either spread a thin layer of red miso over the top of your dough or drop dollops of the miso across the dough. Scatter over the toasted sesame seeds. Proceed to working the folds, mixing the miso and seeds evenly through the dough so that you don't have any big blobs left.

3. Shape the dough as if making Our Ultimate Sourdough Bread, but before putting it into a banneton, bowl or pan, roll it in a bowl of extra toasted sesame seeds to coat the shaped dough. This creates a beautiful sesame crust.

4. Proof and bake the dough just as you would for Our Ultimate Sourdough Bread, following the instructions on pages 194–197.

   Serving suggestion: Hunks of this bread are insane with ramen noodle soup.

THE ALBERT

This loaf is named after my brother. He loves a sliced sandwich loaf as nothing makes a better bacon sandwich – sourdough has too many holes and too crunchy a crust. I decided to devise a loaf that was like a sliced sandwich loaf but still sourdough. We were getting close, but not close enough, then we came across the tangzhong method. This comes from the northernmost part of Japan, Hokkaido, where they grow wheat rather than rice. Basically, it involves making a roux from flour and water, which you then mix in with the dough. We use a combination of yeast and starter and add butter and powdered milk so that you get a simple white loaf with an astonishing softness that is dangerously easy to eat. The Albert has its own cult fan club in the bakery.

MAKES 1 LOAF

- 1½ cups (300g) lukewarm water
- ½ cup (100g) sourdough starter (see page 190)
- 1 teaspoon (3g or ½×¼-ounce envelope) instant dried yeast
- ¼ cup (25g) powdered whole milk
- 4 cups (500g) bread flour
- 3 tablespoons (50g) soft unsalted butter
- 1¼ teaspoons (10g) fine sea salt

FOR THE TANGZHONG

- 1½ tablespoons (20g) bread flour
- ⅓ cup (80g) lukewarm water

1. First, make the tangzhong. In a medium saucepan over a low heat, whisk the flour and water together until it forms a stiff paste. Set aside to cool.

2. Using the ingredients given here, follow the recipe for Our Ultimate Sourdough Bread on pages 193–197, but add the instant dried yeast and powdered milk in the first mix, and then when ending the autolyze mix in the tangzhong, butter and salt. (If you can't find powdered milk, use half water and half milk instead of the water when starting this bread.)

3. We always bake this bread in a loaf pan. Because it is a soft, wet, pillowy dough, you may need to dust with quite a bit of flour while shaping the bread. We plop the dough straight into a well-oiled pan rather than give it any time to rest.

4. Either leave the dough in the fridge to proof overnight or in a warm place to proof for 1–1½ hours.

5. Preheat the oven to 450°F.

6. Bake in the hot oven for 40–45 minutes. Let the loaf cool a little in the pan before easing it out onto a wire rack. Let the bread cool and relax on a rack before slicing; the bread will be too doughy to slice if it is still warm.

Serving suggestion: We use this bread for grilled cheese. Mix up some Dijon mustard, mayo and a bit of sriracha and spread it on one side of the sliced bread. Top with a mix of cheddar, Colby and finely chopped scallions. Close the sandwich and smear a little mustard mix on both outer sides. Toast in a skillet or on a griddle until crispy and oozing.

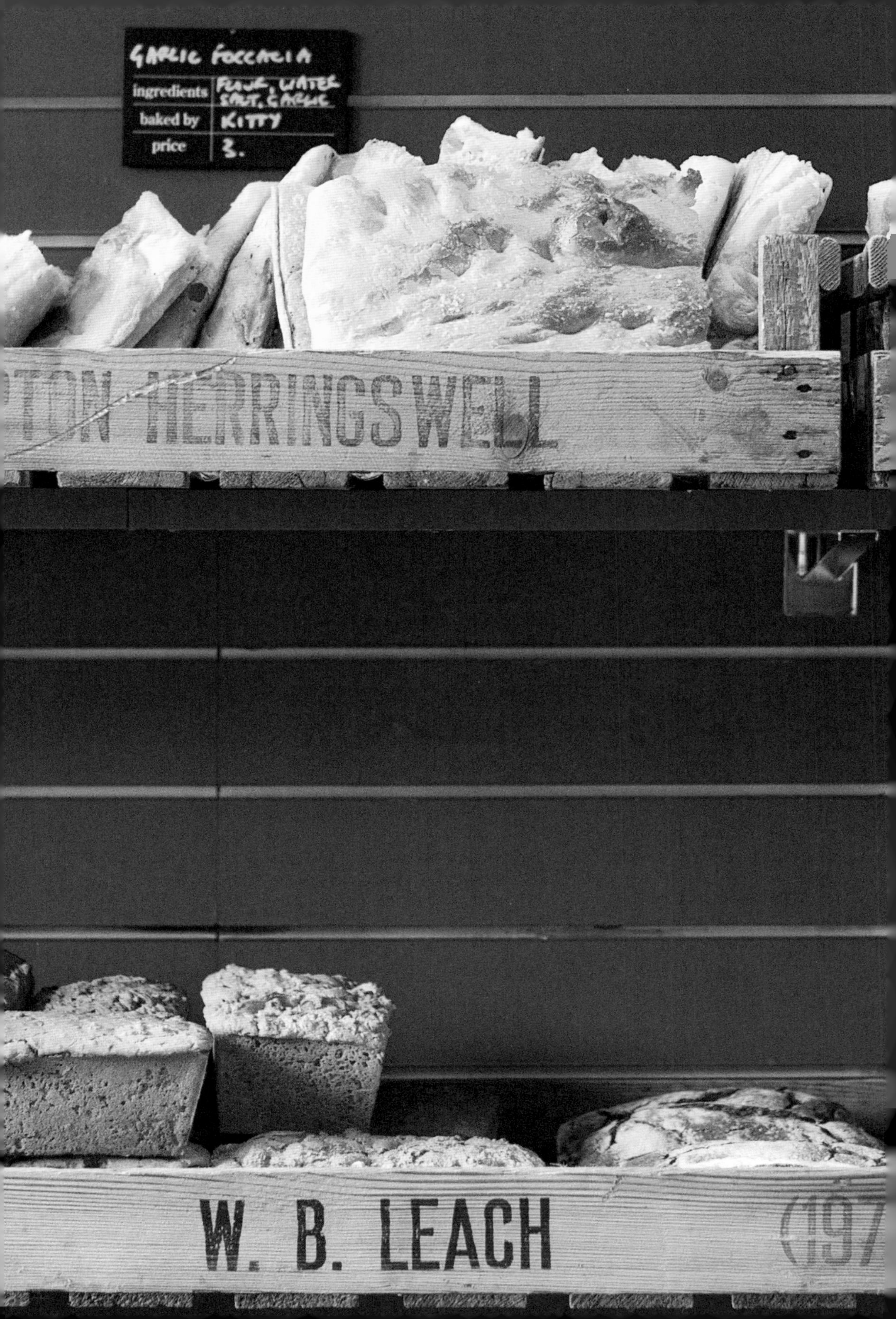

...TON HERRINGSWELL

W. B. LEACH (197

albert
ingredients FLOUR, SALT
MILK
baked by KITTY
price 3

R. J. UPTON HERRINGSWELL

miche
FLOUR WATER
SALT

R. J. UPTON HERRINGS

ULLA'S RYE BREAD

This loaf is named after Ulla, the Danish granny who taught me how to make rye bread. In Denmark you can buy non-alcoholic malt beer for making rye bread. The closest to this in America is malta, a non-alcoholic malted beverage. You could always go for a real beer here – something dark and ruby-ish is good.

MAKES 3 SMALL LOAVES

- 2 cups (500g) malt beer, malt beverage, ruby beer or water (if there is less than 2 cups/500g in the bottle or can, make the rest up with water)
- 1 quantity of rye starter (see below)
- 1½ cups (200g) mix of pumpkin seeds, sunflower seeds, flaxseeds and spelt or rye grains
- 1½ tablespoons (30g) molasses or honey
- 4 cups (500g) whole wheat flour
- 1¾ teaspoons (15g) fine sea salt

FOR THE RYE STARTER

- 1 heaping tablespoon sourdough starter (see page 190)
- 1 cup (125g) rye flour
- ½ cup (125g) lukewarm water

1. First, make the rye starter. In a large mixing bowl, stir together the sourdough starter with the rye flour and warm-ish water. Leave this somewhere warm to ferment for a couple of hours.

2. Next, pour the malt beverage or beer (mixed with water to make it up to 2 cups/500g, if necessary) into the bowl with the rye starter. Give everything a good stir.

3. Add the mixed seeds and whole grains – you can decide on your favorite blend – along with the molasses. Stir everything together. At this point, the mixture will look sloppy and, quite frankly, disgusting. Don't worry. That's a good thing.

4. Cover the bowl and leave somewhere coolish to proof overnight. The fridge might be a bit too chilly, but you don't want this dough to over-ferment.

5. The next morning, add the flour and salt. Stir the mixture well. It will thicken up, but it will still be pretty wet. Leave to rest for 1 hour and then scoop the mixture out into a well-buttered loaf pan. We prefer to use the smaller 1-pound (450g) loaf pans for this bread. You should get three small loaves out of this mixture. You can get everything into a 2-pound (900g) loaf pan but it just needs a bit longer to bake.

6. Wet a dough scraper with a little water and use it to smooth over the tops of the loaves, then sprinkle over some rye flour. These loaves need a good couple of hours to proof. During this time, you'll notice the flour on top starting to crack like a small earthquake has taken place.

7. Preheat the oven to 400°F.

8. Bake in the hot oven for 1 hour or until dark on top but not burnt (1 hour and 20 minutes if cooking in a 2-pound pan). Turn the loaves out onto a wire rack and leave them to cool for at least 5 hours. Many people say that you shouldn't eat rye bread until the next day, but it requires real restraint and patience to stick to that bit of advice. The positive flip side is that this bread lasts for ages.

Serving suggestion: This bread cuts thinly if you have a sharp bread knife. It means you can go to town on the Danish open sandwich (smørrebrød). Butter a slice and then layer with cold cuts (ham, pastrami), boiled eggs, avocado, mayonnaise or a bit of horseradish. If you're going for fish, put your herring on first or try a slice of smoked salmon. Even better, top it off with shrimp and a squeeze of lemon juice. Cornichons are a must, as are crispy onions, and we like potato chips. If you're going veggie, thin slices of cheese and tomato come to life, brilliant with some fig preserves or caramelized red onions. It can look like a work of art or a complete mess, it doesn't matter – it will taste incredible.

SOURDOUGH BURGER BUNS

We wanted to make burger buns that have the softness of brioche but don't fall apart in your hands. The tangzhong method we use to make The Albert on page 203 works really well here. The egg and butter give the rolls another layer of richness, making them perfect for burgers or fish sticks. Once baked, I love squashing the rolls and watching them bounce back to their original shape.

MAKES 12 ROLLS

- 4 cups (500g) bread flour
- 1 cup (250g) lukewarm water
- 2 teaspoons (7g or a whole ¼-ounce envelope) instant dried yeast
- ¼ cup (50g) sourdough starter (see page 190, optional)
- 3 tablespoons (50g) soft unsalted butter
- 1 large egg
- 1 tablespoon honey
- 1¼ teaspoon (10g) fine sea salt

FOR THE TANGZHONG

- 1½ tablespoons (20g) bread flour
- ⅓ cup (80g) lukewarm water

TO FINISH

- 1 egg lightly beaten with 1 tablespoon milk, for the egg wash
- a generous tablespoon sesame seeds, for sprinkling

1. First, make the tangzhong. In a medium saucepan over a low heat, whisk the flour and water together until it starts to thicken. Once you have a smooth, thick gloop, take the pan off the heat and set aside to cool.

2. In a large mixing bowl, combine all the ingredients for the dough with the tangzhong and stir together until there are no visible patches of dry flour left.

3. Tip your dough onto a lightly floured work surface and knead by hand for 10 minutes or in a stand mixer fitted with a dough hook for a good 5–6 minutes. Once the dough is smooth and elastic, put back into the bowl, place a damp kitchen towel over the top and leave to proof for 1 hour or until doubled in size.

4. Tip out your dough and cut it into 12 equal pieces, each weighing roughly 4 ounces (120g). Roll each piece into a ball and place on the lined baking sheet, spacing them 2 inches (5cm) apart. Put the kitchen towel back over the top and leave to proof for a further 30 minutes.

5. Preheat the oven to 425°F.

6. Brush the rolls with the egg wash and sprinkle some sesame seeds over the top. Bake in the hot oven for 20–25 minutes or until nice and golden. Leave to cool on a wire rack.

burger bun hotline

SOURDOUGH DISCARD

Ditching so much of your sourdough starter every time you feed it feels very indulgent, especially when you have had to work quite hard to get things going in the first place. Rather than using freshly fed starter, the couple of recipes that follow actually work best when made with the older discarded starter that you would otherwise tip away.

TRASH CRUMPS

This recipe is inspired by the wicked sourdough witch, Martha de Lacey, who is a brilliant breadmaker. You can buy crumpet rings (also called muffin rings) online or, alternatively, using a set of round biscuit cutters is fine. You'll end up with a range of crumpet sizes but that's part of the charm.

MAKES 7-10 CRUMPETS
(DEPENDING ON
RING SIZE)

- ⅔ cup (150g) discarded sourdough starter
- ⅔ cup (75g) all-purpose flour
- ⅓ cup (75g) lukewarm water
- ¼ teaspoon (3g) fine sea salt
- 1 teaspoon baking powder
- olive or cold-pressed rapeseed oil, for greasing

1. In a large mixing bowl, whisk together all the ingredients into a smooth batter. Transfer the mixture into a pitcher (this isn't strictly necessary, but it makes pouring easier) and leave to rest for 20–30 minutes.

2. Grease your crumpet rings or biscuit cutters with some oil. Heat a large frying pan over a medium–low heat and grease with a little more oil. Put your crumpet rings in the pan and give them a minute to heat up.

3. Spoon 2 tablespoons of batter into each ring – the crumpets will rise quite a lot, so don't over-fill the rings. Cook for 7–8 minutes until the top becomes firm and speckled with tiny holes. Flip the crumpets over and fry for a further 1 minute on the other side.

4. Take the first lot of crumpets out of the pan and remove the rings – they will be hot, so we use a kitchen towel and a knife. Smother the hot crumpets in butter. Eat the first ones while you stand over the pan and fry up the rest of them.

Serving suggestion: With melted butter and Marmite. (I also recommend wearing a bib.)

KNÄCKEBRÖD

This is the brilliant Swedish name for sourdough rye crackers. The coolest thing about these crackers is that the longer you leave them to ferment before baking, the more interesting the flavor becomes. Za'atar spice is a mix of sesame seeds, a variety of thyme and salt. If you have a local Middle Eastern grocer, look for it there where it is often sold in generous bags. If you store these crackers in a ziplock bag, they last for ages. Knäckebröd are amazing, especially loaded with cheese (everything is).

MAKES 10-15 CRACKERS

- ⅔ cup (150g) discarded sourdough starter
- 1 cup (125g) bread flour
- ⅔ cup (75g) rye flour
- 3 tablespoons plus 1 teaspoon (50g) lukewarm water
- ¼ cup (50g) olive or cold-pressed rapeseed oil
- ½ teaspoon fine sea salt
- 1 tablespoon sesame seeds or za'atar spice mix

1. In a large mixing bowl, mix all the ingredients together until they form a stiff dough. You can use it straightaway, but we like to leave the dough for a day for the flavors to sharpen up. Drape a kitchen towel over the bowl and leave at room temperature for 24 hours.

2. Preheat the oven to 350°F and line a baking sheet with parchment paper.

3. On a lightly floured work surface, roll out the dough as thin as you can (around 1/16 inch or 2mm thick). Don't be afraid of dusting the dough with more flour if things get a bit sticky.

4. Using a sharp knife or pizza cutter, cut the rolled-out dough into rectangular strips about 2 inches (5cm) wide. Prick the strips all over with a fork and transfer them to the lined baking sheet.

5. Slide the pan into the hot oven and bake for 12–15 minutes until they have tanned nicely. Put onto a wire rack to cool completely and then store the crackers in something airtight, like a ziplock bag.

    Serving suggestion: The sour sharpness of these crackers works really well with a gooey cheese like camembert or cambozola and a few cornichons on top or a smear of fig preserves.

1. Albert   2. Aggie   3. 'Shop' Katie

4. Kitty   5. Al   6. Justin's wooden shop sign   7. 'Wife' Katie

SWEET DOUGH

FIKA BUNS

If we all ate fika, I think the world would be a much better place. Fika is a Scandinavian ritual, like afternoon tea. Traditionally, a range of buns are served that you share with your neighbors, people you work with or friends (imaginary or otherwise). It's such a great custom and even the mighty Volvo plant in Sweden stops for fika every day. What follows here are the recipes for three different flavor buns, all made from the same dough, but with different fillings (butters) and glazes. We recommend the Milky Way glaze with the cinnamon bun, the coffee glaze with the cardamom and orange bun and the orange glaze with the Nutella bun, but it's totally up to you. We've given quantities for the butter and glaze recipes, but to be honest, you can adjust them depending on whether you want a subtle hint of flavor or a big mouthful, so don't feel tied down to the measurements.

MAKES 15 BUNS

FOR THE DOUGH

- ¾ cup plus 1 tablespoon (200g) warm whole milk (as warm as a relaxing bath)
- 1 egg, beaten
- 2 teaspoons (7g or a whole ¼-ounce envelope) instant dried yeast
- 4 cups (500g) bread flour or all-purpose flour
- 1¼ teaspoons (10g) fine sea salt
- 2½ tablespoons (30g) granulated sugar
- 1 tablespoon ground cardamom (optional, if making buns with cinnamon butter filling)
- 9 tablespoons/1 stick plus 1 tablespoon (125g) soft unsalted butter, cubed
- zest of 1 orange (if making buns with Nutella butter filling)

1. In a small bowl, whisk together the milk, egg and yeast. In a separate large mixing bowl, combine the flour, salt, sugar and ground cardamom, if using. (The ground cardamom is optional for the cinnamon butter buns, but it gives them a subtle Scandi flavor.) Make a small well in the flour, pour in the milk mixture and stir together until it forms a rough dough.

2. Tip the dough onto a lightly floured work surface and either knead by hand for 8–10 minutes or in a stand mixer fitted with a dough hook for 4–5 minutes, gradually working the cubes of butter into the dough as you knead until it is smooth and glossy. Put the dough back into the bowl, place a damp kitchen towel or shower cap over the rim and leave to proof for 1–1½ hours until the dough has almost doubled in size. Alternatively, refrigerate the dough (still covered) for anywhere between 4 hours and overnight. It will still proof, just more slowly, and the dough will be much easier to handle.

3. Tip your puffy dough onto a lightly floured work surface and roll it out into a 12×8-inch (30×20cm) rectangle that is roughly ¼ inch (5mm) thick. Transfer the dough to a baking sheet and put it in the fridge for 10 minutes or so. (Chilling firms up the dough, which makes it easier to spread over the butter filling during the next stage.) Meanwhile, prepare your chosen butter filling (see overleaf).

4. Once the dough is chilled and the butter filling is ready, lay the dough rectangle on the work surface with a longer side facing you. Spread your butter filling across the first

two-thirds of the dough, fold the naked one-third toward you into the middle over the top of the buttered third and then fold the buttered third nearest to you over the folded layers. You now have a long triple-decker sandwich of layers of dough and butter filling, which will give your buns their signature lamination.

5 . Again, roll out the dough into a 12×8-inch (30×20cm) rectangle with a longer side facing you. Using a sharp knife or pizza cutter, slice the dough into 15 equal strips, each roughly ¾ inch (2cm) wide, so that your dough looks like a picket fence.

6 . Take one strip of dough and coil it up from one end so that it looks like a snail's shell. Stretch the last ¾ inch (2cm) of the strip, wrap it over the top of the coil and then tuck it underneath – your snail now looks like it is checking its undercarriage. Repeat for all the dough strips. Place the coiled buns on two baking sheets lined with parchment paper, spacing them an inch or so apart. Cover with a damp kitchen towel and leave somewhere warm to proof for 30 minutes.

7 . Preheat the oven to 350°F.

8 . Bake in the hot oven for 15–20 minutes or until golden brown. Leave on a wire rack to cool for 15 minutes, then brush with your chosen glaze.

BUTTERS & GLAZES

CINNAMON BUTTER

- 7 tablespoons (100g) soft unsalted butter
- ½ cup (100g) superfine sugar
- 1 heaping tablespoon ground cinnamon

Combine all the ingredients in a mixing bowl and beat with a wooden spoon until fully combined into a smooth paste.

CARDAMOM AND ORANGE BUTTER

- 7 tablespoons (100g) soft unsalted butter
- ½ cup (100g) light brown sugar
- 1 heaping tablespoon ground cardamom
- zest of 1 orange

Combine all the ingredients in a mixing bowl and beat with a wooden spoon until fully combined into a smooth paste.

NUTELLA BUTTER

- ¾ cup (175g) of Nutella
- 1 tablespoon tahini, or to taste

This is the easiest of all – no mixing, no measuring, just use Nutella for the butter filling (this is plenty but I promise you'll end up adding a bit more which is why you should have the rest of the jar on standby). If you're feeling adventurous, you can add some tahini – this adds a really nice extra nuttiness. Simply dribble the tahini over the top of the Nutella when spreading it over the dough.

MILKY WAY GLAZE

- 7 tablespoons (100g) whole milk
- ¼ cup (50g) granulated sugar

Warm the milk in a small saucepan over medium heat, add the sugar and stir until it has all dissolved.

Brush or spoon the warm glaze over the cooled buns and leave to set. The glaze adds a thin icing but also soaks through into the dough, adding another layer of flavor.

COFFEE GLAZE

- 7 tablespoons (100g) black coffee (espresso or filter)
- ¼ cup (50g) light brown sugar

Warm the coffee in a small saucepan over medium heat, add the sugar and stir until it has all dissolved.

Brush or spoon the warm glaze over the cooled buns and leave to set.

ORANGE GLAZE

- 7 tablespoons (100g) orange juice
- 1 heaping tablespoon orange marmalade
- 1 tablespoon roughly chopped hazelnuts (optional)

Warm the orange juice in a small saucepan over medium heat, add the marmalade and stir together until you're left with a mouth-watering syrup.

Brush or spoon the warm glaze over the cooled buns. Scatter over a few chopped hazelnuts, if you want.

EVERYTHING DOUGH

We use this dough for pretty much everything, hence the name.
It's more enriched with butter, eggs and sugar than the dough
used for the Fika Buns (see pages 219–20), which gives it the feel
of a brioche. For the savory recipes made with this dough – the
End-of-the-Week Pull-Apart-Bread (see page 232), Béchamel,
Ham and Sausage Breakfast Buns (see page 231) and Za'atar,
Feta and Honey Buns (see page 234) – just cut back the sugar
to 1 tablespoon (10g).

MAKES 1 QUANTITY

- ¾ cup plus 1 tablespoon
  (200g) lukewarm whole milk
- 2 teaspoons (7g or a whole
  ¼-ounce envelope) instant
  dried yeast
- 4 cups (500g) bread flour or
  all-purpose flour
- ⅓ cup plus 1 tablespoon
  (80g) granulated sugar
  for a sweet dough or
  1 tablespoon (10g)
  granulated sugar
  for a savory dough
- 1¼ teaspoons (10g) fine
  sea salt
- 2 eggs
- 9 tablespoons/1 stick plus
  1 tablespoon (125g) soft
  unsalted butter, cubed

1. Gently warm the milk in a small saucepan. Remove the pan
   from the heat and whisk in the yeast. Set aside and leave
   to bubble for 5 minutes.

2. In a large mixing bowl, combine the flour, sugar and salt.
   Make a small well in the flour, pour in the milk and yeast
   mixture, crack in the eggs and stir together until it forms
   a rough dough.

3. Tip the dough onto a lightly floured work surface and either
   knead by hand for 10 minutes or in a stand mixer fitted
   with a dough hook for 4–5 minutes, gradually working the
   cubes of butter into the dough as you knead until it is soft,
   silky and stretchy. Put the dough back into the bowl, place
   a damp kitchen towel or shower cap over the rim and leave
   to proof for 1 hour until the dough has almost doubled in
   size. Alternatively, refrigerate the dough (still covered)
   overnight, ready to bake the next day. If you can plan for
   this extra proofing time, it really helps as the dough is much
   easier to work with when cold.

MAPLE, BACON AND PECAN BUNS

This is a really nice fusion of sweet and savory. We can never quite work out which camp this bun would feel most at home in. It's a little bit fiddly at the end, but even if it doesn't quite come off you'll end up with lots of gorgeous debris which you'll have to polish off because that just helps with the washing up, doesn't it?

MAKES 15 BUNS

- 1 quantity of Everything Dough (see opposite)

FOR THE FILLING
- 1-2 tablespoons maple syrup (depending on your taste)
- 8 slices of bacon, cooked until crisp, sliced

FOR THE TOPPING
- 2 handfuls of whole pecans
- 1 tablespoon light brown sugar

1. On a lightly floured work surface, roll out the dough into a 12×8-inch (30×20cm) rectangle that is roughly ½ inch (1cm) thick. This is much easier to do when the dough has proofed overnight in the fridge and is still cold.

2. Lay the dough rectangle on the work surface with a longer side facing you. Brush the surface of the dough with the maple syrup and scatter over the bacon pieces.

3. Starting at one long edge, roll the dough into a log. Using a sharp knife or length of thread, slice the dough crossways into 15 equal slices, each roughly ¾ inch (2cm) wide.

4. Line two baking sheets with parchment paper. Spread the pecans over the baking sheets and sprinkle with the brown sugar. Place your dough slices on top of the pecans, cut-side down and spaced 2 inches (5cm) apart. Place a damp kitchen towel or plastic cover over the top of the pans and leave in a cozy area to proof for 40–45 minutes or until doubled in size.

5. Preheat the oven to 350°F.

6. Bake in the hot oven for 20–25 minutes or until golden brown. Leave the buns to cool on the pans for 5 minutes. Using the parchment paper, lift the buns from the pans and transfer them to a wire rack. After a further 5–10 minutes, rest another baking sheet or chopping board on the buns and then flip them over so that the sticky pecan side is now facing upward. Peel away the parchment paper. This can be a bit tricky, but you'll feel very proud of yourself when you pull it off (literally and figuratively).

NEXT-LEVEL CHELSEA BUNS

Chelsea buns are the UK's version of sticky buns. They get their name from a bakery in Chelsea and legend has it that when they first came out the queue was in the thousands. I wonder if they got queue nibbles? I used to hate them; I just couldn't see the point of anything where raisins were involved. However, after a lot of requests for Chelsea buns, mainly from customers of a certain vintage, I decided to have a go. Like in Roald Dahl's *Danny the Champion of the World*, I soaked the dried fruits. This made them plump and juicy. This, together with adding thinly sliced apple, results in an amazingly soft bun that is now one of the bakery favorites (even with our customers under the age of 70).

MAKES 12 BUNS

• 1 quantity of Everything Dough (see page 222)

FOR THE FILLING

• 1 cup (150g) raisins or a mixture of dried fruits
• 1 teaspoon garam masala
• 1/3 cup (50g) dried cranberries (optional)
• 1 tea bag (English breakfast or Earl Grey)
• about 7 tablespoons (100g) boiling water
• 3 tablespoons (50g) unsalted butter, melted
• 1/4 cup (50g) light brown sugar
• 1 tablespoon ground cinnamon
• 1 apple, thinly sliced (optional, but recommended)
• zest of 1 lemon (optional)

FOR THE GLAZE

• 3 tablespoons (50g) water
• 1 tablespoon orange marmalade or apricot preserves

FOR THE GLACÉ ICING

• 1 cup (100g) confectioners' sugar
• 1 tablespoon water

1. In a mixing bowl, stir together the raisins or the mixture of dried fruits and garam masala (and the cranberries if you want). Add the tea bag (English breakfast is fine, but Earl Grey adds a really nice fragrance) and pour in enough boiling water to cover. Set aside to steep for at least 15 minutes or overnight.

2. On a lightly floured work surface, roll out the dough into a 12×8-inch (30×20cm) rectangle that is roughly ½ inch (1cm) thick. This is much easier to do when the dough has proofed overnight in the fridge and is still cold.

3. Lay the dough rectangle on the work surface with a longer side facing you. Brush the surface of the dough with the melted butter, sprinkle with the sugar and cinnamon, then lay the apple slices on top.

4. Drain the fruit in a colander and remove the tea bag. Scatter the plump fruit over the dough along with the lemon zest, if using.

5. Starting at one long edge, roll the dough into a log. Using a sharp knife or length of thread, slice the dough crossways into 12 equal slices, each roughly ¾ inch (2cm) wide.

6. Line a deep baking sheet with parchment paper. Place the dough slices cut-side down on the pan, spacing them ½ inch (1cm) apart. Place a damp kitchen towel over the top of the pan and leave in a warm place to proof for 40–45 minutes, or until doubled in size.

7. Preheat the oven to 400°F.

8. Bake in the hot oven for 18–20 minutes or until golden brown. Check the buns halfway through the cooking time. If they are cooking unevenly, then turn the pan around. If they are browning too quickly, drape a sheet of foil over the buns – any exposed raisins may burn and you don't want the bitterness that brings. Leave the buns to cool in the pan for 5 minutes and then transfer to a wire rack.

9. To make the glaze, warm the water and marmalade or preserves in a medium saucepan over a medium heat. Generously brush the glaze over the buns. You can hold on to any spare for later use as it will keep for several days.

10. To make the glacé icing, whisk together the confectioners' sugar and water in a small bowl or pitcher until it forms a silky paste. Once the buns are completely cool, drizzle over the glacé icing.

QUEUE NIBBLES

I started to do these because I felt guilty about people waiting
in line for our shop on Saturdays when we could only allow one
person in at a time. That, and I'm a bit of a feeder.

MAKES 20 NIBBLES

- 1 quantity of Everything
  Dough (see page 222)
- 3½ ounces (100g)
  chocolate, chopped (we like
  Snickers, Twix or Terry's
  Milk Chocolate Orange Ball)
  or you can also use crushed
  graham crackers, mini
  marshmallows and chocolate
  chunks for s'more nibbles
- 1 egg lightly beaten with
  1 tablespoon milk, for the
  egg wash
- pearl sugar (optional, but
  great if you have some)

1. Divide the dough into 20 equal pieces. Press a piece
   of chocolate bar into the center of each piece. Pull the
   edges into the middle, enclosing your chocolate chunk
   inside, and roll around in the palms of your hands. Place
   seam-side down onto lined baking sheets, spacing them
   2 inches (5cm) apart.

2. Brush lightly with the egg wash and sprinkle with pearl
   sugar. Cover with a damp tea towel and leave to double in
   size for 30 minutes.

3. Preheat the oven to 400°F.

4. Bake in the hot oven for 10–15 minutes until golden. Leave
   to cool for 5 minutes and then eat while still hot.

SEMLOR

Semlor buns are eaten by the Swedes in the same way we eat pancakes – on Shrove Tuesday at the start of Lent. At some point along the line, though, they decided that it is just as okay to eat semlor the whole way through to Easter – an excellent idea. I've added roasted rhubarb to my recipe as hot house rhubarb is in season at the same time and I love to cook with it, but it's entirely up to you. Semlor are very more-ish – there's a great story about a Swedish king who passed away after eating 14 one after another – so you have been warned!

MAKES 10 BUNS

- 1 quantity of Everything Dough (see page 222) with 1 tablespoon ground cardamom added to the flour before mixing
- 1 egg, lightly beaten with a pinch of salt, for the egg wash
- confectioners' sugar, for dusting

FOR THE ALMOND FILLING
- 1 cup (100g) almond flour
- ½ cup (100g) granulated sugar
- 3 tablespoons cold water
- 1 teaspoon almond or vanilla extract

FOR THE VANILLA CREAM
- 1 cup (250g) heavy cream
- 1 tablespoon confectioners' sugar
- 1 teaspoon vanilla extract
- 1 teaspoon ground cardamom (optional)

FOR THE ROASTED RHUBARB
- 2-3 stalks of rhubarb
- ⅓ cup (70g) granulated sugar

1. Begin by preparing the dough. Once it has proofed and doubled in size, scoop it out of the bowl and cut into 10 equal pieces. Roll each piece into a tight ball and place them on lined baking sheets, spacing them 2 inches (5cm) apart. Cover with a damp kitchen towel and leave to proof somewhere cozy for 1–2 hours or until doubled in size.

2. Preheat the oven to 400°F.

3. Cut the rhubarb into 1¼ inch (3cm) long pieces and spread out in a roasting pan. Sprinkle over the sugar, cover with foil and roast for 10 minutes. Then remove the foil and continue to roast for a further 5 minutes. Let cool.

4. Brush the buns with the egg wash. Bake in the hot oven for 15 minutes or until golden. Leave on a wire rack to cool.

5. Distract yourself from the enticing smell of the fresh buns by preparing the fillings. Blitz all the ingredients for the almond filling to a smooth paste. In a separate bowl, whisk together all the ingredients for the vanilla cream. Once thick, spoon the cream into a pastry bag fitted with a plain tip (or use a freezer bag and snip one corner to make a piping tip) and set aside.

6. Now, my favorite part: the scooping (which reminds me of pumpkin carving). Using a sharp knife, cut a triangle out of the top of each cooled bun. Save the triangular hats and scoop out a little of the flesh from the middle of each bun to create a well. Spoon in the almond filling, top with pieces of roasted rhubarb, then pipe on some vanilla cream. Put the triangular hat on top, dust with confectioners' sugar and go.

TOP TIP
If you don't want cream and confectioners' sugar all over your face, use the triangular hat to scoop up the cream.

BÉCHAMEL, HAM AND SAUSAGE BREAKFAST BUNS

These are a homage to my dad's breakfast pie. Years ago, Dad decided to perfect a breakfast pie; layers of baked beans, blood sausage, sausage and egg all wrapped in flaky pie pastry – it nearly worked (the bean juice was the error that made the pie collapse). But after seeing a breakfast bun at 10 Belles in Paris, I loved the concept and decided to have a crack. These are perfect for on-the-go breakfast – move aside Belvita. There seems to be a lot going on here, but the béchamel sauce can be made ahead of time and used for all sorts of things later.

MAKES 12 BUNS

- 1 quantity of Everything Dough (see page 222) made using 1 tablespoon (10g) of sugar because this is a savory dish
- 6 thin slices of ham, cut in half
- 2 cooked sausages, cut into small chunks
- 1 egg, lightly beaten, for the egg wash

FOR THE BÉCHAMEL SAUCE

- 1½ tablespoons (20g) unsalted butter
- 2 tablespoons (20g) all-purpose flour
- ¾ cup plus 1 tablespoon (200g) whole milk
- 1 tablespoon grated sharp cheddar
- ½ teaspoon ground black pepper
- ½ teaspoon fine sea salt
- ½ teaspoon Dijon mustard (optional)

1. Tip the dough onto a lightly floured work surface and cut into 12 equal pieces. Roll into balls and place onto two lined baking sheets, spacing them 2 inches (5cm) apart. Drape a damp kitchen towel over the top and leave to proof for 30 minutes.

2. Preheat the oven to 400°F.

3. Once your buns have risen and are bouncy to the touch, using the back of a spoon or your fingers, make a deep well in the center. Make sure the well is really good and deep because it tends to rise up and might end up tipping your ingredients out if it is too shallow. They're now ready for the big assembly – see below.

4. First, make the béchamel sauce. In a medium saucepan over a low heat, melt the butter and stir in your flour to create a roux (this takes a minute or so).

5. Whisk in the milk bit by bit, stir until smooth and thick (this takes about 5–7 minutes). Mix in the cheese, pepper, salt and mustard until everything is melted in and smooth. Take off the heat and leave to cool for 5–10 minutes before using (it will keep happily in the fridge for a couple of days, and you can always use anything left for a cheesy pasta dish).

6. Next, assemble the buns. Spoon the béchamel sauce into the center of each well, then place some ham and sausage pieces on top. Brush with the egg wash.

7. Bake in the hot oven for 15–20 minutes and let cool a little, but try to eat them warm with a nice cup of tea or coffee.

END-OF-THE-WEEK PULL-APART BREAD

This is a great way of using up what is left in the fridge. Shape your rolls into rounds and place them quite close to each other on a baking sheet and that way they'll quietly fuse during proofing, making the pull-apart bit work.

MAKES 12 BUNS

- 1 quantity of Everything Dough (see page 222) but made using 1 tablespoon (10g) of sugar because this is a savory dish
- whatever you have in your fridge or store cupboard (see below for flavor suggestions)
- 1 egg, lightly beaten, for the egg wash
- sesame or poppy seeds, for sprinkling (optional)

1. Tip the dough onto a lightly floured work surface. Using a sharp knife, cut the dough into 12 equal wedges.

2. Flatten each wedge down and place your chosen fillings in the center. Seal in your fillings by folding up the sides of the dough and pinching them together.

3. Line a deep baking sheet with parchment paper. Place the rolls seam-side down on the pan, spacing them ½ inch (1cm) apart. Brush with the egg wash and sprinkle with sesame seeds, poppy seeds or leave naked. Drape a damp kitchen towel over the top of the pan and leave in a warm place to proof for 40–45 minutes, or until doubled in size.

4. Preheat the oven to 400°F.

5. Bake in the hot oven for 20–25 minutes or until golden. Leave to cool for 5 minutes then eat while still hot.

FILLINGS
These are some of the things that we've tried and work really well:
► Leftover black bean chili and cilantro
► Pesto, chorizo and crispy potatoes
► Cheese, olives and crispy fried onions (we love the ones you can buy in packages from supermarkets)

1.+2. End-of-the-Week Pull-Apart Bread → opposite   3. Za'atar, Feta and Honey Buns → page 234
4. Peanut Butter, Banana and Chocolate Buns → page 235

ZA'ATAR, FETA AND HONEY BUNS

← PICTURED
ON PAGE 233

You might be starting to spot my Middle Eastern food fetish by now. I love the blend of spices and herbs and za'atar is pretty much my favorite. You'll find lots of different blends of za'atar depending on where it has been made, but basically it will include thyme, sesame seeds and sumac. These buns are shaped just like the Fika Buns on page 219. They go brilliantly with soup.

MAKES 12 BUNS

- 1 quantity of Everything Dough (see page 222) made with 1 tablespoon (10g) of sugar for a more savory dough
- 1 tablespoon olive oil
- 2 heaping tablespoon za'atar spice mix
- 3½ ounces (100g or approx. 1 cup, crumbled) feta
- sesame seeds, for sprinkling

FOR THE HONEY GLAZE
- 3 tablespoons (50g) water
- 1 tablespoon honey
- juice of 1 lemon

1. Tip the dough onto a lightly floured work surface and roll it out into a 12×8-inch (30×20cm) rectangle that is roughly ¼ inch (5mm) thick. Brush the dough with the olive oil and sprinkle the za'atar over two-thirds of the rectangle. Crumble over your feta.

2. Just like you do when making the Fika Buns on page 219, fold the bare third into the center then once more over the last third of the rectangle; you should now have a beautiful, laminated piece of dough.

3. Roll out the dough once more into a 12×8-inch (30×20cm) rectangle with a longer side facing you. Using a sharp knife or pizza cutter, slice the dough into 12 equal strips, each roughly ¾ inch (2cm) wide. Take both ends of one strip, twist then coil it like a snail's shell, tucking the end over the top of the coil and then underneath. Repeat for all the dough strips. Place the coiled buns on baking sheets lined with parchment paper, spacing them an inch or so apart. Sprinkle with sesame seeds, cover with a damp kitchen towel and leave to proof in a warm place for 1 hour.

4. Preheat the oven to 400°F.

5. Bake in the hot oven for 15–20 minutes or until golden.

6. Meanwhile, in a saucepan, boil up the water and stir in your honey and lemon juice. Once the buns are out of the oven, brush them with your honey-lemon glaze and leave on a wire rack to cool for 10–15 minutes.

Serving suggestion: These buns are awesome with hummus or baba ganoush or as a fancy roll alternative with a nice soup.

PEANUT BUTTER, BANANA AND CHOCOLATE BUNS

← PICTURED
ON PAGE 233

Something about these buns completely overrides your off switch. My dad hates banana and peanut butter but out of all the buns I make, these are his favorite. Make sure you give the buns a chance to cool a little before putting on the bittersweet chocolate ganache coating. The sea salt makes it.

MAKES 12 BUNS

• 1 quantity of Everything Dough (see page 222)

FOR THE FILLING

• ⅔ cup (150g) peanut butter (creamy or crunchy)
• 1 banana, peeled and chopped into 12 slices

FOR THE CHOCOLATE COATING

• 3½ ounces (100g) bittersweet chocolate
• 3 tablespoons (50g) unsalted butter
• 2 tablespoons heavy cream
• flaky sea salt, for sprinkling

1. Tip the dough onto a lightly floured work surface and divide into 12 equal pieces. Between the palms of your hands, flatten each piece into a round(ish) patty.

2. Spoon 2 teaspoons of peanut butter into the center of each patty and put a banana slice on top. Pinch all the edges into the center, enclosing the filling.

3. Place the buns seam-side down on a lined baking sheet and cover with a damp kitchen towel. Leave in a warm place to proof for 1 hour or until doubled in size.

4. Preheat the oven to 400°F.

5. Bake in a hot oven for 15 minutes. Leave on a wire rack to cool for 5 minutes.

6. Next, make the chocolate coating. In a heatproof bowl set over a saucepan of boiling water, melt the chocolate with the butter until silky smooth. Remove the pan from the heat and whisk in the cream.

7. Holding the bottom of each bun, dip the tops in the chocolate ganache to coat. Leave the coating to set slightly for 5 minutes – you may want to put them in the fridge to help this along – then sprinkle over the flaky sea salt. Finally, shove them directly into your mouth (it's the best way to eat them).

SAFFRON CORGI BUTTER BUTTS

Someone sent me a picture of some buns that looked like a Corgi from behind. Corgis have, how do we say this politely, a generous peachy bottom and these buns are unmistakably Corgi. I've used a bit of saffron for color here (I adapted the recipe from a saffron bun recipe our lovely Swedish neighbor Marianne gave us) but it will still be lovely without.

MAKES 10 BUNS

- scant 1 cup (220g) whole milk
- ⅔ cup (120g) granulated sugar
- a large pinch of saffron threads
- 4 cups (500g) bread flour or all-purpose flour
- 2¾ teaspoons (10g or 1½ × ¼-ounce envelope) instant dried yeast
- 1 teaspoon fine sea salt
- 1 teaspoon ground cardamom (optional, but adds an extra dimension)
- 3 eggs
- 3 tablespoons (50g) sour cream
- 8 tablespoons/1 stick (120g) soft unsalted butter
- ½ cup (100g) chocolate chips, currants, raisins or golden raisins (optional)
- 1 egg, lightly beaten for the egg wash
- pearl sugar, for decorating
- 3 tablespoons (50g) cold salted butter, for dotting

1. In a saucepan, whisk together the milk, sugar and saffron. Simmer for 6 minutes over the lowest heat and then set aside to cool.

2. In a large mixing bowl, stir together the flour, yeast, salt and ground cardamom, if using. Make a well in the flour and pour in the sweet saffron milk. Crack in the eggs and add the sour cream. Mix gently until there are no visible patches of dry flour left. Gradually add the 8 tablespoons butter bit by bit until it is largely mixed in and then knead the dough either by hand for 5 minutes or in a stand mixer fitted with a dough hook for 3 minutes.

3. Slowly incorporate any chocolate chips, currants, raisins or golden raisins if using. Knead for a further 3 minutes by hand or 2 minutes by mixer, until your dough is beautifully glossy and smooth. Drape a damp kitchen towel over the rim of the bowl and leave in a warm, cozy place to proof for 40 minutes or until doubled in size.

4. Scoop out your dough onto a lightly floured work surface and cut it into 20 equal pieces. Roll them into rounds or 'cheeks' and then couple them up on a lined baking sheet, like perky little bottoms.

5. Brush the 'butts' with egg wash and sprinkle some pearl sugar over the top. Cut up 10 small squares of cold salted butter and place in the middle of your 'butts'. Place a damp kitchen towel over the pan and leave to get nice and plump for 30 minutes. The butter should have sunk in a little.

6. Preheat the oven to 400°F.

7. Bake your butts in the hot oven for 15–20 minutes then leave to cool on a wire rack.

DOUGHNUTS

These doughnuts are inspired by a recipe from what is, alongside *Tartine*, probably our most well-thumbed and dough-splattered cookbook of all – *Bread, Cake, Doughnut, Pudding* by Justin Gellatly, who set up the bakery Bread Ahead and is famed for his doughnuts. We use a similar dough, but then make smaller doughnuts that we roll in flavored sugars. When I realized that you could wrap the dough around a chunk of chocolate, well, it was like I had reinvented the wheel (at least in my mind). A whole world of possibilities opened up – Terry's Milk Chocolate Orange Ball, Chocolate Kisses, Snickers Bites. I hand this baton on to you – the challenge is now yours.

MAKES 25 DOUGHNUTS

- 4 cups (500g) bread flour
- ⅓ cup (80g) granulated sugar, plus extra for coating
- 2 teaspoons (7g or a whole ¼-ounce envelope) instant dried yeast
- 1¼ teaspoons (10g) fine sea salt
- zest of ½ lemon or orange (optional)
- 4 eggs
- ⅔ cup (150g) water
- 9 tablespoons/1 stick plus 1 tablespoon (125g) soft unsalted butter
- chunk of your favorite chocolate bar (optional)
- vegetable or sunflower oil, for deep frying

1. In a bowl, combine the flour, sugar, yeast, salt and citrus zest, if using. Crack in the eggs and pour in the water. Give everything a good mix and then knead for 4 minutes until you have no visible patches of dry flour left. This is a very wet dough, so an electric stand mixer is the best option.

2. Gradually incorporate the butter (a small chunk at a time) until your dough is smooth and elastic. Place a cover over the top and leave for about 1 hour, or until doubled in size. Knock back the dough and place in the fridge for 4 hours or overnight. This dough really needs to be chilled before you handle it.

3. Take your dough from the fridge and cut it into 25 pieces, each about 1–1½ ounces (30–40g). Roll each piece into a ball. If you want to add a hidden chocolate filling, simply roll the ball of dough around your chosen treat. Place the balls on a floured baking sheet with plenty of room between them so they can proof without merging. Cover loosely with plastic wrap and leave in a cozy place to proof for 2–3 hours.

4. Fill a heavy-bottomed saucepan or deep fryer halfway with vegetable or sunflower oil. Heat the oil to 350°F. Working in batches, deep fry the doughnuts until well browned (about 1 or 2 minutes) and then flip them over with a fork to cook on the other side. Drain well on paper towels and roll in a bowl of granulated sugar until well coated. If you want to go really fancy, you can flavor the sugar with some cinnamon or ginger, but plain sugar is still brilliant.

HAPPY BREAD

Happy Bread was the result a freak coincidence that led to one of my proudest creations of all time. One day I overestimated the amount of doughnut dough I needed, so I put the leftover amount in a focaccia pan and smothered it in extra caramel sauce from some buns I'd been making. The moment it came out of the oven, golden and bubbling, I knew it was going to be a counter hit. When we first started at the bakery, a local business asked if we could sell their CBD (the chemical extracted from marijuana that can give a high, which is legal in most places). We had a sample pot and at first we would dab a bit of CBD onto the bread before baking, hence the name Happy Bread. I think you'll find it makes you pretty happy anyway, without any chemical assistance.

MAKES 8 SLICES

• ½ quantity of Doughnuts dough (see page 239)

FOR THE CARAMEL SAUCE
• 1 cup (200g) light brown sugar
• 4 tablespoons (60g) soft butter (either salted or unsalted)
• ½ cup (120g) heavy cream
• a pinch of flaky sea salt (optional)

1. Line a small baking sheet, roughly 8×6inch (20×15cm), with parchment paper. Tip your dough onto the pan and gently flatten it out to reach the edges and into the corners. It should be about 1½–2 inches (3–5cm) thick. Cover the pan with a kitchen towel and leave it somewhere cozy to proof for 1–2 hours. (If the dough has been stored in the fridge, this will probably take a couple of hours.)

2. Meanwhile, make the sauce. Put the sugar, butter and cream in a large, heavy-bottomed saucepan and simmer over a low heat while stirring or whisking continuously. After about 5 minutes, the sauce will start to thicken slightly. Keep cooking for a further minute and then take the pan off the heat and let the sauce cool – it will continue to thicken off the heat.

3. Once your dough has risen nicely, preheat the oven to 425°F.

4. Gently dimple the dough with your fingertips or the end of a wooden spoon, just like you would for focaccia. Pour over the caramel sauce so that the dimples get filled. If you want a nice, salted caramel taste, sprinkle over a little flaky sea salt.

5. Bake in the hot oven for 25–30 minutes. After 20 minutes, check that the caramel isn't burning. If the caramel is turning a bit dark, put a sheet of foil loosely over the pan. Leave in the pan to cool for 5 minutes before lifting the bread out of the pan using the parchment paper. Transfer the bread to a wire rack and leave to cool completely.

TOP TIP

You can keep the caramel sauce in a sealed jar in the fridge for at least a week, so you might decide to double the quantity and use some over ice cream later.

MINI PANETTONE BUNS

Every Christmas the most disappointing present would be a panettone. It feels really Christmassy, it normally comes in a beautiful, big box, it looks like some strange cupcake on steroids, but then you cut it open and it's nearly always a stale, rather dry cake with an occasional mouthful of fruit. I was determined to capture the flavor I thought it should have. So I came up with these.

MAKES 12 BUNS

FOR THE DOUGH

- 4 cups (500g) bread flour
- ¼ cup (50g) granulated sugar (Golden Sugar, if you can get it)
- 2 teaspoons (7g or a whole ¼-ounce envelope) instant dried yeast
- 1¼ teaspoons (10g) fine sea salt
- zest of 1 orange
- 2 eggs
- 1 egg yolk (save the white for the topping)
- ⅔ cup (150g) warm whole milk
- 1 tablespoon rum, brandy or amaretto (optional)
- 7 tablespoons (100g) soft unsalted butter
- 1 cup (100g) raisins or bittersweet chocolate chips
- ⅓ cup (50g) diced candied peel
- ⅓ cup (50g) dried cranberries

FOR THE TOPPING

- 5 tablespoons (40g) almond flour
- ⅓ cup (70g) superfine sugar
- 1 egg white
- a handful of sliced almonds
- confectioners' sugar, for dusting (optional)

1. First, make the dough. In a mixing bowl, stir together the flour, sugar, yeast, salt and orange zest. Make a well in the flour and crack in the eggs and egg yolk, then add the milk and rum, brandy or amaretto, if using. Mix until there are no visible patches of dry flour. Spoon in the butter, raisins or chocolate chips, candied peel and cranberries.

2. Next, knead the dough. We recommend using a stand mixer fitted with a dough hook as it's a sticky dough. Mix for a good 8–10 minutes or until the dough comes clean away from the sides of the bowl. Leave in a warm place to proof for 1½ hours or in the fridge overnight (this'll give it a much richer depth of flavor).

3. Tip your dough onto a lightly floured work surface and chop it into 12 equal pieces. Shape each piece into a little round and place on one or two baking sheets lined with parchment paper, spacing them 2 inches (5cm) apart. Put a damp kitchen towel over the top and proof in a warm, cozy place for at least 2 hours or until doubled in size.

4. Preheat the oven to 400°F.

5. Meanwhile, make the topping. In a small bowl, whisk together the almond flour, sugar and egg white. Brush a thick layer of the topping over your buns and then scatter the sliced almonds on top. (You can freeze any leftover topping for the next time you bake these buns.)

6. Bake in the hot oven for 15–20 minutes or until golden and crisp. Transfer to a wire rack and leave to cool. Dust with confectioners' sugar, if you want, and then wait for Father Christmas to arrive.

HOT CROSS BUNS

This is another example of something I never really liked when I was little, but once you make hot cross buns yourself you realize what everyone else was on about. They are soft but chewy, wonderful fresh but even better toasted and slathered with cold salted butter. The apricot glaze makes all the difference here – just the right level of sweetness for the bun.

MAKES 14 BUNS

- 4 tablespoons (60g) unsalted butter
- 1 cup (250g) whole milk
- 4 cups (500g) bread flour
- ½ cup (100g) granulated sugar
- 2 teaspoons (7g or a whole ¼-ounce envelope) instant dried yeast
- 1 heaping teaspoon fine sea salt
- 2 teaspoons ground cinnamon
- 1 egg
- zest of 1 orange
- 1 apple, cored, peeled and grated (optional, but lovely)
- dried fruit and/or bittersweet chocolate chips (optional)

FOR THE PASTE
- ⅔ cup (75g) all-purpose flour

FOR THE APRICOT GLAZE
- ¼ cup apricot preserves

1. In a saucepan over a low heat, melt the butter and then pour in the milk. Set aside to cool.

2. Sift the flour into a large mixing bowl and stir in the sugar. Add the yeast, salt and cinnamon and give everything a mix.

3. Make a small well in the flour and crack in the egg, pour in the buttery milk, then add the orange zest and grated apple, if using. Using your hands, mix everything together until you have a shaggy clump of dough with no visible patches of dry flour.

4. Tip the dough out onto a lightly floured work surface and knead it by hand until smooth and elastic (this will take about 5 minutes). Otherwise, put it into the bowl of an electric stand mixer. If you are adding in any extras, such as dried fruit or chocolate chips, gradually knead those into the dough bit by bit making sure they are evenly distributed. Continue kneading by hand for a further 5 minutes (or for 3 minutes in an electric stand mixer) until the dough is silky and elastic.

5. Return the dough to the bowl, cover with a damp kitchen towel and leave to proof in a warm, cozy place for at least 1 hour, maybe 2 hours, or until it has doubled in size.

6. Line two baking sheets with parchment paper. Tip your beautiful pot-bellied dough onto a floured work surface and divide it into 14 equal pieces. Roll each piece into a tight ball and place them on the lined baking sheets, spacing them 1¼ inches (3cm) apart. Put a cover over the top of each pan (reusing a plastic grocery bag is a good option because you can puff it up so that it does not touch the balls) and leave to proof for a further 1 hour.

7. To make the paste for the crosses, whisk together the flour and 5 tablespoons water with a fork until thick and with no lumps. Spoon the paste into a pastry bag fitted with a plain tip (or use a freezer bag and snip away one corner to make a piping tip). Pipe the paste in the shape of a cross on top of each bun.

8. Preheat the oven to 425°F.

9. Bake in the hot oven for 20 minutes or until golden brown. Leave to cool for 5 minutes on a wire rack.

10. Meanwhile, make the glaze by adding a few tablespoons of water to your preserves in a little saucepan and mixing everything together into a liquid as you warm it through. Slather your buns in the warm glaze by brushing them all over and then leave to cool completely.

ave being able to support really good lo

Proud to shop LOCAL

We use
LOCAL
flour

Wessex Mill
Strong White
Bread Flour

LOCAL
eggs

LOCAL
milk

CALNANS

ANGELA

TUTU

SO SUSTAINABLE

and our LOCAL shops

HISTORY

Made using a blend of white, wholemeal and a heritage flour grown and milled by Duchess Farm in Hertfordshire. This comes from a mix of ancient grains which is the way bread wheat would have been cultivated before science got involved.

1. Duck eggs from our local supplier   2. Kitty making croissants
3. Our History Loaf, made with ancient grains   4. The shop cash box

PASTRIES

RUFF PUFF PASTRY

We're in Dad's domain here. He uses this ruff puff pastry for making his cheese straws, sausage rolls (the British version of pigs in a blanket), Eccles cakes (see page 255) and all sorts of other recipes. Watching it puff up into flaky layers is still a joy to me.

MAKES 18 OUNCES (500G) DOUGH

- 2 cups (250g) all-purpose flour
- 10 tablespoons/1 stick plus 2 tablespoons (150g) unsalted butter (set aside 2 tablespoons (30g) and put the remaining 8 tablespoons (120g) in the freezer)
- 1 teaspoon fine sea salt
- 1 tablespoon white wine vinegar or lemon juice
- 7 tablespoons (100g) cold water

1. Sift the flour into a large mixing bowl. Add the 2 tablespoons (30g) of butter and work it into the flour until it looks like fine breadcrumbs. We do this in our old Magimix, but you can do it by hand by rubbing the butter into the flour between your thumbs and forefingers.

2. Add the salt and vinegar/lemon juice. Gradually add the water until everything comes together into a smooth but stiff dough. Again, do this by hand or in a stand mixer with the dough hook. Once the dough has formed, put it in the fridge for 1 hour or so if you have the time – cold pastry is so much nicer to work with; however, this isn't absolutely necessary.

3. When you're ready to work the pastry, take the 8 tablespoons (120g) of butter from the freezer and grate it into shreds with a cheese grater.

4. Roll out the dough into a thin rectangle about ¼ inch (5mm) thick. Scatter half of the grated butter over two-thirds of the rolled-out dough. Fold the unbuttered third of dough down into the center, then fold the buttered third on top so that you now have a triple-decker butter sandwich.

5. Sprinkle a little flour over the dough and roll it out again until it is about ¼ inch (5mm) thick. Repeat the buttering and folding process with the remaining grated butter, folding the dough back on itself.

6. Next, roll the dough out again and repeat the folding process, but this time without butter. Repeat this two more times. Basically, what you're doing is creating multiple thin layers of butter within the dough by making five sets of folds in all, two with butter and three without.

7. Wrap the block of ruff puff pastry in plastic wrap or store it in an airtight container. The pastry will keep in the fridge for a good four or five days. Otherwise, put it in the freezer until you want to use it.

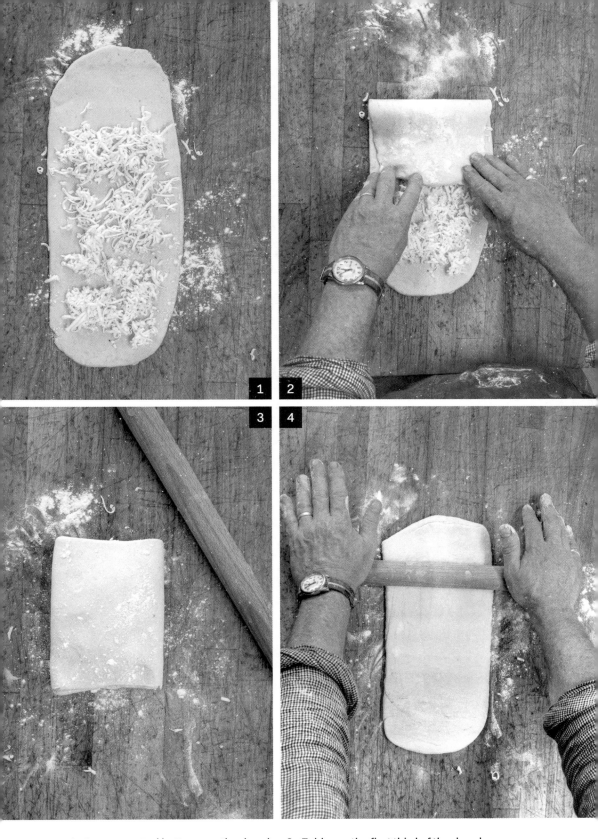

1. Scatter grated butter over the dough
2. Fold over the first third of the dough
3. Fold over the second third of the dough
4. Roll out the dough again, and repeat...

251

CHEESE STRAWS

My granny always makes these cheese straws at Christmas.
They are always excellent, but you can tell if she was distracted
by something especially dramatic happening in *The Archers*,
her favorite radio soap opera, because occasionally the cheese
straws contain enough cayenne pepper to blow a hole in the top of
your head, the ceiling and then the roof after that. Used sparingly,
cayenne pepper gives a brilliant kick.

MAKES 16-20 STRAWS

- 1 quantity of Ruff Puff Pastry (see page 238, thawed if frozen, or use 18 ounces store-bought puff pastry, which is good too)
- 1 heaping teaspoon Dijon mustard (grainy mustard also works; if using English mustard then be a little more sparing)
- 1 cup (100g) grated cheese (we use a mix of sharp cheddar and Colby)
- a pinch of cayenne pepper
- 1 teaspoon paprika
- 1 egg, lightly beaten, for the egg wash

1. Preheat the oven to 425°F and line a baking sheet with parchment paper.

2. Roll out the pastry into a long, thin rectangle that is about ⅛ inch (3–5mm) thick. Cut the rolled-out dough into four equal rectangles. You may need to sprinkle a bit of flour on the work surface to make sure the pastry doesn't stick.

3. Spread half of each rectangle lengthways with an even layer of mustard. Generously scatter the grated cheese over the mustard. Give a few gentle shakes of the cayenne pepper over the cheese and then a few harder shakes of the paprika. Fold the non-mustard half of the dough over the cheese to make a sandwich.

4. Roll out the dough until it is as long as you want your cheese straws to be. Using a sharp knife or pizza cutter, cut each rectangle into four or five long strips.

5. Brush the pastry strips with the egg wash and then pick them up and twist them a few times before placing them on the lined baking sheet. It's up to you how perfectly twisted they are – just remember, they'll taste cheese-tastic whatever.

6. Bake in the hot oven for 10–15 minutes or until crisp and golden. Leave to cool on a wire rack. Don't worry too much if the straws have fused together – once they're a bit cooler, you can easily snip them apart with a pair of scissors.

ECCLES CAKES

After the Chelsea bun raisin revelation, I was keen to explore the world of currants and raisins. Mum read about a father- and daughter-run bakery in Orford (the brilliant Pump Street) who make the best Eccles cakes. We made a pilgrimage to Suffolk. By 6 am I was sitting outside the bakery, hoping to watch them bake. After mildly terrifying a nice woman coming to open the shop, I was told where they baked everything. A couple of miles down the road, the awesome bakers showed me how they use cookie scoops to ball the perfect Eccles filling and shared their secret to getting a caramelized crust on the pastry. This is our version. We add garam masala or, more recently, baharat (a Middle Eastern spice). It adds a bit of smokiness to the raisins, which we really like.

MAKES 10-12 CAKES

- 1 quantity of Ruff Puff Pastry (see page 238, thawed if frozen, or use 18 ounces store-bought puff pastry, which is good too)
- 1 egg, lightly beaten, for the egg wash
- 1 tablespoon turbinado sugar

FOR THE FILLING
- 1¾ cups (250g) mixed dried fruits or raisins
- zest and juice of ½ lemon or orange
- ½ teaspoon mixed spice
- ½ teaspoon garam masala or baharat
- 9 tablespoons/1 stick plus 1 tablespoon (125g) soft unsalted butter
- ¾ cup (150g) light brown sugar

1. Preheat the oven to 425°F and line a baking sheet with parchment paper.

2. Tip the dried fruits into a mixing bowl, then add the lemon or orange juice and zest and spices. Using your hands, scrunch in the soft butter and the sugar – messy but strangely satisfying. Put the bowl in the fridge to firm up the fruit filling a little.

3. On a lightly floured work surface, roll out the pastry to about ¼ inch (5mm) thick. Using a biscuit cutter, cut out 3½ inch (9cm) rounds. (You should be able to eke out 10 or 12, if you reuse the offcuts.) Dollop a generous tablespoonful of the filling onto the center of each round. If you want your Eccles to look really neat, roll the filling into balls a little smaller than a ping pong ball, although a dollop is just fine. Using your finger or a pastry brush, dampen the edges of the pastry with water, bring them into the middle and press together to enclose the filling.

4. Put the Eccles cakes seam-side down onto the lined baking sheet. Brush all over with the beaten egg and sprinkle over a little turbinado sugar. Using a sharp knife, make two small parallel cuts in the top of each cake.

5. Bake in the hot oven for 20–25 minutes or until golden, puffed up and risen – the fruit filling will have bubbled up through the cuts. Leave to cool for 5 minutes before tucking in.

Serving suggestion: Traditionally, Eccles cakes are eaten with British Lancashire cheese, but ALL cheese is good. Personally, I think these are amazing eaten warm with a hunk of sharp cheddar cheese, but it's up to you to find the perfect pairing.

PASTÉIS DE NATA (CUSTARD TARTS)

We are lucky enough to have an amazing dairy near us called Lacey's. They supply us with milk so creamy that you could probably scoop out the top of each bottle and spread it on a scone. Their double (heavy) cream is almost mustard yellow and absolutely delicious. We use a lot of it in this recipe, but it's worth a little artery hardening for the sheer joy of these delicate little tarts.

MAKES 12 TARTS

- 1²/₃ cups (400g) heavy cream
- ¼ teaspoon freshly grated nutmeg
- a pinch of garam marsala
- 5 egg yolks (save the whites to make meringues)
- ¼ cup (50g) superfine sugar
- a couple of drops of vanilla extract
- ½ quantity of Ruff Puff Pastry (see page 238, thawed if frozen, or use 9 ounces store-bought puff pastry, which is good too)

1. Preheat the oven to 400°F and grease a 12-cup muffin pan with butter or oil.

2. In a small saucepan over a low heat, warm the cream with a small grating of nutmeg and the garam masala until it is just starting to bubble around the edges. Turn the heat off and let the spices infuse the cream with all their flavors as it cools.

3. Place the egg yolks in a bowl and stir in the superfine sugar and vanilla extract. Pour the cooled cream into the egg mixture and stir well.

4. Roll out the pastry to about ⅛ inch (3mm) thick. Using a biscuit cutter, cut out 12 rounds at least ½–¾ inch (1–2cm) bigger than your muffin pan cups and gently ease the pastry into the pan to line the cups. (You might need to roll out some of your offcuts to get enough.) Pour the filling mixture into the pastry cases and grate over some fresh nutmeg.

5. Bake in the hot oven for 15–20 minutes or until the pastry is golden brown and the filling is starting to caramelize. Leave the pan on a wire rack and give it at least 10 minutes for the tarts to cool down before gently easing them out of the pan.

CAULIFLOWER GRATIN TARTS

It took me a long time to like cauliflower. I only changed my opinion when I discovered how it tastes when roasted. In this recipe the cauli gets a double roasting – first when it is cooked for the filling and then again when it is finished off in a rich cheese sauce. These tarts are a chance to use up any béchamel sauce you might have left over from making Breakfast Buns on page 231.

MAKES 8 TARTS

- ½ quantity of Ruff Puff Pastry (see page 238, thawed if frozen, or use 9 ounces store-bought puff pastry, which is good too)
- olive or cold-pressed rapeseed oil, for greasing

FOR THE ROASTED CAULIFLOWER

- 1 small cauliflower, broken into small florets
- 1 teaspoon ground cumin, paprika or dried oregano (you can use your favorite ground spice or dried herb)
- 2 tablespoons olive or rapeseed oil
- sea salt and freshly ground black pepper

FOR THE CHEESE SAUCE

- 3½ tablespoons (50g) unsalted butter
- ⅓ cup plus one tablespoon (50g) all-purpose flour
- 2 cups (500g) whole milk
- 1 cup (100g) grated sharp cheddar cheese
- ½ teaspoon fine sea salt
- ½ teaspoon ground black pepper
- ½ teaspoon Dijon mustard (optional)

1. Preheat the oven to 400°F and grease 8 cups of a 12-cup muffin pan with oil.

2. Tip the cauliflower florets into a baking sheet and sprinkle over the ground cumin or other spice or herb. Season with salt and pepper and pour over the oil. Roast for 20–30 minutes until the cauliflower is starting to brown but still has a bit of bite. You might want to give everything a shake halfway through the cooking time.

3. Meanwhile, make the cheese sauce. Melt the butter in a saucepan over a low heat, add the flour and stir until it forms a smooth paste. Keep on cooking the flour mixture for a good minute or so before adding the milk. You might want to use a whisk to get everything smooth. The sauce will start to thicken up as it gets hotter. Once thickened, add the cheese, salt, pepper and mustard, if using. Leave to cool.

4. Roll out the pastry to ¼ inch (5mm) thick. Using a biscuit cutter, cut out rounds big enough to line the cups of the muffin pan with some pastry slightly overhanging the top edge (the pastry will shrink back during cooking). In theory, you should blind bake these pastry cases first; however, we've found that if the pastry is really thin and the oven is hot enough then you can skip that step.

5. Once roasted, add the cauliflower florets to the cheese sauce and stir to combine. (You could always do this ahead of time and leave the filling mixture in the fridge where it will happily keep for a few days.) Spoon the filling into the pastry cases.

6. Bake in the hot oven for 20–25 minutes or until the pastry is a rich golden brown. Leave to cool in the pan for 5 minutes before carefully easing the tarts out of the cups.

ROWIES (AKA ROADKILL CROISSANTS)

Although their proper name is rowies (or sometimes butteries, depending on where in north-east Scotland you are), these pastries go by the brilliant nickname of roadkill croissants. They have the same buttery layers as their classic French cousins and are equally tasty, they're just not quite as beautiful. My great-grandmother came from Aberdeen, which is where rowies hail from. She was also a Kathleen, like me and my mum. I imagine she ate these as a girl and would approve of me baking them now. Don't be put off by the lard in the dough – it's a bit old fashioned, but it works really well with the butter.

MAKES 16 ROWIES

- 4 cups (500g) bread flour
- 1 tablespoon light brown sugar
- 2 teaspoons (7g or a whole ¼-ounce envelope) instant dried yeast
- 1¼ teaspoons (10g) fine sea salt
- 1½ cups (350g) lukewarm water
- 1 cup/2 sticks (250g) unsalted butter
- ½ cup (125g) lard or vegetable shortening

1. Sift the flour into a large mixing bowl and stir in the sugar. Add the yeast to one side of the bowl and then spoon the salt into the opposite side. (Here, it's important to keep the yeast and salt separate at this point as the salt can kill the yeast, which means the dough won't rise.)

2. Make a small well in the center of the flour and pour in the water. Using your hands, mix everything together until you have a rough dough with no visible patches of dry flour. Leave the dough to proof for about 1 hour.

3. Dice the butter and lard, or shortening, into small cubes and cream them together with a fork.

4. Once the dough has doubled in size, knock it back (this is a baker's term for punching the air and gas out of your risen dough so that you can shape it and let it proof all over again). Then roll it out into a rectangle about ½ inch (1cm) thick.

5. Take one-third of the butter mixture and spread it over two-thirds of the dough. Fold the unbuttered third of the dough over onto the first third of buttered side and then fold the final third of the buttered side over onto the other two, making three layers. (Sorry for all the fractions.) Roll the layered dough back to its original size and put it in the fridge on a baking sheet covered in a kitchen towel for 40 minutes.

6. After 40 minutes is up, repeat the spreading and folding process again with another third of the butter. Give the dough another 40 minutes in the fridge. Repeat the process one more time with the last third of the butter and roll the dough out into a rectangle about ½ inch (1cm) thick.

7 . Cut the dough into rounds using a 3¼ inch (8cm) biscuit cutter. (You can re-roll the offcuts to make more.) Place the rounds on baking sheets, spaced apart. Leave to proof for 40 minutes.

8 . Preheat the oven to 400°F.

9 . Bake in the hot oven for 15 minutes or until golden brown. These are very oozy so some people make the sensible suggestion of moving them from the baking sheets onto a wire rack set over the pan so they're not sitting in the fat as they cool. It saves having to pat them dry at the end.

Serving suggestion: Rowies are incredible eaten warm with butter and preserves – just be prepared to dribble melted butter onto your clothing.

CROISSANT DOUGH

The ability to make a good croissant is a skill I envy enormously. You see them all over Instagram – delicate honeycombs of wafer-thin pastry layers. There's a lot of things you need to get right for the perfect croissant: you need the right kind of butter, the correct temperature balance between your dough and slabs of butter, the right lamination technique and, most important of all, the right oven. Even if all of these elements don't fall into place, you can still make a versatile croissant dough at home to use for the different pastries that follow.

MAKES 1 POUND 2 OUNCES (1KG) DOUGH

- ¼ cup (50g) granulated sugar
- ¾ cup plus 1 tablespoon (200g) lukewarm water
- 3 tablespoons (50g) whole milk, warmed to bath temperature
- 3½ teaspoons (12g or 1¾×¼-ounce envelope) instant dried yeast
- 2 cups (250g) bread flour
- 2 cups (250g) all-purpose flour
- 1¼ teaspoons (10g) fine sea salt
- 1 cup/2 sticks (250g) block of unsalted butter (if you can get hold of a high-fat European-style butter, that's great, but normal unsalted butter works really well too, especially for the adapted recipes later on)

1. Combine the sugar, water, milk and yeast in a bowl. Whisk together until all the yeast has dissolved.

2. In a separate mixing bowl, sift together both flours and the salt. Make a small well in the center and pour in the yeast mixture. Either by hand or using an electric stand mixer fitted with a dough hook, knead the dough until it is smooth and elastic. This will take about 15 minutes by hand and 8 minutes in a mixer. Shape the dough into a ball, return it to the bowl and cover with a kitchen towel. Let the dough rise for 1 hour and then put it in the fridge with a kitchen towel draped over the top.

3. Place the two sticks of butter side by side on a sheet of parchment paper. Lay another sheet on top and, using a rolling pin, roll out the butter into a square-ish shape about ½ inch (1cm) thick. If your butter is too cold, you may need to warm it up a little before you roll it out. Once rolled, put the butter slab in the fridge for at least 10 minutes to firm up a bit.

4. Scoop your dough out of the bowl onto a lightly floured work surface and deflate it, pressing it into a rough rectangle. Roll out the dough until it is just wider than the butter slab and slightly more than twice the length.

5. Peel the butter slab off the parchment and lay it in the middle of the dough. Fold the two ends of the dough over the butter and pinch together the edges of the dough so you have a big butter sandwich.

6. Roll out the butter sandwich, making sure the seam is perpendicular to you until it is at least twice as long as before, perhaps as much as three times. Take the short ends of this long rectangle and fold them inward so that they meet in the middle. Bring together both sides of the dough as if you

1. Lay the slabs of butter on the dough   2. Fold the ends of the dough over the butter
3. Roll out the butter sandwich   4. Fold the dough inward to meet in the middle

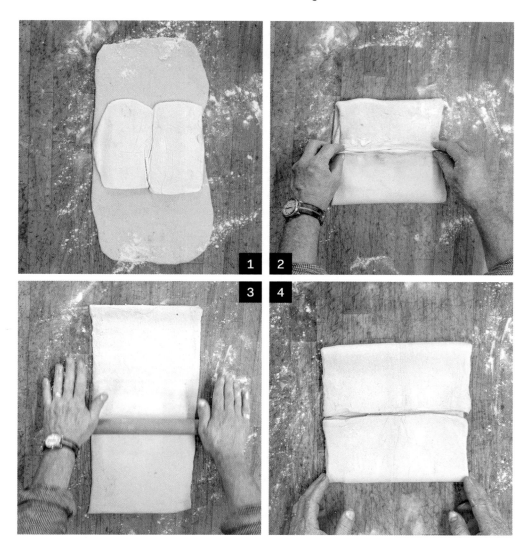

were closing a book to make a narrow rectangle. Cover the dough with a kitchen towel, put in the fridge, set a timer for 20 minutes, settle down with a cup of tea and check Insta.

7. When the timer sounds, repeat the whole rolling and folding process again. Give the dough another 20 minutes in the fridge. Have another cup of tea (if your bladder can take it). Repeat all the folds for a third time and then the croissant dough is ready to use in your chosen recipe. If you're not going to use it straightaway, wrap the dough tightly in parchment paper and store in the freezer.

CROISSANTS

MAKES 9-10 CROISSANTS

- 1 quantity of Croissant Dough (see page 262, thawed if frozen)
- 1 egg yolk, lightly beaten, for the egg wash

1. Line two baking sheets with parchment paper.

2. Roll out the dough into a rectangle 24×8 inches (60×20cm). Using a sharp knife or pizza cutter, cut 9 triangles with a 4¾ inch (12cm) wide base and two long sides across the width of dough. For the tenth croissant, you can fuse together the two half triangles left at each end but this won't look as neat.

3. Gently stretch each triangle from its base so it doubles in length. Starting from the base, tightly roll each triangle into a compact crescent shape with between three and five 'hills'.

4. Place the rolled croissants on the lined baking sheets, spacing them an inch or so apart. Put them somewhere cozy and leave to proof for 1½–2 hours.

5. Preheat the oven to 400°F.

6. Brush the croissants all over with the egg wash and bake in the hot oven for 15–20 minutes or until golden, puffed up and flaky. Eat hot with plenty of butter and preserves.

PAINS AU CHOCOLAT

MAKES 10
PAINS AU CHOCOLAT

- 1 quantity of Croissant Dough (see page 262, thawed if frozen)
- 3½ ounces (100g) bittersweet chocolate, cut into sticks (bittersweet chocolate is best, but you can also use a Snickers, KitKat, in fact any favorite chocolate bar)
- 1 egg yolk, lightly beaten, for the egg wash

1. Line two baking sheets with parchment paper.

2. Roll out the dough into a rectangle roughly 24×8 inches (60×20cm). Using a sharp knife or pizza cutter, cut 10 equal rectangles from the dough.

3. Place the sticks of chocolate all the way across one short end of each rectangle. Roll up the dough to make a neat roll, with the chocolate trapped in the center.

4. Place the rolled pains au chocolat seam-side down on the lined baking sheets, spacing them apart. Put them somewhere cozy and leave to proof for 1½–2 hours.

5. Preheat the oven to 400°F.

6. Check if your pains au chocolat are ready for baking by gently shaking the pans. If the pastries wiggle back, they are good to go. Brush all over with the egg wash and bake in the hot oven for 15–20 minutes or until golden, puffed up and flaky. Enjoy hot for breakfast.

ESCARGOTS

We first came across the Marmite, scallion and cheese versions
of these pinwheel pastries at Pophams in Islington, London,
where they slightly blew our minds. Then, during our bakery
crawl through Paris, we stumbled on the pistachio escargots
at Du Pain et des Idées, looking like bright green Catherine
wheels. Our versions are in homage to these masters. We've
added another slightly Middle Eastern flavored one so you've
got a choice. They all share the same basic method and all are
dangerously addictive – you have been warned.

MAKES 10 ESCARGOTS

• 1 quantity of Croissant
Dough (see page 262, thawed
if frozen)

**FOR THE MARMITE AND
CHEESE ESCARGOTS**

• 2 tablespoons Marmite
or other yeast extract,
for spreading

• 1½ cups (150g) grated sharp
cheddar cheese

**FOR THE FETA, WALNUT AND
FENNEL ESCARGOTS**

• 2 tablespoons honey, for
spreading

• 2 cups (200g) crumbled feta
cheese

• 1 cup (100g) shelled
walnuts, roughly chopped

• ½ teaspoon fennel seeds

**FOR THE PISTACHIO AND
APRICOT ESCARGOTS**

• 2 tablespoons honey, for
spreading

• ¾ cup (100g) shelled
pistachios, roughly chopped

• 8 fresh or dried apricots,
diced

• 1 tablespoon apricot
preserves warmed with
1 tablespoon water, for
the glaze

1. Roll out the dough to a 16×12 inch (40×30cm) rectangle
   that is about ¼ inch (5mm) thick. Depending on which
   flavor escargots you're making, spread the surface of the
   dough with either Marmite or honey.

2. Scatter the other ingredients – cheese, nuts, fruit – evenly
   over the dough and then, starting at one of the short ends,
   roll it up into a very fat log.

3. Line two baking sheets with parchment paper. Cut the roll
   of dough into 10 equal slices and place them on the lined
   baking sheets, spacing them nicely apart. Cover the pans
   with clean kitchen towels and leave to proof somewhere
   cozy for 1 hour.

4. Preheat the oven to 400°F.

5. Bake in the hot oven for 15–20 minutes or until golden
   and flaky. Leave to cool slightly on the pans. If making the
   Pistachio and Apricot Escargots, glaze the pastries with the
   apricot glaze. Eat while still warm for breakfast or cold for
   a mid-morning snack.

1. Our Ultimate Sourdough Bread → page 193   2. Labeling chaos in the shop
3. Oatmeal Bread → page 197   4. The bargain bucket of yesterday's loaves

5. More labeling chaos   6. Kitty with Our Ultimate Sourdough Bread
7. Sparky and Scout

COOKIES
AND
CAKES

CHEDDARS

Cheddar snack crackers are Dad's favorite cracker of all time. He is proud of the fact that he can turn a whole cracker (not a mini one) 360 degrees inside his mouth without it breaking. Sounds easy but have a go and you'll realize why this is his party trick. I made my own version for his birthday – now they're a firm favorite in the shop.

MAKES 8-15 CRACKERS
DEPENDING ON
YOUR BISCUIT CUTTER

• 1 cup (100g) grated sharp cheddar cheese
• 3 tablespoons (50g) soft salted butter, cubed
• ¾ cup (100g) all-purpose flour
• ½ teaspoon fine sea salt
• 1 heaping teaspoon smoked paprika
• a small pinch of cayenne pepper
• 1 teaspoon Dijon mustard

1. Line a baking sheet with parchment paper.

2. In a food processor, mix together all the ingredients. They will go from looking like a fine powder to starting to clump together. If you're worried that the dough isn't coming together, add a few drops of water. If you don't have a food processor, you can rub the butter into all the other ingredients (making sure the butter is softened first).

3. Once a crumbly dough has formed, roll out the dough evenly on a lightly floured work surface to ¼ inch (5mm) thick.

4. Using a biscuit cutter, cut out as many rounds of dough as you can. Depending on whether you want to match Dad's 360-degree party trick, you can vary the size of the rounds. Scrunch any offcuts back into a ball and re-roll the dough.

5. Using a fork, stab the center of your rounds to make a pattern (I like to make a face). Place on the lined baking sheet, spacing them 2 inches (5cm) apart. Chill in the fridge for 30–40 minutes (this makes the Cheddars much flakier).

6. Preheat the oven to 350°F.

7. Bake in the hot oven for 15–20 minutes or until golden and crispy. Depending on your oven. you may need to turn the pan around halfway though cooking for an even bake. Leave the crackers to cool a little on the pan for 5 minutes before attempting to move them, then let cool (ideally on a wire rack) for 10 minutes before eating.

VARIATIONS

For both these flavor variations, follow the same method as given opposite, but tweak the ingredients as follows.

▶ **Cheese and Marmite**
Omit the salt, paprika, cayenne pepper and mustard, but instead add 1 teaspoon of Marmite or other yeast extract.

▶ **Stilton and Walnut**
Replace the cheddar cheese with ½ cup (50g) each of crumbled stilton and grated Parmesan, and add 3 tablespoons (50g) finely chopped walnuts (I use a food processor to blitz them). Omit the salt, paprika and mustard, but do add a pinch of cayenne pepper, if preferred.

STEM GINGERSNAPS

If I were a cookie, I would want to be a gingersnap. They're comforting and warm, but also surprisingly spicy. The perfect cookie for dunking in tea (they don't go soggy too quickly) or for making an ice-cream sandwich.

MAKES 15 COOKIES

- ½ cup (150g) Lyle's golden syrup or honey
- ⅔ cup (125g) light brown sugar
- 2 tablespoons finely chopped preserved stem ginger or crystallized ginger (optional, but it takes things to a whole new level)
- 2⅓ cups (300g) self-rising flour
- 1 teaspoon baking soda
- 2 teaspoons ground ginger
- 1 teaspoon ground cinnamon
- 9 tablespoons/1 stick plus 1 tablespoon (125g) soft unsalted butter

1. In a saucepan over a medium heat, whisk together the golden syrup or honey, sugar and stem or crystallized ginger. Once the sugar has dissolved, take the pan off the heat and set aside to cool slightly. (You don't want the mixture to cool so much that it solidifies – you must be able to pour rather than scrape it into the flour.)

2. In a large mixing bowl, sift together the flour, baking soda and spices. Next, rub the butter into the dry ingredients.

3. Make a well in the center of the flour and butter mixture, then pour in the sugary syrup. Beat together until everything is fully incorporated. Put the mixture in the fridge for 30–40 minutes.

4. Preheat the oven to 375°F and line a baking sheet with parchment paper.

5. Scoop the cookie dough into 15 balls and place them at least 2 inches (5cm) apart on the lined baking sheet. Bake in the hot oven for 15–20 minutes or until crisp on the outside but still a little doughy and soft in the middle. Leave to cool on the pan for 5 minutes before transferring to a wire rack. Eat warm.

ULTIMATE BROWN BUTTER CHOCOLATE CHIP COOKIES

I can get obsessed with things very quickly. When I was 10, it was grilled cheese and I would make one every day after school in Barbara, my Breville sandwich maker. I'd experiment with different kinds of bread, cheese, butters, the cooking temperature and time I'd griddle or fry them for. Cookies are no exception. I have read endless recipes, messaged all my favorite bakeries about their recipes and taken apart every variable of the perfect cookie: how white sugar results in a pale, dry cookie, but dark sugar makes the cookie spread until thin and burnt; how cookies baked straightaway are much crumblier and not gooey at all, while cookies baked from frozen cook too quickly around the edges and are still dough-y in the center. It took months of baking and a lot of chocolate chips, but finally I cracked the perfect chocolate chip cookie – gooey in the center, with a crisp edge and a caramelized nuttiness from the brown butter.

MAKES 12 COOKIES

- 9 tablespoons/1 stick plus 1 tablespoon (125g) soft unsalted butter
- ¾ cup (140g) light brown sugar
- ¾ cup (140g) granulated sugar
- 1 egg
- 1 teaspoon vanilla extract
- 1⅓ cups (170g) all-purpose flour
- 1 teaspoon baking powder
- 1 teaspoon fine sea salt
- ¾ cup (150g) chocolate chips
- a pinch of flaky sea salt
- some chunks of Sweet and Salty Miso Fudge (see page 282, optional, but are a brilliant addition)

1. First, make the brown butter. In a saucepan over a medium heat, melt the butter. Keep stirring until the butter starts to turn brown and gives off a caramelized, nutty aroma. This will take a while. After the butter starts foaming, keep an eye on it because it can switch from brown to burnt quickly. Take the pan off the heat, pour the brown butter into a small bowl and leave to cool in the fridge for 30–40 minutes. Don't worry if there are brown bits at the bottom of your bowl – it's these flecks that make the cookies taste so good.

2. Next, make the cookie dough. In a large mixing bowl, combine the brown butter and both sugars. Beat until smooth and combined (but not too much so that it goes fluffy). Crack in the egg, add the vanilla extract and whisk to a silky paste.

3. Tip in the flour, baking powder and salt. Mix on a low speed until all the dry ingredients have been incorporated. Using a large wooden spoon, stir in the chocolate chips and the miso fudge, if you want.

4. Line two baking sheets with parchment paper.

5. Scoop the dough into 12 balls about the size of a walnut and place at least 2 inches (5cm) apart on the lined baking sheets (these cookies like to spread). Place the pans in the fridge for anything from 1 hour to overnight. (Like sourdough, these cookies develop the best, deepest flavor when they're given a bit of time in the fridge.)

6. Preheat the oven to 350°F.

7. Sprinkle a little flaky sea salt over each ball and bake in the hot oven for 15 minutes or until the edges go crisp but the middle is still gooey. Let the cookies cool on the pans for 4–5 minutes before transferring them directly to your mouth.

1. Deconstructed Snickers cookies on sale in the shop   2. Orange Bakery bag designed by Al
3. Flour delivery to the Scout Hut   4. Kitty, always in dungarees

DECONSTRUCTED SNICKERS

Dad always finishes up each Saturday shift with a Snickers followed by a sleep in the chair outside the old bakery (when it's warm enough). It's his ritual, and it inspired me to come up with this recipe – my own version of a Snickers but in cookie form. I think everything is better in cookie form.

MAKES 18-20 COOKIES

- 9 tablespoons/1 stick plus 1 tablespoon (125g) soft unsalted butter
- 2/3 cup (120g) light brown sugar
- 1/2 cup (100g) granulated sugar
- 1 heaping tablespoon crunchy peanut butter
- 1 egg
- 1 teaspoon vanilla extract
- 1 1/4 cups (150g) all-purpose flour
- 2/3 cup (60g) unsweetened cocoa powder
- 1 teaspoon baking soda
- 1 tablespoon whole milk
- 1/4 cup (50g) bittersweet chocolate chips (optional)
- 1/3 cup (50g) unsalted peanuts (optional)
- 3 1/2 ounces (100g or 2×1.7-ounce packages) Rolos or any other chocolate-covered chewy caramel candies
- a pinch of flaky sea salt

1. Place the butter, both sugars and the peanut butter in a large mixing bowl and beat together until creamy and smooth (you don't want to overbeat as your mix will become fluffy and aerated leading to very flat cookies). Beat in the egg and vanilla extract.

2. Sift the all-purpose flour, cocoa powder and baking soda into your mix and combine using a sturdy wooden spoon. Then mix in the milk, chocolate chips and peanuts, if using. Your dough will be sticky and thick. Refrigerate for 1–2 hours.

3. Preheat the oven to 375°F and line two baking sheets with parchment paper.

4. Now comes the fun part. Scoop the cookie dough into 18–20 pieces and place a caramel in the center of each one. Roll them into balls with your caramel snug in the center. Sprinkle a tiny pinch of flaky sea salt on each ball.

5. Place 9 or 10 cookies on each pan, carefully spaced out as they'll spread when cooked. Bake in the hot oven for 16–20 minutes or until crisp around the edges but still gooey in the center.

6. Leave to cool for a few minutes, then eat while still warm. The caramel centers will still be molten and the chocolate lovely and melty.

CHOCOLATE, TAHINI AND HALVA COOKIES

These cookies are inspired by a favorite recipe from another very well-thumbed book, *Honey & Co. The Baking Book* by Sarit Packer and Itamar Srulovich. We pick up the halva from the lovely Maroc Deli on the Cowley Road, in Oxford, where it is sold in big tubs. If you can't find any near you, don't worry – the tahini and chocolate combo is excellent anyway, giving the cookies a soft, melting, fudgy texture. Delicious.

MAKES 16 COOKIES

- 7 ounces (200g) bittersweet chocolate (we use one with 60% cocoa solids)
- 2/3 cup (70g) all-purpose flour
- 1 tablespoon unsweetened cocoa powder
- 1/2 teaspoon baking powder
- a pinch of salt
- 4 tablespoons (60g) soft unsalted butter
- 3/4 cup (150g) light brown sugar
- 2 1/2 tablespoons (30g) granulated sugar
- 2 eggs
- 1 teaspoon vanilla extract
- 2 tablespoons tahini
- 3 1/2 ounces (100g or approx. 1 cup) crumbled halva
- 1/2 cup (100g) bittersweet chocolate chips (optional)
- sesame seeds, for rolling

1. Melt the bittersweet chocolate in a heatproof bowl, either using a microwave or set over a saucepan of boiling water, making sure the base of the bowl doesn't touch the surface of the water. Once melted, let the chocolate cool slightly.

2. In a separate mixing bowl, sift together the flour, cocoa powder, baking powder and salt. Set aside.

3. In the bowl of an electric stand mixer, beat together the butter and both types of sugar. Once smooth and creamy (but not aerated), whisk in the eggs and vanilla extract. Continue to beat on high speed for 1 minute. Pour in the melted chocolate and beat for a further 2 minutes.

4. With a sturdy spoon, stir the dry ingredients into the chocolate mixture. When there is no flour left, gently fold in the tahini, crumbled halva and chocolate chips.

5. Put your cookie dough in the fridge for 20 minutes to firm up a little. This also gives you a good amount of time to lick the spoon.

6. Preheat the oven to 350°F and line two baking sheets with parchment paper.

7. Scoop the cookie dough into 16 golf ball-size balls, roll them in the sesame seeds and place them 2 inches (5cm) apart on the lined baking sheets to let the cookies spread while baking. Bake in the hot oven for 10–12 minutes or until the centers are really nice and gooey, like a brownie. Leave to cool on a wire rack for 10 minutes and then enjoy.

SWEET AND SALTY MISO FUDGE

Miso is a regular star player in our breads. Made from fermented soybean paste, it has a really different kind of saltiness, which I love. I became obsessed with salt after watching Samin Nosrat's *Salt, Fat, Acid, Heat* and seeing her sprinkle salt on top of ice cream to intensify its flavor. I immediately started adding salt to everything (my favorite is a little pinch in a glass of cold chocolate milk). Here the red miso adds a subtle earthiness to this fudge, which transforms it into the most more-ish snack ever. This fudge is awesome chopped up into little chunks and baked into cookies, brownies and banana bread.

MAKES 12 LARGE
SQUARES OR KEEP IT
AS ONE BIG SLAB AND
BREAK OFF CHUNKS TO
SUIT YOUR APPETITE

- 1⅓ cups (400g or 1×14-ounce can) sweetened condensed milk
- 2 cups (400g) light brown sugar
- 8 tablespoons/1 stick (120g) soft unsalted butter
- ⅔ cup (150g) whole milk
- 2 tablespoons red miso paste
- a pinch of flaky sea salt

1. Line a small roasting pan roughly 6×8 inches (15×20cm) with parchment paper, snipping the corners so that it folds neatly into the pan.

2. In a heavy-based saucepan over a low heat, stir together all of the ingredients except the flaky sea salt. Once the sugar has dissolved, turn the heat up to medium and bring the mixture to a bubbly simmer. Simmer for 12–15 minutes, stirring all the time.

3. Once your mixture has reached the soft ball stage (about 240°F), remove the pan from the heat and leave to cool for 5 minutes.

4. Scoop the mixture into the prepared pan and, using the back of a spoon or spatula, press it down and spread it into each corner. Sprinkle a pinch of flaky sea salt over the top and leave to set in the fridge for at least 2–3 hours.

5. Once set, cut the fudge into squares and either store in an airtight container (crazy people) or eat immediately (my type of people).

VEGAN NUT BUTTER AND BANANA COOKIES

I love making these cookies because they're so simple and always turn out delicious, no matter how much you mess up the recipe.

MAKES 15 COOKIES

- ½ cup (125g) mashed banana (1 large banana or 2 littlies)
- ½ cup (125g) crunchy peanut butter
- ⅔ cup (125g) light brown sugar
- 1 cup (125g) all-purpose flour
- 1 teaspoon baking soda
- 1 teaspoon baking powder
- ½ teaspoon fine sea salt
- ½ cup (80g) vegan bittersweet chocolate chips (optional)
- a pinch of flaky sea salt

1. In a large mixing bowl, beat together the banana and peanut butter until creamy. You can use either a handheld electric mixer or the paddle attachment on a stand mixer. Stir in the sugar and mix again until all combined.

2. In a separate bowl, sift together the flour, baking soda, baking powder and salt. Add the dry ingredients to the banana-peanut butter mixture and mix well. Throw in the choc chips, if using. Gently roll the dough into a ball, cover with plastic wrap and put it in the fridge to chill for 1 hour.

3. Preheat the oven to 375°F and line two baking sheets with parchment paper.

4. Scoop the cookie dough into 15 even-sized balls and place at least 2 inches (5cm) apart on the baking sheets. Using the tines of a fork, flatten each cookie by making a crisscross pattern on the top. Sprinkle over a pinch of flaky sea salt and bake in the hot oven for 10–15 minutes or until the edges go crispy but the middle is still gooey. Let cool for a few minutes then eat.

BLONDIES WITH A MARMITE GLAZE

During our trip to Copenhagen, we visited Hart Bageri, which was set up by a genius called Richard Hart (he is royalty in the bakery world). They were kind enough to let us see behind the scenes and that's where we met Talia. Before falling in love with a Viking and heading to Denmark, Talia had worked as a pastry chef at Claridge's. At Hart Bageri she oversees a range of bakes – her favorite creation is a blondie topped with a Marmite glaze. Talia's mum sends her massive tubs of Marmite from England. This blondie recipe pays homage to Talia. You can omit the Marmite glaze, but I promise you'll be missing out on something very special if you do.

MAKES 10 BLONDIES

FOR THE BLONDIES

- 1 cup plus 2 tablespoons (225g) light brown sugar
- 8 tablespoons/1 stick (115g) unsalted butter, melted
- 1 egg
- 1 teaspoon vanilla extract
- 1¼ cups (150g) all-purpose flour
- ½ teaspoon baking powder
- ½ teaspoon baking soda
- ½ cup (50g) pecans (or any nuts you like), roughly chopped
- 2 ounces (50g) milk chocolate, roughly chopped

FOR THE MARMITE GLAZE

- 1 teaspoon Marmite or other yeast extract
- 2 tablespoons water

1. Preheat the oven to 350°F and line a brownie pan roughly 12×8 inches (30×20cm) with parchment paper, leaving some excess paper overhanging the edges of the pan.

2. In a large bowl, whisk together the sugar and melted butter until combined. (If you're feeling adventurous, brown the butter as for the Ultimate Brown Butter Chocolate Chip Cookies on page 276 – not essential but you'll love the extra nuttiness in the blondies if you give it a try.) Let the mixture cool a little and then crack in the egg, add the vanilla extract and then whisk everything into a silky, glossy batter.

3. In a separate bowl, sift together the flour, baking powder and baking soda. Gently stir the dry ingredients into your batter. Once fully combined, fold in your nuts and chocolate.

4. Scrape your batter into the prepared brownie pan and, using the back of a spoon, evenly spread it out into each corner of the pan. Bake in the hot oven for 25–30 minutes or until golden brown, risen and set on top.

5. Leave the blondie to cool in the pan for 5 minutes, then carefully lift the blondie from the pan using the parchment paper and transfer it to a wire rack to cool completely.

6. Meanwhile, make the glaze. In a saucepan over medium heat whisk together the Marmite and water until completely dissolved. Brush the glaze over the blondie and let it cool completely. The blondie will sink a bit in the middle, but that's fine.

CARAMELIZED BANANA BREAD

We all know what happened with banana bread during lockdown – it went as big as Beyoncé. It's simple, sweet without being too indulgent, and a brilliant way to use up ripe bananas (you almost feel you're recycling when making it). But I always found banana bread to be quite dull and tried to jazz it up by adding anything and everything I could find in the cupboards: among other experiments, there was peanut butter banana bread, cornflake banana bread and Marmite banana bread (that one was not repeated). Then I remembered one of my favorite winter comfort foods – slices of ripe banana, shallow-fried in brown butter and honey until crisp, golden and caramelized. When added to banana bread, the effect of these caramelized bananas is – just like Beyoncé – mesmerizing, and will make you want to twerk a little.

- 10 tablespoons/1 stick plus
  2 tablespoons (140g) soft
  unsalted butter, plus extra
  for greasing
- turbinado sugar, for
  coating the loaf tin
- 1¼ cups (150g) all-purpose
  flour
- 2 teaspoons baking powder
- 1 teaspoon fine sea salt
- 1 teaspoon ground cinnamon
- 1 teaspoon ground nutmeg
- ¾ cup (150g) light brown
  sugar
- 1 tablespoon honey
- 2 eggs
- ¾ cup (200g) mashed banana
  (approx. 2 large)
- nuts (optional)
- chocolate chips (optional)

FOR THE CARAMELIZED BANANA SLICES

- 2 tablespoons unsalted
  butter
- 1 tablespoon honey or maple
  syrup
- 2 ripe bananas, peeled and
  sliced

1. First, make the batter. In a saucepan over a medium heat, melt the butter. Once melted, keep stirring the butter until it turns golden brown and gives off a nutty, caramelized aroma. Set aside the brown butter for 30 minutes to cool.

2. Preheat the oven to 350°F. Lightly grease a 2-pound (900g) loaf pan with butter and coat the sides in a little turbinado sugar.

3. Sift the flour into a mixing bowl with the baking powder, salt, cinnamon and nutmeg.

4. Pour the brown butter into a large mixing bowl, add the sugar, honey and eggs and then whisk together until pale and frothy using a handheld electric mixer. Using a metal spoon or silicone spatula, gently fold in the dry ingredients and mashed banana. At this point, fold in any nuts and chocolate, if using.

5. Next, make the caramelized banana slices. In a saucepan over a medium heat, melt the butter. Once it starts to turn a caramel color and smells nutty and sweet, add the honey or maple syrup. Turn the heat down to low, add the banana slices and gently stir for 2–3 minutes, taking care not to break up the slices. Set the caramelized banana slices aside to cool a little.

6. Pour the batter into the prepared pan, then cover the top with two-thirds of the caramelized banana slices. Bake for 50 minutes or until golden and risen on top – a wooden skewer or toothpick inserted into the center comes out clean.

7. Leave the banana bread to cool slightly in the pan on a wire rack for 20 minutes then ease the loaf carefully from your pan and leave to cool on the rack for another 10 minutes at least. Cut the loaf into slices and serve while still warm with the rest of the caramelized bananas spooned over the top.

VARIATION

► **Bittersweet Chocolate and Peanut Butter**
Add a handful of chocolate chips and a big dollop of peanut butter just after you've added the mashed banana.

EVA'S LOAF

Soon after the shop opened, Eva's mum, Carla, came in. Eva is a fantastic foodie who loves to bake and was born with a rare neurological condition. Her family had set up a charity and Carla asked if we could help with some fundraising leaflets. We decided to go a step further and bake something for Eva we could sell for the charity. Carla gave us a list of Eva's favorite ingredients and we instantly thought tea loaf. We took an old tea loaf recipe and sneaked in some extra Eva favorites. It's very simple yet completely delicious and Eva loved it.

MAKES 2 LOAVES / 10 SLICES

- 1¾ cups (250g) diced dried fruit (we use a mixture of figs, dates, apricots and raisins)
- 1 teaspoon ground cinnamon
- 1 Earl Grey tea bag
- 1 cup (250g) boiling water
- zest and juice of 1 orange
- 2 cups (250g) self-rising flour
- ½ cup (100g) light brown sugar
- 4 cups (100g) cereal or ¾ cup (100g) granola or muesli (we use a mixture of cornflakes and muesli - you want something with a bit of crunch)
- 1 large egg, beaten

1. Lightly oil two 1-pound (450g) loaf pans. (You can use one 2-pound/900g loaf pan, but we prefer to bake two smaller loaves so that we can eat one and sell one.) Cut two long strips of parchment paper. Drape one paper strip over the base of each pan and then up and over the sides. (The overhanging ends can be used to ease the cooked loaf out of the pan.)

2. Put the diced dried fruit in a large bowl with the cinnamon. Add the tea bag to the bowl and pour over the boiling water. Leave for a few minutes to steep and then add the orange zest and juice, stir everything together and leave to cool.

3. Preheat the oven to 350°F.

4. Once the mixed fruits have cooled and been infused with the Earl Grey flavors and the orange, drain away the soaking liquid and discard the tea bag. (The tea bag will be well hidden, so you may have to dig around to find it.)

5. Sift the flour into the bowl over the plump, soaked fruits. Add the sugar, your chosen cereal and beaten egg, then stir with a wooden spoon until everything is thoroughly mixed.

6. Spoon the cake mixture into the prepared loaf pans and bake in the hot oven for about 1 hour or until risen and golden on top – a wooden skewer or toothpick inserted into the center comes out clean. If you've gone for a big 2-pound pan an extra 20 minutes should work fine. If it looks as if it is getting too dark on top after an hour just slip a piece of foil over the pan.

7. Let the loaves cool in their pans for 5 minutes. Using the strip of parchment paper, ease each cake out of its pan and put it onto a wire rack to cool completely.

INDEX

Page numbers in *italics*
refer to recipes

D

Daisy, Cousin 25, 52-3, 93, 99
Danielle 43, 44, 45, 46, 47
Darren 31
dates: Eva's loaf *289*
deconstructed Snickers 127, *279*
Dodo 122-4
dog biscuits 93
doughnuts *239*
    Happy Bread *240-1*
DR 104
dried fruit
    Eccles cakes *255*
    Eva's loaf *289*
    hot cross buns *244-5*
    next-level Chelsea buns *225-6*
    see also currants; raisins, *etc*
Du Pain et des Idées 60-1, 63, 267
The Duck and The Cat 63
Ducky 63, 65, 66, 115
Dusty Knuckle 198

E

Earl Grey
    Eva's loaf *289*
    next-level Chelsea Buns *225*
Easter 228
Eccles cakes 66, 67, 84, 119, *255*
eggs
    custard tarts *256*
    doughnuts *239*
Eilidh 49-50, 51, 78, 124, 132
end-of-the-week pull-apart bread *232*
escargots 60-1, 63, *267*
    feta, walnut and fennel escargots *267*
    Marmite and cheese escargots 149, *267*
    pistachio and apricot escargots *267*
Eva's loaf *289*
Everything Dough *222*

F

béchamel, ham and sausage breakfast buns *231*
end-of-the-week pull-apart bread *232*
maple, bacon and pecan buns *223*
next-level Chelsea buns *225-6*
peanut butter, banana and chocolate buns *235*
queue nibbles *227*
Semlor buns *228*
za'atar, feta and honey buns *234*

fatayers *178-9*
fennel: feta, walnut and fennel escargots *267*
Ferguson (sourdough starter) 29, 32, 37, 38, 39, 46, 189
feta cheese
    feta, walnut and fennel escargots *267*
    za'atar, feta and honey buns *234*
figs: Eva's loaf *289*
Fika 219
Fika buns *219-21*
Finnish Fannies 70
flatbreads
    fatayers *178-9*
    pita breads *171*
Florin 63-4
focaccia 149
    overnight focaccia *159*
    sourdough focaccia *198*
Focaccia Day 198
Fotherby, Susan 39, 96
Frederick 105, 106, 107
free-form bakes 65
French toast *161*
fudge, sweet and salty miso *282*

G

garam masala
    Eccles cakes *255*
    next-level Chelsea buns *225-6*
Gellatly, Justin, *Bread, Cake, Doughnut, Pudding* 239
gingersnaps, stem *275*
Ginny 128, 132-3
Gladwell, Malcolm 16
glazes *221*
Gold, Ollie 63, 64
golden syrup: stem gingersnaps *275*
The Granary Café 128
grass pesto 95
Grimm's Fairy Tales 126
Guinness soda bread *168*

H

Haig, Matt 102
halva: chocolate, tahini and halva cookies *281*
ham: béchamel, ham and sausage breakfast buns *231*
Hamblin, Kate 65
Hamblin Bread 65
Happy Bread 128, *240-1*
Harriet 52

T

AUTHORS' BIOS

Kitty Tait and her dad Al live in Watlington, Oxfordshire, and between them run the Orange Bakery. From the most original flavored sourdough (miso and toasted sesame, fig and walnut) to huge piles of cinnamon buns and Marmite and cheese swirls, the shop sells out every day and the queues stretch down the street. In 2018 Kitty was at school and Al worked at Oxford University, but when Kitty became so ill she couldn't leave the house, the two discovered bread baking and, in particular, sourdough. Chronicled in Kitty's Instagram @kittytaitbaker, they went from a small subscription service to pop-ups to a high-street shop – all in two years. Along the way Kitty got better, a Corgi got involved and Al realized that he was now a baker not a teacher.

THANK YOUS

AL

I've long planned this part of the book as much of this would have never happened without so many people. First our families; Katie and I are both one of four and have a lot of nieces and nephews, so we started with a big team on our side. A special mention to Ben, my man Friday. And also to Katie's mum, Patience, who would have loved this whole adventure. She died in the middle of lockdown and is much missed. To all our friends and generous crowdfunders and of course Watlington – the school, the shops, the Memorial Club, our customers and our very patient neighbors. Then the baking community for allowing us to be part of this amazing world.

To Jane, for going with us even when we wanted a pop-up book with moving parts, and gently guiding us on. To Rowan and Kitty from Bloomsbury for really understanding us and to Ellen and Don for running with all Kit's publicity ideas. To Lisa for her brilliant eye for detail and to Sandra for capturing the joy of *Breadsong* in her design.

All the photos were taken by Mark, who never thought any idea was too mad, and were styled by Nicki, who went around our house finding all the props.

To Aggie and Albert, who I am so very proud of in every way.

And finally to my wife, Katie, who is my strength and stay – she will understand the reference.

KITTY

There is no part of what has happened that I wouldn't choose to do again, but I also know how incredibly lucky I am to have the family I do. If Mum and Dad had listened less and imposed more then I would have spent the past few years in and out of school and most probably hospital.

I remember Mum telling me that at one of our CAMHS sessions she had been taken to one side and told about different types of parenting. It was normally the sort of thing that puts her teeth on edge, but she did listen. There was the ostrich who ignores all problems and hopes they go away, the kangaroo who picks you up and puts you in their pouch so you are safe but can't move, the rhinoceros who uses force and logic to bulldoze their way through and the jellyfish who cannot hide their transparent fear at the distress you are going through. There was also the terrier who constantly nags and cajoles (Sparky was not happy with that one). The ideal parent animal that you are meant to be is a mixture of the dolphin and the St Bernard. The first to swim with you, sometimes in front showing you the way, but more often alongside nudging you along and sometimes behind because they know you can do it. The St Bernard was there to give you hope and compassion, warmth and calmness. A solid presence that is unfailing.

Thank you, Mum and Dad, for being a dolphin called Bernard.

BLOOMSBURY PUBLISHING
Bloomsbury Publishing Plc
1385 Broadway, New York, NY 10018, USA

BLOOMSBURY, BLOOMSBURY PUBLISHING, and
the Diana logo are trademarks of Bloomsbury
Publishing Plc

First published in Great Britain 2022
First published in the United States of America
2022

Text and illustrations © Orange Bakery, 2022
Photographs © Mark Lord, 2022

Library of Congress Cataloging-in-Publication
Data is available.

ISBN: HB: 978-1-63557-804-1
eBook: 978-1-63557-805-8

10 9 8 7 6 5 4 3 2 1

Project Editor: Lisa Pendreigh
Designer: Sandra Zellmer
Illustrator: Al Tait
Photographer: Mark Lord
Prop Stylist: Nicki Barley
Indexer: Vanessa Bird

Printed and bound in China by C&C Offset
Printing Ltd.

To find out more about our authors and books
visit www.bloomsbury.com and sign up for our
newsletters.

Bloomsbury books may be purchased for business
or promotional use. For information on
bulk purchases please contact Macmillan
Corporate and Premium Sales Department at
specialmarkets@macmillan.com.